The Shark Net

The Shark Net

Memories and Murder

Robert Drewe

HAMISH HAMILTON · LONDON

HAMISH HAMILTON LTD

Published by the Penguin Group
Penguin Books Ltd, 27 Wrights Lane, London W8 5TZ, England
Penguin Putnam Inc., 375 Hudson Street, New York, New York 10014, USA
Penguin Books Australia Ltd, Ringwood, Victoria, Australia
Penguin Books Canada Ltd, 10 Alcorn Avenue, Toronto, Ontario, Canada M4V 3B2
Penguin Books (NZ) Ltd, Private Bag 102902, NSMC, Auckland, New Zealand

Penguin Books Ltd, Registered Offices: Harmondsworth, Middlesex, England

First published in Australia by Penguin Books Australia Ltd 2000
Published in Great Britain by Hamish Hamilton Ltd 2000

1 3 5 7 9 10 8 6 4 2

Printed in Great Britain by Clays Ltd, St Ives plc

A CIP catalogue record for this book is available from the British Library

ISBN 0–241–14085–4

For Jan and Bill

Oh, the shark has pretty teeth, dear,
And he shows them pearly white.
Just a jack-knife has Macheath, dear,
And he keeps it out of sight.

BERTOLT BRECHT, *THE THREEPENNY OPERA*
AND LOUIS ARMSTRONG, 'MACK THE KNIFE'

You can only predict things after they have happened.

EUGÈNE IONESCO, *RHINOCEROS*

*One night at a time when people were being mysteriously mur-
dered where we lived, and the police had just fingerprinted
my father and me, he started singing an old Bing Crosby song on
our way home from the police station.*

Where the blue of the night
Meets the gold of the day,
Someone waits for me.

*It gave me a start. He didn't sing very often and in the circum-
stances it sounded bizarre. I wondered whether his mind had
snapped.*

*Our lives at this stage were in a chaotic condition. Our peace-
ful neighbourhood was in an uproar, and for its own reasons my
family was in a state of shock.*

*A boy I knew had been one of the murder victims. One of the
murder weapons had belonged to another friend of mine. Everyone
seemed to know someone who had been killed.*

*Of course my father was just crooning an old song, one with a
different, romantic, meaning to the one which had struck me . . .*

PART ONE

COMMITTAL

It's a different sunlight – harsher, dustier, more ancient-looking – that enters courtrooms. Streaked by this ominous light, guarded by two big uniformed cops and hunched in his old-fashioned blue pin-stripe suit with the curling lapels, the prisoner looked different too. He was uglier, smaller, and, with the eyes of the courtroom on him, even more self-conscious than usual. He looked like a criminal in a B-movie or in *Dick Tracy*. He really was the stereotype of a crook. Even so, for my own reasons I was having trouble fitting the headline *Maniac Killer At Large* to him.

The hearing droned on, the murder evidence piled up, and the voices of authority and retribution slid back into the warm hum of a Perth spring afternoon. In the dusty sunbeams my Pitman's shorthand symbols danced before my eyes. I was writing something down, recording some legal side-issue which the prosecutor and the magistrate were batting back and forth, and my sentence just petered out. I stared at my notebook thinking how strange those hieroglyphics were, those funny upward-and-downward chicken scratchings. And then they didn't seem odd at all. I didn't see them any more.

I was so keyed up, so confused, depressed and, yes, also elated by recent events, so tired of experiencing the extremes of emotion, that my mind had given up and drifted off into a semi-conscious daze. For a while I forgot where I was, what I was doing, what was happening.

It felt like I'd been out to it for at least an hour but it must have been only a minute or so before I snapped awake. The tapping of the court typist, accusingly loud, brought me round. Then everything flooded back. The dry legal voices rang louder in my head. I heard again the car horns out on the street, the trucks rattling over the Barrack Street Bridge, the screech of a train's brakes in the station below.

How could I do that? I felt my heart pounding. Had I fainted? Had anyone noticed? It didn't seem so. Up there in front of me again was the focus of all the room's – and the city's – attention and emotion. Of course he hadn't gone away; he wasn't going anywhere.

Everyone believed he was as good as convicted of multiple murder. I was trying to stay objective, but I thought so, too. Then again, I told myself, put anyone in the dock and they look guilty of something; especially those middle-class first-timers who sprang blithely up the steps – the spruce church wardens, scoutmasters and stockbrokers. The instant they gripped the dock rail and faced the music their faces went red or ashen.

This instantaneous blushing or blanching – like the ominous

sunlight – was one of the many interesting courtroom observations I'd made in my short time as an apprentice reporter on the *West Australian*. From my Press-table vantage point as assistant to the police-courts reporter, Jim Dollimore (a shorthand wizard of twenty-three), I'd noticed how the most minor petty-sessions court, the most trivial charge, had the same humbling effect. Even a negligent-driving charge in the Fremantle traffic court would do it. It didn't take the presiding presence of a magistrate or judge. Well before the start of proceedings, the courtroom's stern demeanour and furnishings and coat of arms – that powerful combination of law, history, punishment and varnished timber – had awed and mystified them. As much as by their current adverse circumstances they looked crushed by important-looking wood.

This certainly applied to the small, frowning figure in the dock. Only because I knew him, and he was sitting up there in front of me, living and breathing and looking anxious (if oozing criminality!), was I able to still give him, if only for a second or two, the benefit of the faintest doubt.

The odd thing was that after nearly two days of undramatic and convoluted detective-speak ('Whilst in attendance I ascertained that a male person had been shot in the head whilst lying in bed by a person in that immediate vicinity'), and the prosecutor's low-key delivery, it was strangely, cruelly, easy to forget that the charge he faced involved someone else I'd known, a boy who was now dead.

But then, like some legal afterthought, the victim's name would suddenly come up again in proceedings. *Oh, yes . . . him.*

And with a sickening shock I'd remember that the subject of the police photographs on the court clerk's table, Exhibit 14 – the shattered head, the blackened mess of blood and matter – was a friend of mine.

Throughout the first day of the committal hearing in the Perth police court the top photograph of Exhibit 14 was visible from my seat. It wasn't one of the more grisly ones. This wasn't one of the full body or head shots. It was a 10 x 8 inch glossy print of my friend's narrow wooden bed on the back veranda of the student boarding house where he was shot that summer night – the evening of Australia Day – while he was fast asleep.

I couldn't stop glancing towards the photo even though members of his family were in the court and I felt bad about them catching me looking.

The sheets, mattress and pillow in the photograph were black with his blood and more blood was pooled on the cement floor. The veranda was narrow, more an open porch leading from the kitchen door to the laundry and lavatory, and the bed-head was only about three feet from the lavatory door. There was barely room for the bed and a small table and a couple of unmatched cane chairs at the foot of the bed. It was rudimentary student accommodation, and hot-weather student accommodation at that.

In front of the bed a clothesline had been strung between two veranda posts, and a sheet was pegged to the line as a makeshift curtain, perhaps intended to give a little privacy to the outdoor sleeper but more likely in this case, I thought, to keep the sun's rays from waking him too early after a late night.

To get uninterrupted access to the boy on the bed, some person had hurriedly twisted the sheet up on the line rather than remove it altogether. It hung there like a chrysalis. I wondered if this person had been a detective or an ambulanceman. Or the murderer.

For efficiency's sake the authorities had decided to try the prisoner on this particular murder charge alone. In the unlikely event that it failed they had plenty of other charges to fall back on. During the first day and a half of the hearing I almost forgot about the other murders.

I was also forgetting the detailed confession. I remembered it, however, late in the afternoon of the second day. The prosecutor was outlining how cooperative the defendant had been, how thoroughly he'd re-enacted his crimes for the detectives, how willingly he'd revisited all the murder scenes and even recalled the exact light stanchion (No. 324) nearest to where he'd thrown one of the rifles from the bridge – enabling the police divers, after three hours' effort in sixteen feet of water, to recover it from the silt of the riverbed.

As this helpful act was revealed – the barnacle-encrusted rifle was lying there on the exhibit table, next to a bloodstained dressing-gown – a strange expression spread across the defendant's face. In my experience of courts, brief as it was, your average alleged murderer would have shaken his head at this point, or frowned, or simply looked blank. But this one looked grateful. His frown vanished and his mouth twisted into a modest but comradely grin. He nodded his head in agreement. As odd as it seemed, he cheered up.

More than anything his manner reminded me of one of those unspectacular but useful utility players interviewed by a sportscaster after a winning football game. One of the team at last, and quietly pleased and proud to have his efforts finally recognised.

For security, I supposed, as much as for architectural reasons, the windows of the Victorian building housing Perth's petty-sessions and committal courts, as well as the State's police headquarters, detective bureau and central police station, had been built high in the thick stone walls, about twelve feet off the floor.

Opening onto a grim asphalt yard, where the prisoners brought from Fremantle Prison were unloaded from the Black Marias and taken to the courts' holding cells, the windows faced west over the lockup and a phenol-smelling toilet block and along Roe Street, infamous since the eighteen-nineties' gold rushes as the street of police-sanctioned brothels, and only recently closed down.

Although the panes were smeared by years of grit and soot from the adjoining traffic bridge and railway station, by mid-afternoon on the second day of the hearing the defendant was sitting in the dock wreathed in sunshine. The dock faced west, too. Now and then he'd patiently inch his chair out of the glare and his guards would look more alert for a moment and make self-conscious adjustments to their own chairs and postures and already grim facial expressions. He had to squint into a stream of rays to see me sitting below the windows, bent over my notebook.

Suddenly I felt him staring at me. I'd been avoiding his eyes, hoping he wouldn't recognise me, but a moment later he winked. I winked back, then I felt a hot wave of embarrassment that quickly turned into anger at myself. I hoped that no one, not the magistrate or the other reporters, and especially not the victim's family, had seen me.

I told myself I should have ignored his wink and looked away. But in the split-second when I'd weighed up my response, I decided he was in such deep shit that it would be uncharitable and somehow treacherous not to wink back.

And there was another thing, something pretty horrible: part of me had also responded gratefully to recognition from a celebrity – even from the worst type of celebrity. For a second I felt recognised, in the centre of things. To be a participant instead of an observer went totally against my training as a reporter. But I liked the feeling.

It also made me feel hot and rattled that this was so. This was a pretty far step removed from the impulse to join all the other posterity-craving names scratched into the varnish of the Press table. (On my second day in court I'd succumbed to this one.) It sickened me that anyone should think my wink indicated I was on his side.

I hated how my feelings were so easily swung around. But at least now we'd made eye contact I could study him more openly. And I couldn't get over his appearance of patient contentment or his late-in-the-day change of manner. He wasn't wearing a tie, and his suit and shirt were creased and grubby. In the circumstances, looking so shabby could hardly help him. I guessed he must have been roused for court very early that morning because by late afternoon his black five o'clock shadow gave him that look of a minor gangster or a stubbled saloon extra in a Western.

Now he reminded me of some movie character in particular. Who was it? Yes, Burt Lancaster's deaf-mute sidekick in *The Crimson Pirate*. They had a lot in common: dark wavy hair, small but athletic physiques, shrewdness, agility, obvious disabilities. But Burt Lancaster's offsider had to be smarter. As our eyes met I thought: Didn't it dawn on you that while the police were praising your memory just now they were nailing you down?

While he sat there looking calm and flattered, he was an open and shut case. He wasn't required to plead but it didn't really matter. You didn't need to hear him speak. At the end of the hearing the magistrate could only decide he had a murder charge to answer.

Even in a short time I'd come to realise that most murderers looked more like bank tellers or economics teachers or crayfishermen. But he didn't. When he smiled and preened like that he looked like a murderer.

The magistrate appeared to agree. He was a twinkling, bow-tied cynic who every day telegraphed his feelings on the disreputable passing parade with snorts of repressed laughter and conspiratorial glances towards the Press table. But this afternoon there were no quips and arched eyebrows. He didn't once look at us. His eyes moved only from the prosecutor to the man in the dock and to the witnesses and exhibits before him, and his decision was never in doubt.

'You are committed for trial for murder,' he said. His voice was brisk and cold and the usually shrewd eyes were flat behind his rimless glasses. Our jovial magistrate looked more like a Nazi intelligence officer.

As he announced his unsurprising decision, the defence lawyers were already bundling up their papers. Their faces didn't show much expression either; only that they knew they had a job ahead of them with this one.

When, four years after the murders began, the long-awaited announcement of the arrest finally came, the front-page photograph of the small hunched figure, a blanket thrown over his head, being led by detectives from the lockup through a handful of intensely curious onlookers to the court holding cells, was greeted by a mass exhalation of breath.

The government, the police and the suburbs sighed with relief. *Thank God!* Now life could go back to normal.

I was one of the onlookers standing in the asphalt court-yard between the lockup and the holding cells. I was just in the picture: on the edge of the newspaper photograph leaning in. I was barely in the frame. I was a left ear, a nose tip, a cheek, a piece of jaw, a jacket shoulder, a sleeve, a hand, a notebook. I was present, but only just. I was made of gradations of grey dots.

When they opened the cell door and bustled the prisoner

outside, a whiff of carbolic acid followed him from the lockup into the courtyard. A detective threw a cell blanket over his head to thwart the photographers. (They'd make sure there wouldn't be any chance of a mistrial because of over-exuberant publicity.) As we thronged towards the small hooded figure the high carbolic stink almost knocked me over.

Already a legendary monster, he was there, shuffling past us, and then he was gone. His shuffle across the courtyard, the bustle of captors and onlookers, the snapping of photographs, the flash of Speed-Graphics, had taken no more than twenty seconds. The photograph of course captured the tension and excitement of the moment but rendered us all – prisoner, police and press – immobile.

I wasn't much more than a slice of nose, chin and notebook but I couldn't stop looking at this photo, too. It reminded me that while life seemed tumultuous to me at the moment, my existence was marginal and my inactivity was probably permanent.

After the committal proceedings, however, with the assignment completed, the story filed (forty-five paragraphs, seven of them written by me), the news editor satisfied, the time-book signed, the next day's assignment noted, the feeling that I'd always be standing dumbly on the periphery of things was the least of my worries.

The 'alleged' murderer had been committed for trial. Without doubt, he'd be convicted. The murders had stopped. Life would go on. But it was clear that my life wouldn't continue as normal.

I'd not long before come to a decision of my own, with hardly any thought or discussion but with complete certainty and no consideration of alternatives. And, it now occurred to me, in the face of grief and wrath and chaos, with no consideration of repercussions.

While life itself was swirling like a sandstorm around everyone's heads, my decision had been clear. This was even though I could see and hear myself and my girlfriend, Ruth, as if in a dream or from afar, sounding and behaving unnervingly like Troy Donahue and Sandra Dee in *A Summer Place*, a corny movie drama that I scorned.

How could I feel so vague and at the same time behave so definitely? I was a day-dreamer; thinking was what I normally seemed to do all day. So what was the matter with me that I couldn't think any more? And why couldn't I even keep this question in my head for more than a second before it flicked away?

After the committal, as I drove my mother's tiny old pale blue Renault that evening across the Narrows Bridge towards Ruth's house in South Perth, I had no imagination or wisdom left to deal with the next few hours. I felt incapable of talking or reasoning. I'd been dreading this evening and now it had arrived and my mind was a desert. I felt sick just being inside the Renault. Halfway across the bridge, a nerve in my right eyelid started twitching. When I checked in the rear-view mirror, however, my face was unusually white but the eyelid was quite still.

In a trance, I drove across the bridge, part of me marvelling at the miracle of the Renault pottering along in the correct lane, avoiding the oncoming headlights, not tipping over the side of the bridge into the river. I couldn't wait to see Ruth. I couldn't wait to make love, to forget this day and this evening and this week and lose myself. Still in a daze, I drove off the down-ramp. Without it registering, I drove down Mill Point Road, past the block of flats where the first woman had been murdered.

In my right mind I was the sort of person who always made mental notes of macabre places like that – like reporters were supposed to, I told myself – but I only remembered the murder flat a few blocks further on when I passed the South Perth Zoo and heard the lions roaring.

I didn't know why I made the connection. I certainly didn't feel the usual eerie but not unpleasant feeling the lions' roars gave me: of being safely uneaten, therefore sharply alive. It wasn't as if I felt safely unmurdered. The only sensation I felt, apart from my eyelid dancing like crazy, was an uneasy, false calm. Not the lull before the storm; the storm was well and truly raging. I felt like I was in the eye of the storm.

But I pulled up. Perhaps I thought I was grabbing the reins for a moment and doing something definite. I stopped the car, turned around and drove back past the murder scene in Mill Point Road – the first of the eight murder scenes – past the ground-floor flat where the sleeping woman, Patricia Berkman, had been stabbed in her bed.

She was the victim some of the papers – not the *West Australian*, of course – had referred to as the 'naked divorcee' to distinguish her from the 'beautiful socialite-heiress', the 'shapely brunette' and the 'studious babysitter', with the disapproving inference that any woman wanton enough to be both divorced and to sleep without nightclothes was asking to be murdered. What's more she'd sold cosmetics at David Jones's department store and had a Greek boyfriend who was a radio announcer. This got the gossip mills humming. Like the other women, she was young and attractive. This had been another count against her.

I turned the car around again, stopped under a street light and, with the engine still running, looked at the flat for a while. *So this was where he started. Where things stepped up a notch.*

I didn't know what I was doing there. Taking my mind off things? Trying to see something of portent in the surroundings? Soaking up the macabre atmosphere? There wasn't any. It was just an ordinary two-storey block of flats. It didn't seem ominously seductive or anything. It didn't look like the sort of place an attractive divorcee who slept naked would live. Even knowing what I knew, there was nothing there to help me imagine the murder that night or the mayhem that followed.

A light was on inside No. 1, the murder flat. I guessed a new tenant was living there now. Of course, it was more than four years since the murder; a string of tenants could have passed through the flat. I wondered what sort of people they could be. How could anyone live where someone had been murdered? Sleep in the same room? Bad vibes, I said to myself.

A middle-aged man in a straw hat was watering the garden and at the Renault's throaty clatter, more like the sound of a Lambretta than a car, he glanced up and glared at me – suspiciously, I thought. He gripped the hose like a weapon. He looked like he was trying to commit the licence-plate to memory. He probably took me for a crime-scene pervert, a nut case. Maybe I was. The duck-egg blue Renault wouldn't have helped.

I hoped it wouldn't stall as it often did when idling in inconvenient places. I didn't want to have to get out of the car outside the flat and crank-start it. It was always breaking down. (You couldn't get the proper spare parts in Perth. The local Renault dealer always insisted they were on a ship arriving any moment from France.) This time it didn't falter, however, and I took a deep breath and drove away.

As I headed off again, the realisation struck me. I was driving to Ruth's out of old habit, and I was going to the wrong place. Ruth didn't live in South Perth any more. At this moment she was probably lying in a negligee in my sister's room in Circe Circle. Around her, people were pale and grieving. Strangers were in the house performing our familiar functions. Suddenly no one was where they were supposed to be.

I felt as if I were speaking aloud to myself, voicing a single thought: I'm only young but this is how I'll feel forever. Dazed, randy, mentally paralysed and swept along by events.

I turned around again and headed back along Mill Point Road towards the Narrows Bridge, towards the evening's appointment. I was anxious about it. I suspected what would happen. Weren't death, murder and birth enough? Now I had to deal with guilt as well. Before the thought broke up and spun away, I wondered, vaguely: What happened?

PART TWO

1

BLACKBOYS

The plane took twelve hours from Melbourne to Perth and my mother cried most of the way. She dried her eyes and bought me barley sugar when we landed to refuel at Adelaide, and when we refuelled again at Kalgoorlie she recovered for a moment when the brilliance of the desert sunset made her catch her breath. By the time we arrived in Perth, it was pitch dark and she'd put on fresh lipstick, brushed her hair and stopped crying.

I thought it was strange she was so unhappy when she'd spent weeks telling me how wonderful this would be. But I was too excited and mystified to think about it for long.

I was six and my little brother Billy was almost two. Before we left Melbourne she'd damped down our hair for farewell photographs with our grandparents, Nan and Pop, and our uncles Ian and Jack, her younger and older brothers. The adults took it in turns to work the camera and line up in two puffy-eyed rows in the garden adjoining the Yarraville branch of the

State Savings Bank of Victoria. Pop had recently been made the manager of this inner-city branch after years of managing country and outer-suburban bank branches and we'd been staying with them in the bank 'residence'. The adults took it in turns to cry, too. Just as one adult bucked up and began to smile bravely, another would start sniffing and soon be blubbing away.

The bank garden itself always made me feel sad. It was tired and wintry and churchy. Even the dirt in the garden beds looked old and apologetic. It was grey and crumbly and birds shunned it. Not surprisingly, for a threadbare oasis in a grimy industrial suburb, its plants and thin lawn were dusted with soot. Sick-looking black snails clung to the creeper on the common wall on whose dusty upper bricks the faint word UTCHER and a bull's and a sheep's face could still be seen. The only flowers were old-ladyish blue hydrangeas and some sort of lilies that made me think of graves.

Even though Ian worked in a bank as well (a different bank, the Commonwealth, and so did Jack), he was too young and jokey to call uncle. He still lived at home, in the Yarraville bank residence. He was only seventeen years older than I was, young enough to join in my games. After hours, when Pop was at his bowling club, Ian would sometimes unlock the connecting door from the living quarters and we'd creep, whispering, down the brown linoleum corridor, falling respectfully silent as we passed the formidable Chubb safe with its silver steering wheel, and into the echoing bank office.

We went there to play with the typewriters. The bank had two of them. The office might have been solemn and dull, with its pious smell of inkwells and locked-up money, but the typewriters were the most impressive things I'd ever seen. I couldn't get over their clever clatter. Ian would write 'The quick brown fox jumps over the lazy dog' and 'Now is the time for all good men to come to the aid of the party' and I'd try to copy them. But I preferred my lines of jumbled letters, numbers and wriggly shapes. I loved the endless combinations of symbols and the way I could peck out a crisp line of these crazy black marks until a bell rang. And then do it again – unless, at the touch of a lever, I chose to miraculously change all these shapes to red.

One evening my mother tiptoed with us into the bank. Her ease with general office equipment was impressive enough, but her confidence in the typist's chair was the real eye-opener. Who was this brisk person? Her upright posture, the way her nimble ten-fingered typing effortlessly produced one neat line after another, made her seem a different woman. It was as if she'd suddenly revealed a talent for a rare musical instrument.

It always gave me a peculiar feeling to catch a glimpse of my parents' lives before I was born. She loved to spring old skills on us: suddenly putting down her cigarette to do a cartwheel, or writing perfect shorthand or casually picking up a ping-pong bat and performing a backhand smash. Then she'd go about her ordinary business with a twinkle that said: There's more to this mother than meets the eye.

As well as our after-hours bank raids, she and Ian and I shared another confidence – my imaginary friend, John Gordon. My mother accepted John Gordon without fuss but Ian was always asking after him, even when my friend wasn't there. He was always offering to hold John Gordon's hand when we crossed the road. He was sorry for spilling John Gordon's glass of water, or eating the chocolate meant for him, or accidentally tripping him on the stairs.

'Whoops, there he goes,' said Ian. 'All the way to the bottom. Terribly sorry, John. Let me give you a hand.'

Ian and his girlfriends used to take John Gordon and me to the beach with them on the tram. Once, two years before, when I was four, he'd taken us to a newsreel theatrette in Collins Street where one of the short features was an episode of the series *Crime Does Not Pay*. I had no trouble understanding it. It was about a family from out of town – mother, father and two little kids – who moved into a city apartment and were almost gassed to death in their sleep by a leak which their crooked landlord was too mean to fix.

The gas hissing into the children's bedroom as they slept affected me right away. (*Wake up, you kids!*) Only a random phonecall from a drunk dialling a wrong number woke their father on the twelfth or thirteenth ring. (*Wake up, mister, wake up!*) Roused by the telephone in the nick of time, the father stirred, shook his groggy head, smelled the gas, threw open the windows and saved his family's lives.

They took a lot of waking, however; especially the smallest child. My own heart was beating fast from the suspense, and also from trying to hold my breath in the cinema against the escaping gas. The gas was so evil I could smell it. I could almost see it, too, and in the recurrent nightmares that followed, I did. It was orange.

John Gordon didn't survive the gassing. He just disappeared. My mother asked after him once or twice. I said, 'He had to go away,' and I didn't think about him any more.

But after that whenever I saw red-haired, teasing Ian ('Danny Kaye's twin', my mother called him), I thought about the *Crime Does Not Pay* family. Seeing Ian the day our family was moving across the continent brought back more vividly than ever the little gassed family from out of town. As we left the bank for the airport I looked up and down the street, half-expecting to see the coughing kids in their pyjamas stumbling out of an orange cloud into the Yarraville traffic.

It made me anxious, but somehow not enough to overcome the excitement of catching a plane all the way to Western Australia. Anyway, in the daytime, if not in my night-time dreams of orange gas, I knew the *Crime Does Not Pay* family was all right in the end.

On departure day, however, my mother's mood about our destination never wavered. In the middle of the farewell photo session, she cried out, 'It might as well be Africa!' This confused me. Reading to me from a brochure on Western Australia just the week before, when she was still cheerful, she'd said it was the size of India and Pakistan combined. She also read out that Perth was the world's most isolated city.

In my opinion, that made the journey more scary but more interesting. This was my first plane trip, heading towards my father and his new job and our new home. Everything I saw was the Great Unknown.

The place that I knew, the ordered Melbourne world of

frosty lawns and trimmed hedges, of grandparents and shoes and socks and winter overcoats, of our green Austin A40, of the zoo, Brighton Beach, the Botanical Gardens and the asphalt playground of Bentleigh East State School – even the intriguing world of bank typewriters – fell away as soon as I looked out the cabin window at the sharp mauve sky beside me fading seamlessly into the gold and grey desert below.

Life was suddenly more unpredictable. When we left the plane at Kalgoorlie to stretch our legs there was a one-legged man balancing unsteadily in the red desert where the tarmac ended, trying to hit a little fox terrier with his crutch. Where the dog's fur was supposed to be white it was pink with desert dust. The man was three novel humans in one: the first real-life drunk, the first cruel person and the first one-legged man I'd ever seen.

The pink dog barked and sprang about as if it were mocking the man, and he was swearing and swinging his crutch at it. One wild swing landed him hard on his bottom. I laughed, and Billy copied me and laughed too, and my mother pulled us away. The man swore up at us from the red dirt, and spit flew out of his lips. He didn't try to get up. My mother's mouth tightened and she looked like she was going to cry again but she didn't.

My father met us at Perth airport. He was all smiles and wearing lighter coloured clothes than before. He seemed to have bigger teeth, a louder voice and less hair. It had been six weeks since we'd seen him and I hadn't realised before that his head looked like an egg. He'd gone ahead of us to find us somewhere to live and to settle into his new job as Assistant State Manager of the Dunlop Rubber Company.

There was an older couple with him to welcome us. Jim Chute shook my hand, and his wife, Gladys, kissed my mother and Billy and me as if we were relatives. In a way, it was true. We were all members of the Dunlop family.

Apart from his war years in the airforce, my father had always worked for Dunlop. 'I'm a Dunlop man,' he'd proudly say to people. At seventeen, straight from school, he was even a Dunlop boy, quite an adventurous boy, too, for the Depression year of 1932. If he were going to make rubber his business he decided he needed to 'see the full picture'. At eighteen he left for England to work for two years on the factory floor of British Dunlop's dark and grimy rubber mill in Birmingham, making car, aircraft and bicycle tyres.

He also needed to fix in his mind where rubber came from. On his way to Britain he travelled to Malaya. He wanted to see the actual trees growing in the plantations, the rubber-tappers at work, and the slender sliced trunks seeping their sticky white sap. He wanted to see the milky latex while it was still called *gutta-percha*.

His enthusiasm for Dunlop reminded me of the beaming garageman in the advertisements who saluted and said, 'Today You'll Use a Dunlop Product.' My father was always talking about Dunlop products or Dunlop people or the Dunlop office or the Dunlop factory or things made of rubber. Most things were, apparently.

He'd met my mother at Dunlop, of course. This was soon

after she joined the company as a stenographer-secretary at the main Melbourne factory at Montague. The occasion was the annual staff ball. Her partner was the dark-haired Davis Cup and Wimbledon tennis hero Adrian Quist. In their photograph in the staff magazine they made an attractive and neatly arranged couple. She was pretty, dark-haired and olive-skinned herself and, at five feet three, petite enough to make even Quist, only five feet seven at full-volley, look tallish. At the staff ball, as far as my father was concerned, Adrian Quist was just another smooth salesman from the sports department. Even if he was the only salesman with his signature embossed on the Dunlop Maxply racquet handles.

'Who's the brunette with Quist?' my father asked his cronies, and soon his name was on her dance card.

As a former employee herself, my mother knew all his work colleagues, all those Stans, Wals, Clarries, Horries, Syds, Lens and Alfs. When they visited our house she kissed them like friends. She understood his constant Dunlop talk.

Every night after dinner my parents would sit at the kitchen table talking solemnly about my father and Dunlop while they finished their glasses of beer and last cigarettes (before ashing them in an ashtray enclosed in a small Dunlop tyre, complete with distinctive tread). I'd lie on my mattress on the bedroom floorboards of the new house the young couple had just built and were gradually furnishing at No. 1 Melosa Avenue, East Brighton, and fall asleep as their voices murmured into the night. They seemed very proud of how my father was getting on in the world of rubber.

This day I understood that rubber had even greater clout than I'd imagined. Dunlop had the power to separate you from your family. It could send you all – one in a state of teary fatigue with her shoes off, one passed out in her lap, and the other sucking barley sugar and staring in a trance out the cabin window – twelve hours and two thousand miles west.

We were booked into the Palace Hotel in the city for a couple of days until we could move into the house he'd found for us. The Chutes insisted, however, that after our long journey we should come home to their house in South Perth for supper.

The adults were soon all drinking beer and laughing, even my mother. 'What a trip!' she said. She seemed to have perked up. Now she wasn't moaning that it might as well be Africa. She was telling the story of the one-legged man and the pink dog. She was swinging an invisible crutch and making it seem an amusing experience.

Billy passed out on the lounge-room sofa. My mother said I was exhausted too, so I was put to bed in the Chutes' bedroom. As she settled me down I sniffed suspiciously about the room. 'Is there gas in Perth?' I asked her.

'Nothing to worry about,' she said.

'Is this Africa?'

'Hardly,' she said, and patted my head.

As she left the room, Jim Chute appeared, holding his glass of beer, in the doorway. He had a dry, drawling voice and combed-back, oiled hair, and he wore his pants belted high over his pot belly. He was shorter, plumper and older than my father. And now he had a new younger boss from head office.

'Sleep tight, sonny,' he said to me. He gave a sly grin and cocked his head towards the window. 'Watch out. There's a lot of blackboys out there in the garden.'

It *was* Africa. Why did she lie to me?

Outside in the dark, something rustled against the fly-screen. I lay above the covers on the double bed in a strange bedroom on the far side of the country, thinking about the tribes of natives creeping around the garden. Twice I crept to the window, took a deep breath and peered out. It was too dark to see them but I could hear their whispers and the soft rattle of their spears.

I was going to call out to the adults but I could hear my father's voice confidently asserting something and Jim Chute's voice drawling something else and everybody laughing as if they were all going to get on fine. West Australian rubber products were in good hands. Then I heard my name mentioned, and Billy's, and everyone chuckled, and I fell asleep.

PEOPLE OF THE DUNES

We moved into a house in the dunes. Everyone lived in the dunes. From King's Park, on top of the highest dune, you could look down and see the whole city spread along the coastal dunes and around the sandy river flats, from the ocean to the ranges.

Something strange happened in the south in the late afternoon. When you looked south from King's Park the whole sand plain and the farthest suburban roofs and treetops joined the clouds in a dense purple mirage which imitated a European forest. It was a gloomy storybook place of tall, angry-looking trees and hills and castles. But in real life we were all living in bright sunlight and on flat, dry sand.

Some people lived in the loose white sand near the ocean. Even though everyone in Perth lived in the dunes I thought of them as the Sand People. Every afternoon the fierce sea wind, which they dismissed as The Breeze, blew their sand into the air and scalloped and corrugated their properties.

Sun and wind had rearranged the appearance of the Sand People, too – tanned, freckled, scabbed and bleached them. With their darker skins, red eyes, raw noses and permanent deep cracks in their bottom lips, they looked nothing like Melbourne people. Some were as eroded as the cliffs, their noses and ears worn and peeled away, so that grown men had the snubbed features of boys. Around their edges – noses, ear tips, cheeks, shoulders – they were pink and fraying. Shreds of skin poked up from their general outline and fluttered in the sea breeze. Boys bled if they smiled too fast.

From a distance most of the adults seemed stained a smooth reddish-brown – my paintbox burnt sienna – but close-up at the beach, walking behind them down the wooden ramp to the sand, you saw they were stippled like people in newspaper photographs, spotted with hundreds of jammed-together freckles and moles – brown and black on a pink background. There were women with chests and backs like leopards.

The men and boys all looked tough but relaxed, even sleepy. My mother said they were half-dazed from the sun. They were indeed slow smilers, but I could see it was because they were being careful of their split bottom lips.

I was impressed that all the males and some of the younger girls went bare-legged and barefoot most of the year. From my sandalled perspective it seemed clear that life in all of Western Australia, not just near the sea, revolved around bare feet. There was obviously something important going on with feet.

Foot knowhow seemed the key to belonging. Feet were an

instant giveaway for a newcomer. Only mothers' boys and English kids – or Melbourne boys – wore sandals in summer. Or, worse, shoes and socks. So said Miss Langridge, my new second-grade teacher, when I relayed to her my mother's message that despite Miss Langridge's advice to the contrary she would be continuing to send me to school with 'covered feet'.

Miss Langridge attempted to mask the bitter plump redness of her face with overlapping layers of powder which subdued her colour to pink. She bent down and hissed at me, 'Does your mother think her little darling will get a cold in the tootsies?' The force of her words dislodged tiny clumps of powder from her cheeks and they floated in the air between us.

The heat was just part of the daily contest for feet. Boys merely wandering home along the road felt bound to compete at withstanding the searing sand, melting bitumen, rocky road verges, bottle shards and grass prickles with their bare soles. The darker the surface the hotter, but it hardly mattered; everything underfoot was either sizzling, prickly or sharp. Feet, generally, took a thrashing. Those grazed ankles and blackened toenails, the blood-blistered heels, the festering reef-cuts criss-crossing their soles, showed a boy's familiarity with reef, surf and cliff-face. Their feet were painted so boldly with Mercurochrome and flavine antiseptic they looked like they were wearing red and yellow socks.

Their brave bare toes gripping their verandas, the Sand People were forever squinting into the summer sun and wind, the winter rain and gales. Whenever we drove along the coast road I'd follow their gaze out to sea and wonder what they were looking at. There was nothing out there. They seemed so proud of their views but all I could see were straight lines of sand, water and sky, the speck of Rottnest Island on the horizon and the wind forever chopping the ocean.

They acted like they owned the weather and the coastline, too. But my father told me knowledgeably that their situation depended on limestone. 'They'd be lost without it.' They'd had to build high limestone foundations to stop their houses sliding down the sandhills, and they'd had to erect limestone battlements against the onslaughts of the wind – called the Fremantle Doctor because it brought relief to the sunstruck city. Even so, their houses rattled and whined and their clotheslines bent like trees in the wind. You could see their flyaway front yards streaming down the street. The roads lay under drifts of sand as white and thick as snow. Everything outdoors was faded, pitted and smoothed by salt, sun and sand.

The coastline reminded me of ancient religious backdrops at Sunday School: the Dead Sea and places waiting for a miracle. It looked as old and bare as the moon. It was also like living in a geography lesson here where the land and sea met. The Indian Ocean was supposed to be constantly invading the shore and the land plants forever edging towards the sea. But apart from the wind nothing seemed too busy to me. The only flicker of activity was from blue-tongue lizards rustling in the pigface and a sand-coloured bush whose spidery tumbleweeds blew along the beach faster than I could run. On the sand cliffs above the shore the wind fizzed through a single clump of pine trees. The way the swings creaked and swung in the children's playground even when it was empty made me think little ghosts were playing there. Drowned kids perhaps.

After a while I worked out why the Sand People were always staring over the cliffs and out to sea. They were trying to see Africa. It was an exciting idea that Africa was the next continent, just over the horizon. In the atlas it was a straight line from us to Namibia in south-west Africa or, going the other way, Valparaiso, Chile. We were thirty-two degrees south. That sounded much colder than it was, until you found the places that were the same latitude north: Tijuana, Mexico, and Casablanca, Africa.

Casablanca sounded right to me. From the sea, the houses of the Sand People loomed like Foreign Legion forts. In the sun their quivery roofs melted into Sahara mirages. There was nothing in the straight white coastline to give your eyes a rest – no bays, few trees, to break the line and the glare and the shuddering mirages. Often on hot days the smell of something dead rose from the dunes and filled your head. Perhaps it was a blue-tongue stoned by boys. You became dizzy and got a headache if you looked towards Africa too long on a summer day.

My mother had been given bad information about Western Australia by a great-uncle who'd gone to Kalgoorlie looking for gold in 1902. He warned her of 'boiling brain'. Apparently it was an extreme form of sunstroke. It began with a severe headache. You turned feverish, her great-uncle said, and then delirious, and you saw spots like hundreds of red suns. If an ice-cold bath and a dark room didn't bring you round, you thrashed about and died.

Because she was an outdoor person herself her boiling-brain warnings rang true with me. She'd been a sportswoman: a swimmer, tennis player and horse rider. But Victoria's weather was colder. Her beach experience was in relatively sheltered Port Phillip Bay. At first she was suspicious of the surf and relentless sun. Now we were in a strange, hot, dry land, she was a mother, and she was taking no chances.

I imagined a boiling brain. It looked like a big jellyfish melting on the sand – just a circular outline of smeared and fading slime. For our first few summers, whenever Billy or I made a particular peculiar face on a hot day, or said something odd – and she was the judge of the strangeness of these grimaces or statements – she'd feel our foreheads and stare into our eyes to see if we were delirious. Just in case, she ran a mental check on us.

'Where do you live?' she'd snap. 'How old are you? Where does Dad work?'

'Goodyear,' I cracked once. That earned me a smile. It was lucky he wasn't there then. He would have thought I had boiling brain.

Eventually Billy and I turned the delirium tests into a farce. We cottoned on to the particular strange expression that panicked her: a sort of jaw-dropping, upward eye-rolling and stretching of the face, as if our skin was too tight. And after a day in the hot sun, it did feel ready to burst. We made this

38

moronic stretching face all the time. The shouts of, 'Come quickly, Mum. He's got boiling brain!' palled for her much sooner than they did for us.

At the same time as my mother was testing us daily for boiling brain she scoffed at the local mothers' remedy for sunburn: a potion of brown vinegar, sliced tomato and cucumber. When my new red- and yellow-footed friends padded into our house with tomato skins sticking to their shoulders and cucumber seeds in their ears, she sniffed the spicy air and said, 'It's not only people who don't wear hats who've got boiling brains.'

My father's bald, pale head never went uncovered outdoors, but for reasons of vanity rather than health. According to him, the real beach terror lay in the undertow, the shark: the unruly sea itself. He preferred to keep his distance from the coastline.

For him the coast was under a cloud in any case. He'd just had a shock at work. Head office had suddenly recalled the State manager, Ern Kellam, and abruptly appointed Ken Scrutton, an older Dunlop man from South Australia, in Kellam's place. The Scruttons had moved into a big old house on the wind-buffeted hill above the ocean at Cottesloe. It was a bigger and better house than ours. For my father it was a symbol of head-office injustice. 'You wouldn't catch me living there in a fit,' he said. 'Blowing a gale all day long.'

As Kellam's deputy my father had presumed he'd get the job. But Kellam hadn't gone to bat for him. 'I was knifed, pure and simple.' For weeks this was the drift of my parents' after-dinner conversations. Night after night I heard my mother making soothing murmurs over their last cigarette and glass of beer. She pointed out yet again that he'd been assistant manager for less than a year. 'You're only thirty-five. There's plenty of time.'

But my father was in a hurry. He was on the ladder now. He was working harder and finding it increasingly difficult to relax outside work. When it was hot he sometimes took us to the ocean after work or at weekends, but it was under sufferance, and he regarded it warily. The ocean was such a mysterious, unknown quantity that he even put a veto on us using inflatable tubes and surfboards. We could only use them in the river. He thought a rip would suck us out to sea on our Dunlop products. The irony of Dunlop sweeping his children to destruction was too terrible to contemplate.

Every time we ventured to the ocean, he'd bravely test the waters first. While we squirmed and jumped impatiently on the shore, he'd gingerly dive in, immediately leap up, shake his head and go, '*Whoo!*' Then he'd brush the water back over the skin of his head, smooth back his hair at the sides, stretch out his arms to balance himself upright in the surf, blow his nose, and shake his head in wonderment at the extraordinary phenomenon of wave motion.

In control of events now, he'd frowningly survey the adjacent waters for seaweed. If a piece of kelp bobbed nearby he'd snatch it up and elaborately dispose of it, flinging it far from him, as if he mistrusted its sinister kelpish intentions. From his solemn manner you'd think he was rendering a valuable service to all swimmers. Of course they were all carelessly brown and horizontal, languidly stroking past or riding waves to shore, while he bobbed there, white, serious and vertical, clearing the waterways and gauging the tides. Finally he'd stamp towards us and brusquely motion us in. 'Be very careful,' he'd warn. 'There's an undertow today.'

All this was my parents' Melbourne viewpoint. I didn't find any of these things – waves, weather or the prospect of white pointers – unsatisfactory. I loved the whistling, windy Scrutton house with pine cones thudding on its roof. I wanted desperately to be like the salad-smelling Sand Children.

I envied their rakish red and yellow feet. I envied the vinegary confidence with which they peeled sheets of skin from their shoulders and passed them around for comparison at the Saturday afternoon pictures. The aim was to peel off a perfect unbroken strip of skin from shoulder to shoulder. I was filled with wonder that in this delicate parchment you could see every pore.

Most of all, I envied the superior foods they claimed to live on. Salad was for smearing on their burnt bodies – what they ate was fish and chips, chocolate-coated icecreams, spearmint milkshakes, Passiona drink and hamburgers, the aroma of whose frying grey mince patties and onions attracted both Sand People and outsiders after dark to a stark but oddly thrilling clifftop caravan named EATS.

Some boys also ate themselves. Their scabs, of course – even Melbourne boys ate those – but also nose-skin, cheek-skin, forehead-skin and especially shoulder-skin. By now I was impressed, but not at all surprised, by boys who ate their own flesh. The coast seemed generally strange and risky. In a place smelling of coconut oil, hot human skin, drying kelp and fried onions, I thought anything could happen. Where else but the white sand could there be such prospects for pleasure and danger?

2

SATURDAY NIGHT BOY (I)

What he'd do at midnight was run straight down the hill from the Embassy ballroom with the music still in his head and dive into the river in his Saturday-night clothes and swim across the river from the city to South Perth.

Four Saturday nights one summer he swam fully dressed to South Perth. The way he was feeling, it was even worth risking the new midnight-blue pants and oatmeal jacket. Worth it for the cries and gasps back on the jetty, worth it for their rush to the water's edge and the different – bewildered and curious – feeling of their eyes on him.

Kicking away the lifebelt someone had thrown after him, striking out beyond the jetty lights into the black estuary, gave him a real payback thrill. He didn't care if they were more panicked or impressed. Whether they thought him insane or just wild, it was something to savour, shocking those Nedlands and Dalkeith and Cottesloe girls with their smooth, bare shoulders, those tanned, snobbish shoulders always turned to his face as he came up to them.

When the Ray Le Cornu Octet struck up something racy – first Les Boucher on piano, then Ray himself on drums and Brian Bursey on bass, and the others dropping in one by one – there were always three or four girls huddling on the far edge of the dance floor near the Ladies, heads brushing together and darting sly glances around to see whose groins they were going to be pressed up against next, and by Horrie King's first few moody clarinet notes of 'Caravan' he'd think: That blonde's giving me the eye for sure.

He'd start to saunter over – and maybe he just knew instantly it was a mistake. But the clarinet and the warm desert air held him in an optimistic trance. The song of the sand dunes. He liked the idea of doing it in the sand.

Anyway, all eyes were on him as usual so he had to see this through. He flicked back his hair and moved across the wasteland of floorboards towards the girl. Steadily, inevitably, he moved around shuffling obstacles, side-stepping sarcastic girls and arrogant boys with beery breath. The clarinet began hinting trouble, insinuating little sneers, but he wouldn't be diverted. Sensing competition from everywhere, he stepped up his pace and hurried towards the girl. He felt his palms were damp and wiped them down his pants. George Kirkby's trombone seemed to be blowing raspberries as he got closer. And suddenly, yet surprisingly, he was there at the girl's side, at her actual ear, at her real shoulder, and was so dizzied by the din and the blunt intimacy of her hair and skin that he nearly fainted against her.

The fierce way he was breathing her in through his mouth and nose he could even taste her.

And, because the girl was always frowning away towards the band or the Ladies or somewhere (amazing how interesting they suddenly found the seating, the lights, the Exit signs!), he had to touch her to declare his arrival and intention. The usual choice of safe places, from the small of the back upwards. He'd gently prod her side or elbow, or the material at her waist, or above her hip where the dress flounced out. This time, yes, he'd put his finger on the high, bare part of her back. Or (exactly at the level of his mouth!) brush her naked shoulder, where he could just make out the finest pale gold hairs on a tan of tiny, delicately arranged freckles. No matter where he touched there was the female smell, the silky smell, the underwear, flesh and perfume smell. Perhaps – he loved that slutty touch on posh girls – a bra strap peeking out.

He touched. Tap, tap on her bare skin. The warmth. 'Kews-me-woodya . . . ?'

And then the familiar hateful routine: the whispers, stifled giggles and averted glances, the turned backs. Occasionally a bold face-off: 'What are you saying?' And of course he was trying to fashion a deep sophisticated voice out of the braying air and his own hollow skull.

Horrie King was back on tenor sax and some fans of the band clapped in appreciation.

'What? What? What's he trying to say?'

These girls were so tall and healthy he had to stand on tiptoe to shout his requests into their hair, sniffing (*this close to nuzzling!*) a reluctant scented ear or dodging strand of blonde-ness. Clearing his throat made no difference. Trying to rise above Jack Pope's trumpet, his own sounds came out all clogged and weak.

'Woodya lumph damph?'

And now came down the old and smouldering cloud. As he fought to force it back, his desperate hair tosses and body moves shouted at the girl: Forget the voice, the face, the talking-through-the-nose! You've got it wrong! Announcing the real me, his gestures said: Man of many parts. King of the Embassy. Boss of the ballroom. Also nifty jive-maniac (well-known whirling dervish of the notorious Snake Pit), Scarborough lifesaver, tenpin bowling ace, hockey player, et cetera. To sum up: Loner, smooth operator, sportsman, proven stud. In other words, Joe Cool.

So, said his tapping foot and snapping fingers, how about it?

Baboom, kat-ish! went Le Cornu on the drums. The cymbal still vibrated in his head.

'You must be joking!'

The scorn of those posh girls. But worse – so bad that recalling it in bed at night made the blood pound in his ears and his throat squeeze off his air – were the overheard mutters, the whispers. 'Look out, here comes . . .' He could hardly bear his brain revealing the venomous word. Worse than 'harelip', worse than 'cleft palate'.

'*Birdmouth!*'

The trombone sniggered as the derisive Nedlands girls turned their fragrant shoulder-blades on him.

48

So, even alone again (*especially* alone again) there was an extraordinary charge in leaving the Embassy at midnight, humming 'Golden Wedding' after the band's big wind-up, and running down the William Street hill to the river, shouldering through those laughing bare-armed girls and superior, drunk boys (as if he were going on with them to Bernie's for hamburgers, as if he were their friend), and calling out loud good nights to all and sundry before launching into his final sprint and dive.

He made a splash. Considering the distance from wharf to water, his dive was shallow. He took the sting mostly on his forehead. The water's slap went deeper than his skin; it seemed to smack and burn inside his head. With it came the jarring thought: This time I won't come up. I'll drown. That teenage dive flashed back: thirty show-off feet into the Araluen pool, then blackout, hospital, electrodes, more blackouts, headaches. Hospitals. In the brackish, oily coolness more neon lights fizzed inside his eyes.

But on the surface, light and sound safely separated. The past vanished with the pain. The recklessness, the drama, the late hour, the apparent danger, the *showing them*, got him primed and going again. If you were trained for it, despite the drag and sag of pants and shoes and jacket, the whole gratifying performance was really a cinch. Even at fourteen he'd swum four hundred yards fully clothed for his bronze lifesaving medal. So night swimming in this black but smooth river, in this balmy air, was a snap. The stroke to use was the sidestroke – steady and smooth, no unnecessary overarm flapping.

You stayed compact and the air in the clothes helped your buoyancy. And when the sidestroking arm got tired, you just switched arms.

It was becoming his Saturday-night routine: swimming out three hundred yards or so beyond the glow of the street and jetty lights, then treading water in the dark, letting his clothes billow around him while he got his breath back. The only sound out here was the regular jump and plop of a feeding fish. Under the high moon, he'd float on his back and bask in the way he'd turned things around again. Put himself in the driver's seat.

I showed them all, he thought. It felt good. And now he calmed down by looking up at the backlit war memorial on Mt Eliza and the stationary lamps of the men kingfishing by the brewery outflow, the car lights cruising homeward along Mounts Bay Road and the prawners' lamps slowly dipping and rising along the shore.

When the street lamps went out at one a.m. he slowly swam ashore and walked the half-mile west along the bank to the Narrows. He liked it when the lights shut down for the night. He liked the idea of some old night-watchman at the State Electricity Commission pulling a switch and plunging Perth into darkness. Total darkness gave him an advantage, allowed him to see things other people couldn't. Courtesy of the army, he possessed acute night-vision. During their brief encounter the army had taught him three valuable skills (a skill for each month of service). Of course his record had caught up with him before he looked like getting to Korea, but those three skills were plenty: firearms, motor vehicles and night-vision.

In the river he squeezed his eyes shut and counted the twenty seconds to wipe out their memory of the light and bring his night-vision into play. But two distant cars, their headlights on full-beam now, messed up his gradations of blackness. Their beams blurred his night-time silhouettes.

This was the place where he actually swam the river. No point any more in crossing Perth Water at its widest – two miles across – like he'd done at sixteen, eighteen, to make a point to the old man and a girl or two, people who didn't believe he had it in him. At the Narrows the river was only a quarter-mile across and he still made his point. (Even though without the burden of clothes he could still easily manage the two miles. Probably even *with* his clothes.) The river was so narrow at the Narrows they were planning a bridge there, to relieve north–south traffic pressure on the Causeway, upstream. To bring together the southern and northern shores. That was fine by him. It'd make life easier.

When he reached the Narrows he waded out into the river again and struck out for the pale gleam of the sand-spit on the southern shore. It deepened quickly here – the bottom was dredged out for the Rottnest ferries – and the tides swirled stronger in the channel. But he took it easy, clasping his rolled-up jacket to his chest with his left arm and sidestroking comfortably with his right. The night river didn't frighten him. The noise of the lions coughing in the South Perth Zoo made him smile. Sharks? Not a thought. Everyone knew there were none in the river. He wouldn't fancy treading on a cobbler's spine in the shallows, but then he was OK because he was wearing shoes, wasn't he? What a laugh. Before he knew it his feet were brushing the sand of the spit and he was walking up the beach, clearing his nose, dripping water and crunching mussel shells underfoot, and clomping past the Old Mill and on to Mill Point Road.

He called it a night then. Anyway, he was too soaked to do anything more. It took him five minutes to find and hot-wire a Holden outside the zoo, and in another five or six minutes he was walking through his back door in Rivervale. Taking care not to wake the kids, he stepped out of his clothes and slid into bed beside Sally. ('Slipped off the ferry gangplank, didn't I?') River algae was still in his hair and on his skin. As he dropped off to sleep his head swam with the algae's yeasty smell, all mixed up with the bodies of standoffish girls and the sniggering of brass instruments.

3

YELLOW SAND

We lived in the yellow sand. My father had swapped houses with a Perth family, the Seftons, who urgently needed to move to Melbourne. He thought the house-swap was a neat arrangement. My mother hated it. She was bitter that her new brick veneer house with its big windows over-looking her English flower beds and soft bowling-green lawn in East Brighton had been exchanged for a crumbling 'Californian' bungalow with small leadlight windows and a patchy lawn of buffalo grass whose coarse runners poked up from the sand.

She hated its gloomy interior, especially the dusty home-made bric-a-brac left behind by Mrs Sefton. 'I don't want to inherit her *hobbies*,' she complained. The knitted doilies and toilet-roll covers, the dried flower arrangements and orna-ments of *papier-mâché*, the prissy lamps and vases made of jars and milk bottles covered with finicky little pieces of glued-on coloured paper, depressed her to tears.

Mrs France next door cheerfully told us that Mrs Sefton was a regular patient at the Claremont Mental Hospital because of her obsessive desire to polish the front fence and path in her brassiere and bloomers. The news gave my mother further pause. While she gathered up all traces of Mrs Sefton's occupational therapy and packed them out of sight, she worried what Mrs Sefton was getting up to in *her* house.

The bungalow was at 30 Leon Road, Dalkeith, on the corner of Robert Street, near the top of a dune which rose from the river three blocks back. If you dug a hole in our yard the sand was pale grey for the first few inches, then it turned yellow and stayed yellow as deep as you could dig.

The surroundings were greener than the coastal dunes (they could hardly be *less* green) and the prospects of danger and pleasure required more imagination here, three or four miles upriver. But they were there if you knew where to look.

The front yard had poisonous oleanders which could kill you if you sucked their leaves and maybe if you even brushed against them. (It also had blackboys, which I discovered was the name for grass-trees with spear-like stems.) In the back yard there was a bobtail lizard and a grass snake or two in the lantana hedge and, overhanging Robert Street, a Japanese mulberry tree, big and leafy enough to hide in, which gave both fruit and efficient missiles that struck hard but squashily and left a satisfying indelible stain.

As the neighbourhood boys showed me, the yellow sand was favoured for one of the two popular local customs – digging tunnels. The other craze was for urinating on moss.

Whenever a boy saw moss growing anywhere – on a wall, rock, path or tree – he felt bound to piss on it.

It was second nature. Perhaps growing up in the dry heat among the cardboard-coloured vegetation and pale dunes had given them an aversion to anything lush and green. My new friend Nick Howell was the chief exponent of moss-pissing. He was pleased to have us move into the neighbourhood. He'd already killed all the moss along the lee side of his own house down the road, and the Ivimeys' moss at No. 34. He'd nearly finished Miss Thomas's side fence at No. 35, and the three France girls at No. 32 wouldn't let him anywhere near their walls. He was grateful to have moss access at No. 30.

They called their sand tunnels 'underground cubbies'. When we moved in, all the local boys were absorbed in some stage of the tunnelling process: digging a winding trench, roofing it with tin, cardboard or three-ply, heaping it with camouflaging sand, then disappearing down inside the burrow. In the hot sand they worked with the strange urgency and optimistic flurry of ants, pausing only to gulp water from the garden hose and piss on any available moss.

Tunnel collapses were frequent. The walls or roofs simply caved in, or sometimes the boys forgot where the cubbies were and stepped on them. It didn't seem to dawn on anyone that the speed of construction, the flimsy materials, and especially the loose, unstable sand could be to blame. Gasping boys crawled out from under the rubble, spitting dirt and shaking their heads as if to say, 'How did *that* happen?'

Most tunnellers were painted red and yellow, too, but on

the other ends of their bodies. When I came home with a grazed forehead from a collapsed tunnel my mother shook me angrily. She couldn't believe mothers allowed their children to go to school barefoot, much less risk suffocation by burrowing underground.

Some local kids, even more strongly connected to the landscape, were named after West Australian geographical regions, native animals or plants. There were Kimberleys everywhere, named after the far north. I knew boys (Jarrah) and girls (Karri) with the names of hardwood timbers. Some parents chose to combine both marsupials and local building materials in their children's names. Kanga Jarrah Tuart Wandoo Williams was the class librarian.

The tunnelling craze, according to my father, had probably begun with those prison-camp escape books where cheeky British tunnellers constantly outfoxed their German guards. Then he decided the boys' habit must have been picked up from their parents and grandparents. When the Japanese had bombed Broome, Exmouth, Onslow, Port Hedland and Wyndham, in the north of the State, the residents of Perth had sand-bagged their homes and rushed to dig air-raid shelters in their back yards. He knew all about bombing raids. He'd been a bomber pilot.

'The war's over,' my mother said tartly. She didn't encourage talk about it.

He was probably right. Many of the back yards still had their old air-raid shelters. Ian Hodge's grandfather had one in working order, half-hidden under his orange trees, with a faded sign outside which said, 'Turn Off the Bloody Lights! Tojo Can See Them in Tokyo!'

Eventually I found our shelter. It was covered by the lantana hedge. I'd just seen *King Solomon's Mines* and when I levered up the rotting trapdoor in a Stewart Granger manner, the suspenseful squeak of the rusty hinges and the chance of discovering a treasure – or a skeleton – had me so excited I didn't notice my face was bleeding from lantana scratches.

In the cobwebby space of the shelter lay the treasures the Seftons had chosen to help them withstand the bombs of Japan: some bunches of rusted keys, a corroded torch, a pile of *National Geographics* turned to yellow pulp, a cracked rubber surgical cushion and a jar of dried peas. No diamonds. Not even any of Mrs Sefton's occupational therapy.

Aroused by the disturbance, dozens of red-back spiders scuttled from their nest in the surgical cushion. I'd also just seen *The Treasure of the Sierra Madre* so I didn't need to be told not to return to the shelter. Living in Western Australia, I thought the Sierra Madre landscape looked quite familiar. Humphrey Bogart looked familiar, too, at least when he kept his hat on. Something about his eyes and top lip reminded me of my father.

Forbidden to dig sand tunnels and wary of air-raid shelters, I waged sand battles with Nick Howell and Ian Hodge against our enemies, the Mueller brothers from Viking Road, in what we regarded as our territory, the sandhills and limestone fortresses and bamboo thickets along the river between White Beach and the old Gallop house, a mile and a half east. Here the rich sand-crust broke into handy egg-sized clumps the local boys called *boondies*, which kept their form during flight but which exploded on impact.

Halfway along this riverbank was the Sunset Old Men's Home. On the riverfront below Sunset hot water flowed from an artesian bore into a rudimentary and notorious swimming pool known as the Hot Pool. During the Depression poor families had camped there and taken their baths there every Saturday night. Now it was frequented by old invalids during the day, and at night, according to my mother, who'd heard it from the neighbours, by 'peculiar people who get up to strange things'.

I couldn't imagine what things. Or what sort of people. The old men's home's air-raid shelters were still down there, hidden from Japanese bombs in the bamboos below the home, with swear words and drawings of sexual organs smeared on their sides. Broken bottles and cigarette butts were strewn around and the air reeked of piss. As for the Hot Pool itself, you couldn't have paid any child I knew to swim there. Its time had passed. It was slimy and it smelled like rotten eggs. The only people I ever saw lolling in the pool were sad, creepy old men.

Still, I knew I'd be mightily depressed myself if I were an old person living in a place called Sunset. You couldn't get a blunter name than that. If I understood the name to mean the end of the day, curtains, the light going out, surely the old men got the point, too? How could the people in charge rub it in like that?

When I needed to keep a straight face for some reason, like standing for two minutes' silence on Remembrance Day, I could make myself sad by imagining I was a Sunset inmate. Maybe I'd be like the old Chinese man who nodded up and down twice, bared his teeth at the sky, and then shook his head twice, ceaselessly. This constant compulsive exercise had worn his neck as thin and taut as electric cord; a vigorous sky-smile or head-shake could probably have snapped it. Or the old fat man who inevitably sat next to me on the 201 bus. Every time I saw him get on the bus I'd will him, just this once, to sit somewhere else. Not a chance.

With a whistling snort, he'd plonk down beside me. Where his nose should have been was a gaping hole, like the nose cavity on a skull. He'd grown a walrus moustache to hide it, but to no avail; of course the moustache grew downwards instead of upwards, accentuating both his noselessness and his walrusness.

He made many long, noseless trips into town sitting beside me, and every time I felt sorry for him. But as he breathed his snorting whistle, and his fat thighs took over the seat, and his fingers worried away at the edges of the nosehole until his eyes watered, I inched so far away from him that I was barely sitting. I was teetering on one buttock and I was half out the bus window. I had a crick in the neck from twisting and leaning away and desperately trying to avoid a view of the inside of his head.

One day the news got out that Old Mr Mueller, the Mueller boys' grandfather, had done something to Rosalie France down at White Beach. The Frances had called the police. My parents were, as always, both agitated and silent about 'trouble' but Nick Howell said Old Mr Mueller had lifted her dress and looked at her underpants.

This didn't seem particularly serious to me. Rosalie France's underpants, like those of her sisters, Margaret and Natalie, were made by her mother out of sturdy maroon or purple cloth and were no surprise to anyone. The France girls spent most of the day hanging upside down, or doing head-stands and handstands and cartwheels, with their dresses tucked in their pants. Try as we might, it was impossible for the neighbourhood to escape the sight of the France girls' violently coloured homemade underpants.

No one said anything more in my hearing about the underpants, or Rosalie France either, but two days later she was standing on her head in her front yard with her dress tucked in her purple bloomers as usual and the Mueller family was packing Old Mr Mueller off to Sunset to live with the head-waving Chinaman and the noseless man.

Nick Howell was my link to the scandalous adult world. His mother told him everything he wanted to know, about the Muellers or anything else, and he passed it on to me. Both of them seemed to relish these roles. Mrs Howell knew details of the neighbourhood's latest polio victims, how severely they had the disease and in what limbs. She knew which neighbourhood men were having affairs and which boys were romancing which girls. She knew what most kids' fathers earned and everyone's parents' ages.

She volunteered other things. She told Nick his father's secretary's boyfriend had given his father a heart attack. Nick and I rode our bikes to the private hospital where Mr Howell was recovering. When we arrived his father was sitting up in bed with a black eye and the *Saturday Evening Post*. He hugged Nick with tears in both eyes and said his heart was better now.

'How did he get the shiner?' I asked Nick as we rode home.

'Oh, something about him and his secretary,' he said airily.

Nick's life was different to mine, more sophisticated and strangely intriguing. He had the most freckles and the first crewcut I'd ever seen. Instead of Christmas presents each year his parents gave him a cheque made out to 'Merry Christmas'. His parents slept in separate bedrooms. Mr Howell was a General Motors distributor and loved American things. He scoffed at me one day when I was talking about cars and I referred to the glove box and dashboard. He said, 'It's glove compartment and instrument panel, buddy.' He wore bow ties, read American magazines and spoke in an imitation American drawl which intrigued the ladies. He'd also patented an actual invention: a type of wire coat-hanger in the shape of a sock which he said stopped woollen socks from shrinking. It would make his fortune. Then nylon came in.

Nick was wearing a Davy Crockett coonskin hat his father had brought him back from America the day he told me of the existence of prostitutes, and what they did with Italians and

South Fremantle footballers in Roe Street. 'Oh, sure!' I said. During the Coronation celebrations at school he said it was a fact that Queen Elizabeth had the smallest breasts in the world and Marilyn Monroe the biggest.

He had one blind eye from being shot with an arrow by a boy called Christopher Catchlove after he dared him to. It looked the same as the other eye, just cloudier. After that his mother was fiercely protective of him. He could do no wrong. One day he remarked to me thoughtfully that he wished he could remember what it was like to suck at the breast. I didn't take much notice. He was always saying things like that. Next day he said, 'Well, I found out.'

'What? How?'

He'd asked his mother to remind him.

'You're nine years old!' I said.

'So what?'

'She's old!'

'So?'

There was a fairly long silence. 'Well, what was it like?'

He examined a wart on his thumb. 'OK. No milk, of course.'

Once Old Mr Mueller was safely inside Sunset everyone calmed down again. The adults acted as if he'd been the only blot on Dalkeith's reputation for respectable behaviour. But Nick casually said to me, 'You know the old Gallop house? There was a murder there with an axe.'

'When? Who?'

'Dunno. A long while ago. They found a woman's body. Chopped up,' he added with relish.

'I don't believe you.'

'God's honour. Ask Mum.'

Our mothers could have been from different planets. I was still living down coming home from school with a song for my mother. The official version was on the hit parade. My barefoot friends had been singing the local version in the playground. I ran in the door and sang it for her: *Lady of Spain, I adore you. Lift up your dress and I'll explore you.*

Coming after the Old Mr Mueller Business, my song made her face go blank. She pressed her lips together. 'I think you'd better go to your room,' she said.

Our house rested on foundations of limestone, too. Limestone is only compressed sand, after all. It was easy to carve your initials in the foundations with a stick. Indeed, their bland facade and lemony softness begged to be scratched and scraped, especially the bigger, yellower supporting stones in the front of the house.

My new neighbourhood friends Nick Howell, Ian Hodge and Neil Liddell had all dug their initials in their foundations. But their initials were arrangements of straight lines. When I carved mine with a screwdriver something strange and fascinating happened. The D crumbled instantly and gently into a powdery cave, which engulfed the earlier R. As I watched, almost hypnotised, the cave quickly grew. Out of its mouth dribbled a pale lemon stream and then such a frightening rivulet of sand that I envisaged the whole house pouring into the street in an avalanche.

The foundation stone seemed to be melting. Soon it was more crust than stone. It was behaving like a big hourglass, with a neat heap of fine-grained sand piling up at its base. At the same time, a thin plume of dust rose into the air like a tiny signal of disaster and softly blew away.

In fright, I looked around for a rock or some solid object to plug the hole. The only things in sight were two of my brother's Dinky toys: a Ford Customline (a miniature of my father's new company car) and a red London bus, and my cricket ball. I pushed the Customline in first. It disappeared entirely inside the cave. Then the double-decker bus. It vanished too. I tossed in the screwdriver but still the trickling continued. Desperately, I even offered up my six-stitcher. The cave swallowed it, and sand still trickled merrily onto the ground. As a last resort, I unscrewed the sprinkler from the garden hose and jammed it in, vertically. The sprinkler was metal, about eight inches square. The pace of the trickle seemed to slow. It hesitated and as I held my breath it stopped.

Now I had to put back the lost sand. I tried to scoop up the mound but it was so fine it fell through my fingers. I needed to wet it. The hose was nearby, but by now logic was beyond me. Addled by destruction and panic, my brain instructed me to urinate on the pile of sand. (Of course! That's how they did things around here.) Then I packed the mud into the cave, jammed it tight over the Ford, the London bus, the cricket ball and the screwdriver, packed it around the sprinkler, threw more mud over everything, patted it down, and waited. The entombed offerings held fast. The plug stuck.

Our foundation stones were made of sand and they rested on sand. My mother made a rule that children weren't allowed to run madly around the house. Running made cracks appear in the walls. So did big trucks rumbling past. For a long time I lived in fear; not so much that we'd all be buried under a limestone avalanche – that seemed inevitable – but that the house, agitated by some racing boy or delivery van, or my father's temper, would one day pop its cork and spit out the evidence of my evildoing.

Growing an English lawn, English roses and deciduous trees on dry sand in a place of water shortages was hard work. So even moderately successful gardeners liked to grow their front lawns right to the road, without a fence, to display their good intentions. Having a front fence was considered standoffish, in any case. It could prevent Sunday drivers from admiring your home. Similarly, people who didn't keep their lawns green were thought to be of low moral fibre. Not to try to overcome the odds was regarded as 'letting the street down'.

In order to boast greener grass in a place of constant water restrictions and infertile soil some people sank bores in their back yards. These places were easy to pick. Their sprinklers whirred at hours when everyone else's were forbidden. Instead of the usual cardboard-coloured buffalo and couch grass their lawns were an eerie Technicolor green and the walls of their houses looked bloodstained from the iron in the bore water.

It was during one of our first summers in this place of anguished gardeners, when we thought we'd grown accustomed to living in the sand (after my mother had hysterically axed her first grass snake), that our neighbours began to shyly ask my parents whether our garden hose was trying to escape.

'Hmm,' said my father.

They had heard stories of this problem, the neighbours said, and now their own hoses had tried to make a run for it. The hoses seemed to be attempting to tunnel down into the earth. As if to freedom. They seemed to have a strange, well, *rebellious* force. When you tried to pull them up, they pulled against you. It took all your strength to hold them. They were straining against their taps and water pipes, some stretching to breaking point like big rubber bands, others bending the pipes and, in some cases, snapping their shackles and diving into the earth.

'Goodness,' my father said.

As the mystery of The Great Hose Escape grew and spread, quiet suburban gardeners began writing whimsical but increasingly anxious letters to the newspapers about their rebellious hoses. What was going on underground? The thinking seemed to be that the hoses were in cahoots. Water diviners and dowsers weighed in with their theories. It was hinted that strange subterranean, even supernatural, forces were at work.

Geologists finally stepped in to solve the mystery. The problem, they declared, was caused by drought – several years of declining rainfall had made the surface of the dunes even drier and looser than usual. The dripping water from any garden tap which was not completely turned off could make a connected hose sink into the deep tunnel it was making. A suction effect was occurring underground. The solution couldn't be simpler: disconnect your hose from its tap after use, and make sure it was firmly turned off.

Dunlop, naturally, was a leading maker of garden hoses. It had recently developed a new lighter, green-coloured plastic hose to compete against the common black rubber hoses that were heavy to haul around, blackened your hands and – bad commercial sense – lasted forever. During the height of the furore my father was telephoned at seven one morning by a reporter from the evening *Daily News* to comment on the phenomenon.

'Dunlop garden hoses will not run away,' my father, in his pyjamas, declared firmly. 'Their behaviour is impeccable.' Indeed, our own new hose, even then coiled obediently and motionlessly in the rose bed, hadn't moved a muscle during the fracas.

'What advice do you have for people whose hoses are trying to tunnel underground?' asked the reporter.

'The culprits are your older, heavier rubber hoses – those out-of-date ones that soil your hands. My advice is to buy a new Dunlop plastic garden hose immediately. And, of course, one for the back garden.'

When he was pleased with himself he reminded me of the English film comedian Terry-Thomas, all teeth and moustache. He put down the phone and, carrying his cup of tea with two Granita biscuits, his Turf cigarettes and the fresh copy of the *West Australian* (whose crumpled disorder, bad odour and steamy dampness would soon make it untouchable by any other member of the family), he disappeared happily into the bathroom.

Over the following few weeks the word 'hoax' came into my vocabulary. It cropped up for a while, among gusts of laughter and mild protests from my father, during their drinks parties.

———

It was in Leon Road that the lions began to come into our house. Once or twice a week I'd catch a glimpse of a lion padding down the hall, another one climbing through the dining-room window, its mane disturbing the curtains. Sometimes I'd hear them breathing before I saw them. They had a chesty wheeze like Ian Hodge's asthma. Their visits were quiet and unfussed. I was the one they were interested in. They didn't act ravenous or angry but I naturally presumed they wanted to eat me.

Sometimes it was just a single lion, big-maned and yellow.

Other times a whole pride of lions and lionesses would come sauntering into our yard, looking for a way into the house. It didn't take them long. They jumped in through the windows or pushed their way in the back door. Soon they were padding through the house with that thin-hipped, quiet urgency that lions have.

I didn't waste time hiding. It didn't matter which room I was in, I knew they'd find me. Often they found me lying on my bed in the sleep-out. The sleep-out's louvres and fly-wire screen opened right onto the side garden with its overhanging mulberry tree. They padded straight over and surrounded me, studying me and weighing things up. They stood so close I could feel the warmth coming off their flanks and the meaty heat of their breath on my cheeks.

It was at that moment, just before they decided to open their jaws and devour me, that I took control of the situation. No matter where I was, even if I was outside in the garden, I lay down, closed my eyes and kept very still. I didn't blink or move a muscle. I played possum. I said to myself: *I am a dry twig. I am a cold rock. I am dull grass.* And it worked. The last thing I'd remember before I sent myself to sleep was the lions sniffing my body in bewilderment.

Then I'd wake, my heart thudding, lying in my actual bed in the sleep-out. I'd escaped again.

Lying awake at dawn in the filtered green light of the mulberry tree, I could hear a lion roaring across the river. At this quiet hour the river carried the sounds of hunger and frustration from the South Perth Zoo across the glassy estuary to me in my sleep-out on the farthest bank. Beside my cheek the mulberry branches rustled against the fly-wire. The lion kept up its rhythmic moaning cough until it faded into the waking hum of the day.

My lion anxiety affected this new pleasure I'd discovered: going to the pictures. I loved the Saturday children's matinees at the local movie theatre, but there was a price to pay beyond the admission charged by Mr Palmer, the proprietor. I was scared of the MGM lion.

The start of any film by Metro Goldwyn Mayer had my heart beating faster. The afternoon's main feature stood a good chance of being an MGM film, and it was always preceded by three or four MGM *Tom and Jerry* cartoons. That was a lot of lions. I spent a great deal of time ducking down in my seat or pretending I'd dropped the money for my OK Peanut Bar on the floor. Of course I didn't let on to anyone that I was scared of Leo the Lion. But only when the trademark stopped roaring, turned into silent profile and faded into the opening credits could I begin to relax and enjoy myself.

But not fully. A source of general anxiety was Mr Palmer himself. To all the local boys he was Dalkeith's most important and frightening citizen. Running the picture theatre was an awesome privilege. Mr Palmer took it very seriously, at least on Saturday afternoons.

During his evening – adult – sessions he was a cordial host. On Saturday afternoons, however, his mood ranged from stern to ferocious. He never relaxed. Every week before starting the matinee he stood in front of the screen, blew on a silver whistle, issued dire threats and declared his rules. No whistling or cat-calling, no feet on the seats, no throwing sweets, no changing seats. Then, glowering along each row, as if committing the face of every boy to memory, he strode to the back of the theatre and grudgingly signalled the projectionist to begin.

The cacophony of whistles and cheers that greeted the lights going down was thrilling in its crazy courage. Another surge of joyful defiance greeted the first cartoon. (This was the cue for me to stop whistling and duck down to avoid the lion.) Depending on Mr Palmer's degree of surprise at this weekly occurrence, he'd either blow several furious bursts on his whistle and threaten us again, or stop the film, turn the lights up and toss out four or five suspected catcallers.

A whispery hubbub followed this disturbing turn of events. For minutes there was a restless stalemate. Eventually both audience and proprietor subsided enough for the matinee to begin. For the rest of the afternoon Mr Palmer prowled the aisles, matching whistles with us, daring us to challenge the rules and cheer at the exciting bits or groan at the love scenes, raging at us while his torch beam sought the most piercing whistlers, the most abject groaners, the feet-on-the-seats heroes.

It was hard to completely give yourself over to Abbott and Costello, or Jeff Chandler as Cochise, the gallant Apache leader, in *Broken Arrow*, when Mr Palmer could materialise beside you, blow his whistle in your ear, shine his torch in your face, and growl, 'Name, sonny?' I loved the pictures but I always reeled out into the sunlight with a headache.

Mr Palmer resembled the high-waisted actor Buster Crabbe, whose ancient serials he was still screening. Buster Crabbe was a former American sports star but he made us snigger because in his tight safari shirts and interplanetary spacewear he displayed what we called 'bosoms'.

Bosoms or no bosoms, he had the hero profession sewn up. One Saturday he'd be on the screen playing Jungle Jim, the next, Flash Gordon or Buck Rogers. Put a snug shirt on him and he was in business. Most Saturdays you were sure of seeing Buster Crabbe jiggling his way through some cliffhanger or other. He even played Tarzan a couple of times but we were loyal to Johnny Weissmuller and weren't interested. We didn't like the idea of seeing him with his shirt off.

Mr Palmer didn't like us laughing at Buster Crabbe's bosoms either.

We were loyal to Johnny Weissmuller but we permitted Lex Barker to play Tarzan as well. I was a big Tarzan fan. Not a Tarzan film went by when Tarzan wasn't pounced on by an angry lion or two in my full view. Strangely, while I hid from the trademark lion at the start of MGM's Tarzan pictures, once the film got going I could boldly face every pouncing, slavering lion they threw at him – and at me. Actually, they helped me over my problem. Perhaps because Tarzan quickly despatched them. They looked like moth-eaten stuffed lions in no time.

On the weekdays following each Tarzan matinee I'd hurry home from school, take off my clothes and put on my school PE shorts, as the garment most approximating Tarzan's loincloth. Then I'd pad around to Noeleen Ivimey's house, climb into the jacaranda tree in her back yard and commence to beat my chest and give the Tarzan jungle cry.

Eventually Noeleen would appear at her laundry door wearing her swimming costume and with a monkey puppet on one hand. She would join me in the jacaranda, and we'd pat the monkey, re-enact the previous Saturday's film and indulge in a 'Me, Jane', 'You, Tarzan' domestic routine for a while, until, as if at some silent signal, we'd jettison the monkey, climb down from the tree and assume the game's next positions.

My position was the fence on one side of the yard, hers the other. Between us stretched the Congo in all its lion-infested savagery. Calling each other's name, arms outflung, oblivious to vines, rivers and wild beasts, Tarzan and Jane would run through the jungle towards each other, until they met in the middle with a jarring impact and kissed on the mouth.

This stage of the Tarzan game, the urgent running at each other and the kissing, was vital to our plot. I found it strangely exciting – yet not quite as thrilling as I'd anticipated. The movies had made me expect something more of kissing on the mouth. Although honour demanded that I groan at film stars' love scenes, I didn't hate them at all. They just made me curious. I wondered whether Noeleen and I were romancing properly. Maybe you needed to be older than nine. I thought we should be running faster at each other, but we could hardly collide with any more force than we were already. Even at our present speeds we were getting headaches and bleeding lips.

Nevertheless I would have happily played our secret Tarzan game every day if Noeleen hadn't spilled the beans. She gave Rosalie France the details. That was embarrassing enough. But Noeleen didn't mention Tarzan. She said our game was called Sophisticated Lady. My ears burned just thinking about it. If Jane was the point of the game I didn't want to play it any more.

———

For the first time I began to notice the way my parents behaved in the outside world and the way we lived together. Against the brighter, lighter background they seemed to stand out more.

My mother had more rules than before. In the summer they were mostly to do with avoiding polio. Stay away from crowds. Don't swim in the river. Don't eat shop-handled pies, hamburgers, fish and chips or sandwiches. Don't touch things if you don't know where they've been. Try not to handle coins. Don't breathe strangers' breath on the bus. These were hard ones.

The worst, however, under the no-crowds rule, was her ban on films. I could hardly bear it. Every Saturday Nick Howell sauntered off to the matinee shaking his head at my plight. Every week he generously dropped in on his way home to tell me why it was the most bloodthirsty or the funniest movie ever made. The memory made him shiver in wonder or brought tears of laughter. 'You would've loved it!' he insisted. He seemed to be resisting polio very effectively. He acted out *The Lawless Breed* and *Seminole* and *Abbott and Costello Meet the Invisible Man* with such relish I wouldn't have minded his legs withering and his arms going floppy then and there.

Polio completely changed my mother's attitude to the outdoors. Polio took over from boiling brain. Now she said all the time, 'Go outside and get some fresh air,' although 'outside' could be a hundred degrees. Even when the regular summer polio epidemics waned, the cinema ban wasn't lifted so much as modified. Now I was allowed back, but only every second Saturday. She didn't say why, but I presumed she thought it was halving my polio chances.

It was torture watching the trailer for the next week's film, then listening to my friends excitedly anticipating it all week. The alternate-week rule ruined movie serials for me forever. That was the end of *Superman*, *Batman*, *Hopalong Cassidy* and *Buck Rogers*. Buster Crabbe was history.

My mother had more rules than before, but my father's behaviour was like a different person's. He was much more the boss. She told me he was now a big fish in a small pond. He seemed to me to be one of the people running Western Australia. When they struck oil in the north-west at Exmouth Gulf he was so excited I thought he'd won the lottery.

Considering he was only home for a couple of waking hours in the morning and evening he made his presence felt more. Everything about him was *more*. His voice and laugh were louder, his opinions firmer and his anger greater. You even had to wait longer in the morning before you could face going into the bathroom after him.

For the first time I noticed his mysterious morning ritual. It began with him locking the bathroom door and immediately flushing the toilet. Then he urgently tore up sheet after sheet of toilet paper. The tearing sound went on for so long it reminded me of the nesting frenzy of Ian Hodge's ferrets. He tore up enough paper to wallpaper the room. He had to be lining the seat before he sat down. He must be giving himself a cushion of paper a foot high, I thought. But who else sat there? Only our family. He was protecting himself against the germs of his wife and children, shielding himself against the tender bottoms of his own babies! I was offended on behalf of us all.

I looked at my mother. She shrugged. 'It's something to do with the war,' she said.

He also seemed to have acquired new sayings for the new place and his new job. He said *for crying out loud!* when he was getting agitated and *by the same token* when he was disagreeing with someone but wanted to appear reasonable. If someone had some knowledge, experience or skill, they were *a full bottle*. He was a full bottle on the rubber industry and the business world. He was also a full bottle on company behaviour and the unfairness of being passed over.

He never swore in front of us, but where other men with

hurt feelings might respond with curses, he had an odd retort when he felt hardly done by or criticised. He delivered this peculiar saying with a fierce smile. It stung and then it stuck in your mind like the worst swearing.

Why don't you go and dip your left eye in lukewarm fig jam?

When he directed his fig-jam reply at someone else it sounded weird but harmless enough. The first time he said it to me it still seemed silly but it didn't make me laugh. It froze me in my tracks and it made me feel strange. I wondered if it was what the Baptists said instead of cursing.

It was dawning on me that my parents each had two names to suit their two personalities. There was Roy or Royce, and there was Dorothy or Dot.

My father's name was Royce but he liked Roy. It was chummier and fitted the business world. The only ones who called him the longer Royce – his family in Melbourne – also called my mother the shorter, more common, Dot. On the other hand, my mother's family had always called her Dorothy, which she preferred.

He looked like a Roy. He gave a distinctive Roy whistle, *Whee-whew* – like a wolf whistle with a shorter final note – when he came in the door each evening. We all whistled back at him, so there were these friendly *Whee-whews* coming at him from various rooms. When I was younger I liked to meet him before the whistle. I'd wait for him at the gate. He'd stop the Customline and I'd get in and sit on his knees and steer it into the garage.

He was never more a Roy than when he was speaking

funny German after dinner, all guttural and sputtery, pretending to be Hitler in a fit. He was very much a Roy, too, when we persuaded him to play 'Bye Bye Blackbird' on the harmonica or 'I'm Looking Over a Four-Leaf Clover' on the ukelele. We loved these rare boisterous times. Roy suited the gap in his front teeth, his loud laugh, sandy moustache and high-domed head. Roy was a full bottle on male games – poker, pontoon and punting. Roy patiently let our new baby sister, Janet, play hairdressers with his sparse locks. He didn't complain when she brushed so hard over the skin of his head that it left scratches. She was the apple of his eye.

Roy called his workshop under the house the Doghouse. Descending into the Doghouse after Sunday lunch, Roy's catch-cry was, 'Help your mother with the washing-up.' Emerging again, he impressed us with his carpentry: his bookcases, homework desks and cupboards. Like the wicked spin of his table-tennis serve, his eye for darts and carpet bowls, this skill seemed to arrive from nowhere.

Roy recalled for us boyish motorbike adventures in England. Roy had tapped rubber trees in Malaya. Roy had broken low-flying regulations to buzz my mother's house and flash romantic messages to her while in pilot training. Roy had kept a pet sugar-glider possum in New Guinea. Roy talked about his possum but was quiet about the risks of being a bomber pilot in the New Guinea Highlands. In photos from the war zone he stood amongst feathered tribesmen and bare-breasted women cuddling piglets. He wore a jaunty cap, shorts, no shirt, a handlebar moustache and a pistol on his belt. The Flight-Lieutenant posing in front of his Boston Bomber was thin and brown. Dashing Roy.

Where Roy was most at home was in Saturday saloon bars with horseraces booming on the radio. Roy left me in the car with the Shell road map and Ford service manual while he strolled whistling into the din. The pilot relaxing after a tough sortie.

I became familiar with the asphalt carparks of many suburban pubs. Dalkeith's boundaries were the Nedlands Park Hotel, with its mysterious sign, *Biergarten*, and the Continental Hotel ('Mine Host Happy Harry Ward'). But I also knew the carparks of the Ocean Beach, Highway, Captain Stirling, Mosman Park, Brighton and Cottesloe hotels, even the Raffles across the river. Most of the Saturday carparks had views of glinting water – the river, the ocean, yachts and joyful swimmers. Slumped on the car seat, I watched excited children run by the car, taking short cuts across the carpark and through the stacked beer kegs, yelping at the hot asphalt underfoot, hurrying through the heat mirage to the water.

Roy called going into pubs 'doing business'. He'd say, 'Just going to see a man about a dog. I'll only be a minute.' He meant an hour or two. He brought out glasses of raspberry lemonade. It wasn't too bad – he parked me in the shade.

We still had to watch ourselves, and were careful not to disagree with him, but it was usually all right when he was Roy. The one to look out for was Royce. Royce was Roy when agitated.

Royce came home late and brittle. ('Oh, no!' we'd whisper.

'Whisky!') The Dewar's made him glittery and cool. Royce waited for an affront – but not for long – so he could let loose. Usually he found one in her silence. Then, with relief, it seemed, he took offence and huffed and stamped around the house while Billy and I lay low.

His specialty was indignantly departing rooms, then returning and leaving again, and slamming doors so hard that sand ran down the walls. The area of his agitated comings-and-goings would quickly expand, first the room, then the house, and eventually the district, as he leapt into the Customline in high dudgeon and sped off with tyres squealing for a circuit of the suburb, thinking up new grievances for his return – and departure again.

I didn't block my ears. I strained to hear the Royce voice in the night. It made me more unsettled than scared, like a bad dream. I quickly recognised the pattern: his late and jovial homecoming, her silence, his reaction, the stray word that became an argument, the bitter fight and the second, more savage, silence – the pause after some ultimate insult to his dignity. In this vacuum, while I tried to listen, my breaths became shallow sips of air. There! The slap, the running feet, the slamming bedroom door. I could go to sleep.

She looked both Dorothy and Dot to me – a Dorothy indoors, outdoors very much a Dot. Dorothy was the woman, the wife, the suburban mother, the Mrs Dunlop at the business functions. At breakfast, the silent one at the stove. Two thousand miles from home. Cooking but not eating. Who'd been crying.

In Dorothy mood she murmured to a friend on the telephone: '. . . Yet he's never let a night go past when he hasn't put his arm around me when we go to sleep.' Overhearing this surprised me, considering the row the night before, but it made me feel better to hear it.

I didn't know why she favoured Dorothy to Dot. Dorothy was the unsettled woman; Dot was the girl. Small, dark-haired, very tanned now, Dot ran everywhere. (Sprinting along the shore, she could easily catch me.) Dot made many friends; West Australians were fond of her and Dot loved Perth. Dot swam. Dot cartwheeled on the beach and did handstands. Dot had decided not to fear the sun; she was brown year-round. In the sandy landscape she was a busy little speck.

BUMPERS

By the time my family had dug its own hollow in the dunes and settled into what everyone called the West Australian Way of Life, a certainty had come into my own life. Every Christmas I received a pair of Dunlop Bumpers. Every Christmas Eve I went to sleep knowing the morning would bring the next size in Bumpers, and it did.

Every Christmas morning my heart sank when I saw the parcel and uncovered the familiar yellow and black box. When I opened the box and caught that first sharp rubbery whiff, unwrapped the tissue paper and spied the new Bumpers huddled heel-to-toe inside, I could have cried. But I went through the Christmas motions. 'Oh, good!' I lied. 'New Bumpers. Just what I wanted.'

Bumpers were clumpy-looking 'leisure shoes'. They came in two styles, each with the same thick, creamy yellow rubber soles. These soles were the 'bumpers', the buffers to the shoe. If you counted the in-soles, the soles were two inches thick. For uppers, you had the choice of a navy blue canvas-like material or chocolate-brown artificial suede. Over various Christmases I was given Bumpers in both colours, but I usually received the chocolate fake-suede ones. The navy blue Bumpers had a more daytime, middle-aged, yachting and golfing look whereas the chocolate ones were day-and-evening-wear Bumpers. This was supposed to make me feel better.

It was impossible to convince my parents that in the place, climate, fashion niche, age group and time in which I lived the preferred casual footwear was the desert boot. I even tried the physical-terrain angle. 'We live in the sand, after all,' I said plaintively.

'Bumpers are good in the sand,' my father said. 'Look at those soles, like camels' feet.'

Every Christmas I put in an optimistic request for desert boots. My requests were foolhardy and increasingly provocative. My mother associated desert boots with the vandalism, vulgarity, music and greasy haircuts of 'juvenile delinquents'. My father simply declared, with growing impatience and unarguable logic, 'Dunlop doesn't make desert boots.' Desert boots were made by Clark Rubber. Dunlop made Bumpers. Desert boots were the competition. Desert boots were the enemy.

After five years, aged forty, my father had at last been promoted to State manager. I wouldn't have thought it possible but the promotion had made him even more of a company man, and he and the company sincerely believed that Bumpers were superior to desert boots. When I approached my problem in a roundabout way by suggesting that Dunlop take the plunge and start making desert boots like Clark's, my father shook his head. I was hopelessly misguided. The world of business was not for me.

'Bumpers don't have the bad image of desert boots,' he said reassuringly. He was right.

For some reason he and the Dunlop marketing people thought a wholesome buffoonish image was the smart way of pitching to the adolescent market. Their plan was that Bumpers would bite deeply into the teenage desert-boot market while still satisfying the middle-aged yachting- and golf-shoe market. My father and Dunlop couldn't grasp the essential flaw in their belief that teenage boys aspired to the shoes of their fathers. Maybe even to the slippers of their grandfathers.

I could have warned them this would be the downfall of Bumpers. I could've said I'd never seen another boy wearing Bumpers. I could have challenged my father, mother and the Dunlop board of directors to ask any teenager, especially those who sniggered at my Bumpers at North Cottesloe Beach or at the Claremont, Windsor or Dalkeith picture theatres, whether Bumpers seriously rivalled desert boots. But I didn't. It would have disparaged all those Christmas presents. It would have hurt their feelings. And it would have made my father angry because he made them and sold them.

I couldn't say that unless you thought it suave to have limitless bounce in your step and a safety buffer around each foot, Bumpers had no panache. Or that Bumpers focused undue attention on the feet and dominated the rest of your clothing.

Bumpers resembled Mickey Mouse's shoes. They looked as if you'd inserted your feet in a pair of fairground bumper cars. If I hadn't been wearing them myself *I* would've teased someone wearing Bumpers.

The only apt thing about them was their name. The tragedy was that with soles that thick they were indestructible. There was no escape. You could never move on to a new, Bumper-free life. The only way you could discard a pair of Bumpers was by moving up to another, bigger, pair.

There was another important reason they failed as Christmas gifts. I knew they were just a tick on a docket some-where. No one had actually *shopped* for them, nor had full price been paid. A secretary could fetch a box of Bumpers from the storeroom in five minutes.

To be fair, there was one thing in their favour. They made you two inches taller. For that reason I liked the album pho-tographs of our family taken during a Christmas holiday at Shoalwater Bay. I was about to turn thirteen. I had two favourite before and after shots. In the first, we were all ready for the beach, lined up self-consciously in our beachwear. I was barefoot and my father, who was wearing a pair of strappy leather sandals that embarrassed me, was taller. In the second snap I was dressed up to the nines in that Christmas's pair of Bumpers, my first sports jacket and matching pants. I was smiling down managerially on my father's head.

One Saturday I was caddying for my father at the Cottesloe Golf Club, hauling the Dunlop bag with his Dunlop clubs, Dunlop waterproof windjacket, Dunlop-65 balls and Dunlop golf umbrella. I was wearing my current Bumpers, my sixth or seventh pair, because they would be gentle on the greens. As the afternoon drew slowly on and my interest in the game waned to zero, I was astonished to see two other pairs of Bumpers on the golf course, one on the twelfth fairway, the other on the fifteenth tee, both being worn, apparently willingly, by non-Dunlop personnel or family.

I watched them carefully for as long as I could. Both pairs were the navy blue variety and fitted with golf cleats. I noticed that their owners were well into their forties or fifties: guffawing, big-bottomed business types. My father was also wearing his navy blue Bumpers, so there were four pairs of Bumpers on the course at the same time! I felt like phoning the newspapers.

Mine, however, were the only representatives of the chocolate ersatz-suede, day-and-evening-wear variety. The day was cool and the dew on the fairway soon turned the nap on my Bumpers sleek and black and glistening with what looked like snail mucus.

While I waited in the car for my father and his golfing partners to wind down at the nineteenth hole, I had plenty of time to ponder the effect of dew on artificial suede, and related matters. My Bumpers stayed like that, like wet otter skin, even when they should have dried out. When they were still slimy a week later – as if they had spent much of that time under the house in a bucket of water – I was allowed to throw them away. They were my last pair.

The Bumper Leisure Shoe was just one of the many rubber products that exerted their personality on our family. We wore, played with, slept on, walked on, sat on, floated on, swam in, sheltered under, showered behind, warmed our feet on, and kept our bathwater from going down the plughole with Dunlop products. Naturally, we were conveyed by – in any vehicle you could name – more Dunlop products. I supposed millions of other families were, too, but for them it wasn't compulsory. And I presumed they were blissfully unaware of the fact.

We were a one-hundred-percent Dunlop family. Apart from my Bumper problem I went along with the company all the way. We were mightily impressed by the rubber industry and its offshoots. We were led to believe that everyone else was, too.

As my father liked to declare at drinks parties, when he'd married my mother he'd said to her, 'You know you're marrying Dunlop as well as me.' He'd glance around the group and add self-righteously, 'I said to her, "You know Dunlop will always come first."' The males present, if they were Dunlop employees, nodded sagely over their beers. The women said nothing. My mother gave a faint sociable smile. It was at this time that she taught Junior, our budgerigar, to say, 'Today You'll Use a Dunlop Product.'

We knew that to have Clark desert boots or a Goodyear

tyre or a Spalding tennis ball in your possession, even in your general vicinity, was to commit a crime somewhere between treason and sacrilege. We understood it was disloyal. It breached the faith of my father. We honoured the giant D of the advertisements and the Dunlop colours of yellow and black, selected by Dunlop scientists – my father pointed out – as the most arresting to the human eye.

One day I professed wonder at the huge number of things Dunlop made. 'Gosh, everywhere you look there are rubber goods,' I said.

I thought I was paying my father a compliment. I was surprised at his stern reaction.

'At Dunlop we say "rubber products" not "rubber goods",' he said.

Even things in our house which weren't Dunlop products purposely reminded you of them, especially items to do with drinking and smoking. I thought they were sophisticated and witty. What rakish characters thought up these things? I wondered. What would they think of next?

We had bottle openers, ashtrays, cigarette lighters and drinks trays shaped like miniature tyres, giant golf balls, tiny tennis racquets, little gumboots and tennis shoes and hot-water bottles. We had decks of cards with pictures of Dunlop's Peter Thomson winning the British Open, and Dunlop's stable of tennis players winning Wimbledon and the Davis Cup, and Dunlop's Hubert Opperman winning bicycle races, and Dunlop's Jack Brabham winning the Grand Prix, and other decks of cards, vaguely saucy (and so kept away from children's random glances in a sideboard drawer), of vivacious young women keeping dry in shiny Dunlop rainware.

We had cocktail swizzle sticks designed like little golf clubs (separate woods, irons and a putter), and toothpicks like golf tees, all slotting into a little Dunlop golf bag which was really a martini jug. We had a rubber ice-tray, resembling some sort of invalid's appliance, which froze water into little dimpled golf balls. We had drink coasters like flattened tennis balls, golf balls and the bowls used on bowling greens, and other coasters like bicycle, motorcycle, car, truck, tractor and aircraft tyres. We had a big Dunlop-65 golf ball, hinged in the middle, that opened to display a collection of twelve miniature spirit and liqueur bottles. We had pewter tankards engraved with the names of all the major Dunlop sporting events. And above all these clever party souvenirs the dour, bearded likeness of old John Boyd Dunlop, who invented the pneumatic tyre, grimaced down on us from a shelf collection of beer mugs.

In our house's celebration of rubber and the business world only the small lounge-room bookcase showed evidence of my parents' lives before Dunlop. The top shelf displayed my parents' old school awards: his gold-embossed, leatherbound book prizes from Carey Baptist Grammar School and her plain blue clothbound ones from Frankston High.

My father's prizes, signed by the headmaster, H. G. Steele, MA, had the school badge on the cover, an athlete carrying a torch above the motto *Animo et Fide*. He'd been dux of his class most years from Form IV in 1925, aged eleven (the Oxford edition of *John Falifax, Gentleman* by Dinah Maria Craik), to his final year. In 1927 he'd picked up *The Three Midshipmen* by W. H. G. Kingston. For being dux in 1929, the year the stock-markets crashed, he won *The Romance of Scientific Discovery* by Charles R. Gibson and *Tales of Washington Irving*.

My mother's book prizes, embossed with the Frankston High School badge of a bubble-blowing fish flicking its tail in the air above the motto *Optima Semper*, were *The Plays of J. M. Barrie* and *The Plays of John Galsworthy*. W. J. Bishop, head-master, said inside the cover that Dorothy Watson had been awarded the Citizenship Prize (Gift of The Welfare League) for being school captain.

The top shelf also contained three *Reader's Digest* Condensed Books and the six hardback novels my parents owned (they preferred to borrow best-sellers from the library): *Grand Hotel*, *The Egg and I*, *Doctor in the House*, *Doctor At Large*, *They're a Weird Mob*, and another Australian novel called *Andy*, which I'd care-fully chosen and saved up to buy for my father the Christmas I was eleven because it was about an Australian pilot in the war. I was crushed to overhear him loudly dismiss it as 'just an Australian book – I couldn't get into it'.

Not counting the six volumes of *World War II in Pictures*, the remaining two shelves were all either about Dunlop, sales and marketing techniques, accounting or business management.

The walls told a similar story. Apart from an oil portrait each of my brother and sister (thin, pimply and self-conscious, I'd refused to be painted), the lounge room, dining room, front hall and kitchen all displayed watercolour scenes of the rubber industry.

The framed watercolour prints were my parents' favourite selections from Dunlop calendars over the years. The calendars displayed the works of Australian painters who'd been finalists in the lucrative annual Dunlop art contest. Every year a lot of noted artists delighted the judges by choosing Dunlop's smoky rubber factories at Montague, in Melbourne, and Drummoyne, in Sydney, as their favourite landscapes in the whole continent. This always came as a pleasant surprise to my father. It confirmed his view that 'modern art' couldn't hold a candle to Australian realists.

My parents had both put in time at grimy Montague and come home with black tyre dust on their clothes and, in my mother's case, in her hair. Freshly showered after a Sunday morning's lawn-mowing, beer glass in hand, *Carousel* spinning on the radiogram, my father liked to relax before the roast dinner by humming 'Soliloquy' ('*My boy Bill is as tall and as strong as a tree . . .*') while admiring Bill's and Jan's painted likenesses. Then, stepping back and frowning like a connoisseur at a gallery, he'd contemplate the framed factory chimneys belching into the sky on every wall and say, admiringly, 'You can almost smell the smoke.'

On weekends we were often taken to 'see over the factory' ourselves. This was Dunlop's new West Australian rubber plant, built by my father in the new industrial estate of O'Connor. I found it interesting on the first, and even the second, visit. Quite soon, however, the process from the coagulated milky latex of *gutta-percha* to rubber sheeting was firmly impressed on our minds.

I liked the sweet smell of *gutta-percha*. Its sticky sponginess tempted you to chew it or roll it in a ball and throw it around the factory. You could stretch it into strips like elastic and twang it at each other. But in the end it wasn't edible, and you could only sting each other's legs so many times before someone cried. The latex smell became cloying. It filled your nostrils and then your whole head and you had to run outside into the fresh air.

The Dunlop office was more sedate than the factory. There was nothing to do there but eat biscuits and play with new tennis balls, their yellow nap surprisingly thick and fluffy, provided by Miss Edna Kirwan. She was my father's crisp but kindly secretary, a sturdy, aunt-like figure, fifteen or twenty years older than my father, who wore her hair in a French roll. Miss Kirwan was unlikely to cause a managerial black eye or a heart attack. It was Miss Kirwan, we discovered, who always remembered and bought my mother's birthday, wedding anniversary and Christmas presents.

Unfortunately Miss Kirwan was in hospital for my mother's fortieth birthday so my father forgot it. I remembered her birthday, however, with a tin of MacRobertson's 'Clematis' chocolates with painted purple flowers on the lid. My mother let him suffer for several days while she made a fuss of me. But remembering her birthday did me more harm than good. It sealed my dubious reputation as her gallant young knight.

Dunlop children led busy social lives. At weekends we went on Dunlop picnics and barbecues in the Darling Ranges or we watched Dunlop teams of Alf, Les, Syd, Nev, Stan, Wal,

Alan, Len, Ken and Clarrie playing other firms in sporting events, using Dunlop sports equipment. In one social cricket match, against the Ford Motor Company, Dunlop's spin bowler, my father, injured his knee. He had to have a cartilage operation at St John of God's, arranging with the nuns to keep a supply of cold beer for visitors. The operation wasn't a total success. Thereafter, wounded in Dunlop's service, he walked with a pronounced limp.

The main social occasion was the company's children's Christmas party. Despite the summer heat, it always took place indoors, in the main city showroom at 424 Murray Street. There was no air-conditioning. Rubber fumes rose in waves from the showroom floor and hung over the festivities. To demonstrate the merits of rubber flooring it had been made several times thicker than normal commercial flooring. While it cushioned any pressure, and muffled and absorbed voices and normal office sounds, its sticky surface squelched and peeped at the slightest foot movement. No one could sneak up on you at Dunlop. The showroom floor was like a shifting, rubbery swamp that squeaked a warning before it sucked you under.

This bouncy backdrop compelled us to leap about like spacemen until Santa Claus, played by Dunlop's most rotund executive, Jim Chute, finally arrived, *ho-ho*-ing in his Dunlop industrial workboots. He gave you a present every year until you were twelve. They were proper presents, not rubber products. By the end of the gift-giving all the Dunlop children would be tired of rubber – all of us spread out, red-faced and gasping for air, on the Dunlopillo settees in the reception area – so we appreciated this.

In our own house, of course, Dunlop was ever present. Even when we urinated. Males stood and aimed from two rubber footprints wittily set into the Dunlop bathroom flooring at the approximate average adult firing range. If you were still a child, of course, more often than not you missed and pissed on Dunlop.

Because of their Dunlop connection, and the shortage of social attractions in Perth, famous sportsmen regularly came to our house to eat or, more often, to drink. In a way, Dunlop was like a country. They represented this country in their sport, and my father, as the country's local consul, entertained them at his consulate.

Those tennis players, golfers and racing-car and rally drivers on the payroll, visiting the West to perform with and promote tennis racquets or tyres or automotive products or tennis shoes or golf balls, would sprawl in our lounge room drinking beer in pewter tankards and throwing peanuts into their mouths.

The older ones, especially the golfers and racing-car drivers, would try to flirt with my mother and, in the case of 'Gelignite Jack' Murray, the champion rally driver, simultaneously flirt and explode fireworks in our kitchen. Gelignite Jack had made his name by cheekily lobbing explosives around the countryside during the Redex Round-Australia car reliability trials, and he had a reputation to live up to. Even when he didn't win these rallies he got so much publicity that everyone thought he had. As Gelignite Jack sold many Dunlop tyres, fan belts and batteries in the process, my father chuckled tensely at the flirting and the exploding bungers on the veranda and the catherine-wheel burning the paint off the kitchen door and topped up everyone's drinks.

I was torn. I loved to see these famous adults at close quarters, like newspaper photographs come to life. They were different to the other adults I knew, yet, regardless of their individual sports, very like each other.

I wondered what made them different. I could see that the famous golfers' fingers curled around their drinks were uniformly stubby and thicker than most normal fingers, as if they were all the meaty digits of the same person. And when I passed a plate of bacon crackles to Rod Laver I noticed that while his gingery right wrist was not much thicker than mine, his left was twice as thick. Lew Hoad, meanwhile, had forearms and wrists the size of Popeye's.

They either seemed to be straining on invisible leashes or so relaxed they were almost asleep. I loved to soak up this sporting atmosphere but I hated seeing sportsmen winking and grinning and cracking their knuckles around my mother. I didn't mind them finding her attractive but I disliked them being suggestive. I didn't like their jokes hanging in the air. I wanted them to be polite and chivalrous heroes. I wanted them to look up to her. And I didn't want my father to look bad.

But I took my cue from him, and the high-jinks seemed

tolerable to him. It wasn't as if the flirting sportsman in question was the still lithe and suave Adrian Quist. Within the company their paths crossed constantly but on his many visits to Perth, during which he effortlessly picked up several State singles and doubles titles, Quist was never invited to our house. To the company's delight and my father's annoyance, he'd recently won the Wimbledon doubles again, aged thirty-seven, fifteen years after winning it the first time.

Would he never stop being a hero? My father was still peeved that my mother had kept a racquet that 'Adrian' had personally signed for her, indeed the racquet that had helped Australia win the Davis Cup in 1939. This racquet had trounced the reigning Wimbledon singles champion, Bobby Riggs. My father was happy for me to bash around with it on the street.

When the racquet got chipped on the bitumen and warped from playing French cricket on wet grass, he was good about it. Perhaps surprisingly, so was my mother. She didn't seem to mind at all. So when she mentioned 'Adrian's' latest success in a neutral sort of way, it seemed unnecessary for my father to mutter, 'Little siss!' and to mimic someone prissily combing his hair. It was a bitter gesture which I put down to the sensitive matter of his having no hair himself, except around the edges.

Depending on the specialties of the visiting sportsman, I'd nonchalantly walk into the room swinging a tennis racquet or whatever. I was always optimistic that one of these heroic figures, Lew Hoad, say, or Peter Thomson, would be struck by the coincidence of our shared sporting interest, impressed by the signs of my early promise and praise me generously. This hero was already a guest in our house; there was a good chance we would become friends, I reasoned, and with his encouragement I would rise to the same dizzy sporting heights.

So my fantasy went. But beyond an initial wink, most of them took no notice of me. When we were introduced they shook hands, cracked incomprehensible jokes and turned away. I got their autographs, though. I got the autographs of all the tennis stars, even the non-Dunlop Americans, Pancho Gonzales, Vic Seixas and Tony Trabert. I was a relentless autograph hunter and I followed their careers with keen interest. I was even training my hair into a Kramer cut, the popular hairstyle named after that of the former American tennis champion, Jack Kramer – short on top and swept back at the sides.

One exciting day during the Davis Cup interzone finals my father gave me and Nick Howell tickets to the Players' Lunch at the Adelphi Hotel. We ate in the terse but awe-inspiring company of Rod Laver, Lew Hoad, Ken Rosewall and Roy Emerson. Ted Schroeder, the US team manager and former American player, sat next to me. Businessmen and tennis officials were tucking into jewfish, prawns, crayfish platters and schooners of beer. But none of the players at the Players' Lunch was lunching. They sat around, tense and decorative, sipping orange juice. I was dumbstruck but thrilled. Sitting by himself in the corner of the Adelphi dining room, eating a steak and salad and drinking a big glass of Coke (the first male adult I'd ever seen drinking it), was Jack Kramer.

My eyes settled on this lone figure. Because he was trying to persuade the tennis players to turn professional, none of them could be seen sitting with him. As he was the originator of the Kramer cut, the founder of my very own haircut, I naturally gave his hairstyle the once-over. It was short and brushed neatly forward. It didn't stick up in a rigid flat-top, it lay down. The sides weren't longer and swept briskly back. It was nothing like a Kramer cut! Jack Kramer didn't have a Kramer cut! What was wrong with the world?

But the great Lew Hoad spoke to me this day. Well, not *to* me. *Of* me. After the lunch there were four company cars waiting outside the hotel to ferry the Australian players and sports executives to Royal King Park where they were playing the interzone finals. I had a Dunlop ticket. I was wearing my Bumpers. My father asked Hoad which car he wanted to ride in to the courts.

Lew shrugged. More than ever he looked like Robert Mitchum's sleepier brother. Then he lazily tilted his head in my direction. He said, 'I'll go with Shoes.'

STRANGERS

A stranger showed up in our back yard one day with a shot-gun. Another time one had a tank of poison. It wasn't unusual for a stranger to suddenly appear unannounced. My mother called this 'lurking'. Not surprisingly, she found it threatening. Her 'lurkers' – axe- knife- saw- and scissor-sharpeners, window-cleaners, gardeners, odd-job men, Italian fishermen, Yugoslav vegetable and mushroom growers, manure-men: moody, whiskery, stained and smelly men lump-ing sacks of sheep shit and dripping poultry droppings across the path – often loomed around the corner of the house, tout-ing custom and catching her unawares.

Any man carrying a sack, bin, bucket, spirit-level or tool-box; any man confidently wearing a hat, overalls or a leather apron, could open the back gate, march up the back steps with an air of authority and, in passing, laconically correct the way you were managing your life. By the way, did we realise we'd planted the wrong sort of grass for this soil and climate? What with all the problems his brother-in-law said Ford were having down at the Leighton assembly plant, he'd be buggered if he would've bought a Customline himself.

The sound of a man clearing his throat woke me one winter morning. I heard him spit, then the scrape of his boots and a hissing noise. A high, sweet smell came into the bedroom. I peered out and saw a man crouched in the yard below the window. He looked like a lurker to me. He had a tank strapped to his back and a woollen cap in East Perth football colours pulled down over his ears. He was spraying our back path and stairs with liquid. It was barely dawn and steam was rising from the cold cement where the liquid hit it, and the liquid was running down the stairs and fizzing into the lawn. A vapour mist clung around the man's legs and waist. He frowned up at me and turned back to his spraying.

It was six-thirty. My parents were still asleep. I went outside in my pyjamas and stood there in his vapour. I didn't ask what he was doing but by standing there I was obviously wondering.

After a while he looked up from the mist and said, 'Poisoning Argentine ants, aren't I?'

'Have we got Argentine ants?'

He was spraying so vigorously the poison was splashing as it hit the cement. It was running down the path and pooling under the clothesline and trickling down the stairs into the Doghouse. It smelled like fly spray but sweeter, like DDT mixed with honey. 'Dunno,' he said. 'But I'm spraying for them anyway.'

'What's wrong with Argentine ants?'

'They're against the law. Can't stop to chat. We've got to do every bloody house in town.'

I'd trod on a few ants in my time. I'd even burnt the occasional ant with a magnifying glass out of curiosity. I remembered the little spiral of smoke rising from the squirming body. But I had nothing against ants. I asked him, 'How do you tell an Argentine ant from an ordinary ant?'

He stopped squirting poison for a moment, looked at me and sighed, as if his line of work called for great patience. 'You know when you squash an ant in your fingers it smells like varnish?' He mimed someone doing this.

I nodded.

'Well, an Argentine ant doesn't smell like varnish. It doesn't smell like anything. That's how you tell.'

'Do the ants in our place smell like varnish?' Suddenly I felt quite possessive of our ants. 'I think all of them do smell like varnish.'

'Bugger off, sport,' he said. 'I haven't got time to squash ants.'

The man who burst into our yard with a shotgun was hunting sparrows. This was during the Great Sparrow Panic. There'd been a sparrow sighting reported in our neighbourhood and you couldn't be too careful. He was a Sparrow Ranger from the Agriculture Protection Board and the double-barrelled shotgun made him look very serious.

Sparrow Rangers were allowed to come onto your property and blast away. All they had to do was show their ID and say, 'Official business. I'm hunting sparrows,' and you were supposed to gratefully step aside. That's what he said to my mother while she was hanging up the washing. She laughed at him, then she said, 'I don't want a gun here, thank you.' Anyway, the only bird in our place was Junior the budgerigar so he left.

The State Government, the newspapers, everyone but our family, it seemed, thought this was vital work. The Government declared that Western Australia was the last place on earth apart from the North and South Poles where the sparrow hadn't gained a foothold. Its fear of sparrows was even greater than its fear of Argentine ants. (I never found out why the ants were supposed to be so evil. In any case, despite the ant poison saturating the suburbs, they continued to thrive and the Government eventually gave up the fight.)

Both fears were to do with our isolation. The ants and sparrows were like fruit flies, Ceylon crows and 'conmen' from the 'Eastern States' – that catch-all description for anywhere outside the State border, but especially Sydney or Melbourne. (A car with a distinctive yellow Sydney licence-plate was suspicious enough to be noted by police.) All of them had the potential to make our lives that little bit less harmonious.

West Australians were accustomed to the Nullarbor Plain and the Indian Ocean keeping unpleasantness at bay. Thanks to the desert between us and the rest of the country, and the ocean between us and the rest of the world, there had never been a sparrow in Western Australia. Still, sparrows were at the top of the Agriculture Protection Board's Vermin List. They were an official menace to agriculture, and a potential nuisance to city dwellers because they built their nests in gutters and eaves. They had to be shot on sight.

For once my parents disagreed with the Government. This was remarkable in itself. In our obedient neighbourhood it was almost treachery. My parents reverted to being Victorians. They recalled sparrows hopping around their old streets and parks without their bringing either the city of Melbourne or the State of Victoria's agriculture to its knees.

Over his beer on the evening following the gunman's visit, my father suddenly became quite sentimental about sparrows. 'Cheeky little fellows,' he said. I wondered whether he missed Melbourne. But if nostalgia was driving him, so was territorial instinct. He decided to make a protest to the Government.

First, he tried to drum up a joint complaint with the neighbours. They weren't enthusiastic. 'A bloody nuisance, I agree,' said Bill Stockwell, the dentist, next door. 'But better safe than sorry, eh Roy?'

'By the same token,' said my father, 'what's worse, a sparrow or a public servant with a shotgun?'

Once the Press became stirred up over the 'outbreak', sightings flooded in from all over the State. The 'outbreak' became an 'invasion'. My father began cutting out the newspaper reports and filing them in a manila folder for his protest presentation to the Government. With growing scorn, he read out the latest developments each morning. 'Stop the presses!' he'd say. 'A Fremantle steelworker saw a hen-sparrow eating sandwich crumbs outside his factory canteen. We'll all be ruined!' Next he'd yell, 'Hold the front page! Our steelworker friend has spied a cock-sparrow outside his canteen, pecking at a piece of fruit cake.'

How had the sparrow spotter known their sex? ' "I've seen sparrows before, in England," he reported. "And I know my sparrows." ' Reading this out, my father affected a lugubrious northern English accent and a dark look of suspicion. Armed rangers had hurried to the premises, but although they'd seen many birds in the factory grounds, shot several and scared all the rest away, none was a sparrow. '*Bah goom*, fancy that,' my father said.

The Government was offering rewards for people killing sparrows and Sparrow Rangers were engaged around the clock investigating reports. So far none of the birds had proved to be sparrows. We were delighted. We'd turned into a one-hundred-percent pro-sparrow family. Of an evening we'd spread out the sparrow protest file on the kitchen table and all gather around with newspapers and scissors, laughing at the Government and urging the sparrows on. For once we had something in common: sparrows – or, rather, the complete absence of sparrows.

Although the sparrow file grew thick with news cuttings, the invasion was proving difficult to illustrate. The *West Australian* ran two news photographs of a Mr Healy of East Fremantle. In the first photograph he was pointing at an empty tree where he thought he'd seen a sparrow the day before. He said he'd observed the sparrow in the tree for seven minutes 'before it flew off in a southerly direction'. In the second photograph Mr Healy was pictured pointing in a southerly direction.

My father cut out and filed the photographs of Mr Healy sternly pointing at an empty tree and then at the air. Underneath them he wrote, 'I Rest My Case!'

The Sparrow Panic turned him into a bird lover. He shook his head at the tragedy of all the dead birds piling up in the offices of the Agriculture Protection Board. Shot birds were arriving curled up in shoeboxes and preserve jars. There were heaps of grey whistlers, silvereyes, cuckoo-shrikes, thrushes, finches, flycatchers, shrike-tits, wrens, robins, mudlarks, willy-wagtails, swifts, fantails and honeyeaters. But no sparrows.

A lesser body would have called it quits. The Agriculture Protection Board, however, saw the continued absence of sparrows as proof of the birds' shiftiness as well as their danger to agriculture and domestic guttering. Vigilance must be increased.

The Board decided on a two-pronged attack. Sparrow Ranger Squad Number One was despatched to conduct close surveillance of all suspected sparrow habitats – warehouses, grain stores, railway yards. Squad Number Two was ordered to inspect all ships entering Fremantle harbour from 'sparrow infested areas'. This meant inspecting ships from every port on the planet.

'That'll keep them busy,' said my father.

The Sparrow Panic lasted six months. One dead sparrow was found sealed in a car packing-case which had arrived from England. The Sparrow Rangers never saw one live sparrow.

Everyone but the Agriculture Protection Board soon forgot about the invasion. Even my father's indignation faded. The sparrow protest file lay forgotten in a sideboard drawer until I found it a year later and used it in a geography project. Mr Drake, the geography teacher, failed me. He favoured the Government line on sparrows.

———

The front door was for adult friends of the family, official business or female callers. The back door was for tradesmen and children. From the confident way they acted, it could have been the tradesmen themselves who made the rule. All of them except the butcher, the Watkins man and the Dutch lady baker came to people's back doors.

It would never have occurred to the butcher not to come to the front door: he was a businessman, with two butcher shops. The Watkins man came to the front door because he was middle-aged, wore a tie and was a respectable anachronism, selling from his sedate green van things which people didn't need and which lasted forever: padded coat-hangers and tea-cosies and bottles of vanilla essence.

In hushed tones he spoke the mysterious language of mothers and their products. He was like a mobile church fete. All the women, including my mother, always bought something from the Watkins man, even if it was only a packet of jelly crystals or safety pins.

I was mystified and impressed by the long and serious performances the Watkins man and his customers would act out. 'Anything you need today, madam?' he'd ask. 'Bobby-pins? Hat elastic? Nutmeg?'

The women would rack their brains and finally say, 'Oh, I could do with some cochineal.' And he'd say, 'Blow it! I just sold the last bottle three doors down. Would you like to put in an order?' And they'd say earnestly, 'Yes, I'd better,' and he'd take out his order book from his briefcase and arrange his carbon papers and fasten them securely with a bulldog clip and painstakingly write down their details: Mrs So-and-so, No. 45, Cochineal. And everyone could relax. The cochineal problem was covered.

But it wasn't really. The Watkins man wouldn't be back our way for two or three months. There was no fixed delivery time. If someone needed cochineal at all, they needed it to make pink food in the near future. Anyway, if buying cochineal – or safety pins, or jelly crystals, or a thimble – was a matter of urgency, the shopping centre was only a couple of hundred yards away.

I wondered why the women conspired with the Watkins man's pathetic salesmanship. They had to be humouring him. Perhaps they were pretending they were lonely nineteenth-century farmers' wives living hundreds of miles out in the bush, and the intrepid Watkins man was fording the floodwaters and crossing the desert and climbing the ranges to bring them vital cochineal supplies. Maybe the hopelessness of his endeavours just touched their hearts. Anyway, his business was so eccentric it did quite well.

The women treated the Dutch lady baker with respect, too, considering she was a foreigner and slim-legged and made her bread deliveries wearing short shorts all year round. (Although, being Dutch and fair, and on our side in the war, she was regarded as only semi-foreign.) I admired her after she told me one day about her wartime years. When she was twelve years old, during the Nazi occupation of Holland, she'd crept out every night after curfew, past armed German soldiers, to fossick through garbage heaps for vegetable peelings to feed her family.

'We ate potato peels every night for six months,' she said. They seemed to have done her good. She never stopped running.

She and her husband had bought the bakery in Waratah Avenue. He made the bread and pastries and she did the deliveries. She urged Dutch macaroons and almond pastries on us. I wanted to like her macaroons and pastries because of the Nazis and the potato peels, but even though I kept urging my mother to buy them I thought they tasted strange and I never finished one of them.

When the Dutch lady baker and her husband acquired the bakery business the deal had included the horse and cart. The old draught horse knew the baker's route well but perhaps she didn't know draught horses. One day it went mad at a particular flick of the reins and bolted down the Adelma Road hill, carrying the cart and the Dutch lady baker across Waratah Avenue, and through the window of the grocery store. The horse had to be put down, and she ended up in hospital. When she was better she and her husband sold the bakery, got out of bread deliveries and concentrated on their macaroons. They sold them to people who appreciated them more than I did, and they prospered.

The back door had a sort of tyranny. At the front door the householder was in charge, in a stronger position to decline what was being offered. But the common belief was that locking your doors was ridiculous and showed an untrustworthy, inhospitable nature. It could prevent friends from walking unexpectedly into your home with armfuls of beer.

Not only was the back door never locked, it was rarely closed. Only the swinging fly-wire screen door kept out the world. People appearing at the back door caught the householder unawares, maybe only partly dressed. While the front door was public, the back door was more intimate. The caller was almost over the threshold. A back-door caller couldn't be seen from the street. Any lurker could bowl up to the back door.

The greengrocer was a lurker, but he buttock-bumped the door open with the confident energy of the lover. Wide-bummed and five feet three, with an Errol Flynn pencil-moustache, he bandaged wedges of lemon to his arms and neck to treat his chronic boils, and he lusted after my mother.

I didn't like his chances. He'd stood too close to her for comfort a couple of times, squeezing her hand as she paid for the fruit and vegetables, calling her 'beautiful lady' and brushing his grubby bandage lumps against her.

Fortunately he telegraphed his arrival. Now whenever she heard him grunting up the back steps, wincing as he bumped a boil on the door frame, she dropped what she was doing and broke into a run. I was sent to deal with him and she lay low in the bedroom until he was gone.

I almost felt sorry for him. The proud way he lifted the box of greens from his shoulder and set it down on the kitchen table, it could have been an elk or wildebeest he'd killed himself. He stood there panting, wiping his dripping face on the most convenient of his bandages and waiting with beaming anticipation for something wonderful to happen.

As the seconds ticked by and his spiky breath and body odour filled the kitchen, his smile slowly faded as he realised that the cash in my outstretched hand meant the transaction was over. There would be no appearance today of the desired one.

Lovelorn, he peered abjectly around me into the recesses of the house, craving to enter. 'Again she's not home?' he'd say accusingly. 'Always she's out! I have special present for her of strawberries. She like mushrooms? Rockmelon?' He was desperate now and agitatedly twisting the lemon wedge on the back of his neck. 'Tell me what she like best and I get it! Anything! Tell me and I bring it next week!'

I was quite proud that my mother was attractive to men but one night at Perth's Luna Park it unnerved me, too. We were all enjoying ourselves at the funfair when a young man stepped out of the crowd, touched my mother's shoulder and said, 'If you've already got a fellow it's bad luck for me.'

He was courtly and half-drunk but she was a good sport, laughing and saying, 'Yes, I've got three fellows, and here they are.'

'Well, you're still the best-looking woman in Luna Park, and I'm the best shot. None of these buggers can shoot!' He presented her with the box of chocolates he'd just won at the shooting gallery. 'I want you to have these.'

She smiled blithely. 'Thank you, but I couldn't.'

We ignored him and kept moving. But her declining the chocolates only prolonged his attentions. 'I want you to have them! A girl like you deserves presents. Come with me and I'll show you how to shoot.' I thought: A girl? Doesn't he realise she's getting on?

Our progress was jerky now. He was following us, poking the chocolate box at her and paying her ardent compliments. He was jarring our nerves. Billy looked worried and took her hand.

And now my father turned and took in the young stranger with a quizzical look, as if he were trying to place him. The boy was tall, red-skinned and rangy, with angry acne across his cheekbones, and the look of a farmer or a serviceman in unfamiliar city clothes. My father had a tense half-smile on his face but he was still giving the boy the benefit of the doubt. He said quietly, 'She said she doesn't want them. Thanks, anyway.'

'I'm talking to the young lady, not you,' the boy said.

My father's face went pink. 'But I'm talking to you, son,' he said. His voice was still quiet but his eyes bulged alarmingly.

'My wife's here with her family, trying to have a nice time. Don't spoil it for her.'

The boy was young and big, and in his face you could see his brain ticking over. The cogs were whirring slowly. His jaw clenched and then he gripped the box of chocolates like a weapon. He shifted on his feet while he weighed things up.

Billy whined, 'What's happening? What's gone wrong?'

'Nothing, dear,' my mother said. 'We'll have fun again in a minute.'

The boy blinked and drew a long breath. '*Whew!*' he said. He shook his head as if to clear it. '*Hah!* I get the picture!' He dropped his shoulders, and the chocolate box almost dragged on the ground. 'Sorry to have bothered you, lady. You too, sir.'

'Forget it,' my father said, and moved us off.

'Have a nice evening,' my mother said.

'I don't get down to town much!' The boy's voice trailed after us. 'Still learning the ropes!'

I'd hated him a minute before and now I felt sorry for him.

My feeling about the woman at the bus stop was more complicated. My father was about to drop me off at school one morning on his way to work when he pulled in to a bus stop and picked up a woman. He often stopped to give lifts to people he knew and to friends of mine. Because they'd been expecting a crowded bus, not a comfortable car ride, they were usually pleasantly surprised and grateful.

I thought it was strange this woman didn't seem surprised. She took the lift for granted. I was sitting in the back seat. She gave a small smile as she opened the car door and slid into the front seat beside him. She was buxom and looked quite old to me, but she was probably my parents' age. It was obvious she knew him but they didn't call each other by name and he didn't introduce us.

That evening for some reason I remembered the lift and chattily mentioned it to my mother. I would have forgotten about the woman if it hadn't been for the row that night. He never forgave me.

—

One morning a man I hadn't seen before appeared in our back yard carrying two dining-room chairs and said to me, 'You'll get warts doing that.'

It was the August school holidays and I was kneeling on the back veranda fixing a puncture in my front tyre. (I'd discovered Dunlop bicycle tyres weren't totally invincible.) I had the bike turned upside down, resting on its handlebars and seat. While I was waiting for the rubber-cement to set on the patched tube, I was pumping the bicycle pump against my wrist so it made a squeaky farting noise.

I couldn't understand what he said. I just looked at him, so he said it again. I felt uncomfortable. When I did hear him correctly, I thought: What sort of stupid superstition is that? Warts from a bike pump?

Apparently he worked for Dunlop, and he was smiling, so I couldn't contradict him. Especially because of his appearance and voice. He was about five feet six or seven. He had a harelip and the talking-through-the-nose voice that went with it. You were polite to people who looked like that. No one would have guessed right off he was saying 'warts'. I thought he was saying 'horse'. But then 'warts' wasn't a word you expected to hear from a clear-speaking stranger either.

I pumped out a couple of lesser fart-squeaks on my arm while I considered all this, and then I said, 'I thought it was frogs that gave you warts.' I didn't really think that either.

Was he trying to be funny? He had an odd, half-smiling, half-frowning expression, probably caused by his dark eye-brows almost joining in the middle. 'Don't know about frogs,' he said seriously, 'but a bike pump'll do it.' He trotted nimbly up the stairs in his thin-soled shoes, as soft and as soundless as dancing pumps, and put down the chairs. 'It's the concentrated air pressure on the skin.'

It took me a while to understand that, too.

Then he winked. 'I'm Eric. What do they call you?'

I told him my name and we shook hands. Then he said, 'Back in a sec,' and pattered down the stairs, his wide trouser cuffs flapping. In a minute he returned with another two chairs. 'Phew,' he said. 'Throwing a big dinner party, eh? Where are you off to on the bike?'

'The beach,' I said. Actually, what my friends and I did was ride our bikes up to Stirling Highway, leave them leaning against the fence of Christ Church, and then hitch a ride down the highway to the ocean.

'Which beach?' he asked. The eyebrow and mouth combination was disconcerting. It made his face look apologetic and angry at the same time. I told him North Cottesloe.

'Really?' He looked at me accusingly but still smiling as well. 'That's a Neddies' beach.'

'A what?'

'Where the Nedheads go, the snobs from Nedlands.' Still the smile.

It was just a small ocean beach enclosed by reefs and two wooden ramps, a place to bodysurf. But now I felt uncomfortable that I swam there. I didn't want to do anything snobby or conservative. On the contrary, I was cultivating a rebellious teenage image. I was growing out my Kramer cut. At that moment I was barefoot and wearing tightly pegged jeans with a pink shirt hanging over them.

'It's the closest beach,' I muttered. I was embarrassed and self-conscious, and annoyed that I was.

'Get yourself a motorbike then. Get a Harley like me.'

'Sure.' I hoped it sounded sarcastic. 'I'm thirteen.'

'So?' While he was talking he was taking in his surroundings. We'd finally moved out of Leon Road. On being made State manager my father had bought a block of land in Circe Circle, half a mile away, and built a house. After the crumbling Sefton bungalow my mother was desperate for a 'contemporary home'. Its design had appeared in the architecture section of the *West Australian*. It had pinkish-coloured bricks and a skillion roof and was shaped like an H, with the letter's cross-bar, the veranda terrace where Eric and I were standing now, connecting the living and the sleeping sections of the house. My mother had insisted on big ceiling-to-floor windows.

The boss's house, eh. He looked interested but not overly impressed. It was just a suburban house, built in the modern style. After a moment, he said, 'Scarborough Beach's the best,' and added nonchalantly, 'I'm in the surf club.'

I wasn't too happy with the drift of the conversation although being a 'clubbie', a Scarborough lifesaver, was pretty impressive. The beach was bigger at Scarborough, the surf was better and often more treacherous. That wasn't all. Scarborough was the centre of Perth's teenage myth. It was the home of the legendary Snake Pit, a notorious patch of beach-front cement where older, tougher, more reckless and even more extravagantly dressed teenagers jived to a jukebox. It was where the motorbike gangs congregated at the end of a satis-fying sweep of intimidation along the West Coast Highway or Scarborough Beach Road. Rumours had also filtered down from older boys that it was the best pickup place in the whole city.

Naturally the only time I'd seen the teenage-evil side of Scarborough was in the embarrassing company of my mother. During a hot Sunday drive we'd gone into a barn-like milk bar on the beachfront for drinks and icecreams. Inside, a chunky lout was amusing his cronies, impressing girls and outraging older customers by sauntering among them while combing his hair and repeating in a falsetto voice, 'Rape! Rape!'

118

The word was like an electric shock. I couldn't believe someone was saying 'rape' in public or that I'd heard it in the company of my mother. I hadn't got over seeing the word in print – in my friend Stephen 'Sten' Gunn's father's law books. When Sten's parents were out we pored over them, searching for real-life sex crimes. You had to wade through a lot of boring pages about torts and jurisprudence but now and then there was a payoff.

Astonishing as it seemed, we discovered that women were occasionally convicted of sexually assaulting teenage boys. (We shook our heads in disbelief. *The boys complained?*) And, according to some judge or other, thirteen-year-old boys were too young to be charged with rape. Interesting stuff, although Sten and I were mildly indignant – and personally flattered – at this particular legal decision. We were thirteen. And, boy, were we technically convictable, we told each other.

The boy in the milk bar had more words in him yet. 'Breast!' he said loudly. *'Breassst!'* His hair was thickly oiled and he tousled the front of it so it fell down over his forehead and then he looked up through the greasy curls and brayed, *'Raaape! Breassst! Sexsss!'*

I was in awe of his mad confidence. How could those loaded words be flying around the room without something drastic happening – his instant arrest or the immediate closure of the milk bar? When he'd finished saying them they didn't go away. They had so much thick, sly power they hung in the air like dog farts.

'See what I mean?' my mother muttered, her lips tight, as we fronted the counter. 'Did you see?'

What I could see, through a smoky haze, was tough youths with greased hair and girls indeed with breasts, breasts so pointed they might have had pencils in their bras, all smoking cigarettes and slurping milkshakes. They were also belching competitively like eight-year-olds, shoplifting chocolates, mock-punching, swearing profusely, pawing each other exhibitionistically, jigging to the jukebox and shoving forward to the counter so they could hoot orders to the harassed proprietor.

'What?' I said. The din was incredible. I couldn't credit that I was with my mother in this place. The air stank of body odour, hair oil and sex – smells of danger and excitement. I was self-conscious, embarrassed and generally awestruck. I stared straight ahead and for the first time in my life hoped I looked younger than my age. A welcome thought from primary school flashed back: *No one hits you if you're with your mother.*

'That boy is wearing desert boots,' she said. She rested her case.

For some reason I wanted to regain lost ground now. I wanted to impress Eric the Scarborough lifesaver. 'I'm going for my bronze next year,' I blurted. I was a good enough swimmer for the surf swim but you had to turn fourteen to be eligible to be tested for your bronze lifesaving medallion. 'I've done the drills.'

'That so?' He eyed me up and down. I was taller than he was, but I was skinnier. He'd rolled up his sleeves; his forearms and biceps had mature muscles. He must have been in his late twenties, older than the run-of-the-mill Scarborough bad boys. And, in those elastic-sided shoes and flapping cuffs, a laughably out-of-date dresser. He didn't seem to care. 'Well, well,' he said. 'Hope I'm never drowning. Just joking.'

It was on his third journey up the stairs that he gave my shirt the once-over. It was an old business shirt of my father's, previously white and now dyed shocking-pink. I'd concentrated the dye so it was almost fluorescent. The shirt swam on me; the shirt-tail nearly touched the backs of my knees. My father had said, disapprovingly, 'He looks like a lampshade.' Nevertheless until this moment I'd thought that wearing a billowing hotter-than-pink shirt was a good idea. It was the fashion, the popular rebellious colour. It was the look I was after.

'Fill me in, boss,' he said, confidingly, setting down the chairs. 'What's the deal with the shirt? Are you a commo or what?'

I could feel my face go hot. I felt young and dopey. I thought: You don't look big enough to be a Scarborough life-saver, but I didn't say it. I muttered, 'It's just a shirt.'

He blinked, or maybe it was another wink. 'I don't suppose you could spare a glass of water?' he said.

When I came back with the water he was sitting on my bike although I hadn't replaced the wheel yet. He'd turned it right side up, so it was resting on the front forks. He was straddling it and gripping the handlebars. '*Vroom, vroom,*' he said. 'Here I come. Look out, you little North Cottesloe molls!'

'You'll break it!'

'I'm not putting any weight on it. What do you call this flash sort of bike anyway?'

That uncomfortable feeling again. 'A dirt-tracker.'

'*Very* fancy.'

'I saved up for it.' I wished I hadn't said that. It sounded childish and conscientious. It had taken me two years to save the money for the bike. I suddenly felt differently about it.

He arched an eyebrow. 'Good boy.' He swung himself off the bike and turned it upside down again. He spun the back wheel. 'See you, boss,' he said, and scampered down the stairs.

I watched him go around the side of the house. The yellow-and-black Dunlop truck was too wide for our driveway, and he'd parked it hard up against some of my mother's shrubs.

He had to leap up to get into the cabin. The driveway was uphill to the street and when he reversed he revved the engine and spun the wheels and gravel flew up. He was steering while hanging half out the door to see behind him, and the open door stripped branches from the oleander and bottlebrush. When he swung the truck out onto Circe Circle it left tyre tracks in the lawn. I could see the trademark Dunlop tread in the flattened grass.

After that I saw Eric about once a month. When he wasn't delivering something to our house he was taking something away. My father used to pay the neighbourhood kids for every old car battery they found. Eric would take the batteries back to Dunlop HQ where they re-used some vital part of them. I didn't know which part; once I'd got my cash I couldn't have been less interested in car batteries.

It wasn't the most taxing collection job in the world; some weeks there were only four or five batteries to pick up. Eric would stretch out the time, have a yarn. One afternoon I was practising hockey, shooting for goal. 'Let's have a go,' he said. I handed him the stick and he dexterously spun around, backhanded the ball through my legs and flicked it into the goals. He was good and I said so.

'A-grade,' he said. 'Could've played State, maybe national, but the surf club took up too much time.' Then he skipped off. He liked to leave on an upward note.

The dining chairs Eric had been delivering were for the dinner party that evening for Mr Blackwood, my father's boss from Melbourne. The chairs were old ones re-upholstered for the occasion with Dunlopillo, for maximum seating comfort.

I thought about how Eric and Mr Blackwood were at precisely the opposite ends of the Dunlop spectrum. Eric was a relief delivery driver in the company's most remote branch office. Mr Blackwood was the managing director.

Eric had come around the back of the house. Mr Blackwood was ushered through the front door by my father. In the hallway my mother said, 'How nice to see you,' and he kissed her cheek. After they'd had drinks, as my father showed Mr Blackwood to his seat at the table, I remembered Eric delivering it that morning and thought how the biggest boss and the lowest employee were linked by that chair.

It was a coincidence that both of them talked to me about the beach. Mr Blackwood said to me, 'I hear you're a man after my own heart.' Was I? 'Interested in the seashore,' he said.

'Oh, yes.' I didn't know what I was letting myself in for.

'Excellent. Your dad says you can show me some intertidal platforms.' I could? 'Reefs.'

Mr Blackwood's first name was Robert. When my father was referring to him during company business he called him R. B., but in conversation he called him Bob. He was the big boss but he wasn't the sort of businessman I was used to seeing. He wasn't loud and bossy, he didn't smoke cigarettes and he toyed politely with his drink. He wore rimless glasses, smoked a pipe and knew the names of twenty kinds of limpet. He was the first intellectual I'd ever met.

When bigshots came across the country to inspect their western territory and address the troops my father wined and dined them. He'd give a cocktail party and dinner at the Esplanade Hotel. On another night there would be the dinner party at our house. Sometimes he'd also organise a golf day at the Cottesloe Golf Club or, in summer, an evening's sailing on the river.

Bob Blackwood didn't want to play golf or go sailing. He'd been plucked out of Melbourne University to be Dunlop's boss, and his manner was solemn and thoughtful. What he wanted to do after hours was roll up his trousers and paddle along the seashore.

At the end of his first day in town, my father came home shaking his head in a bemused way. He poured a beer for my mother and himself, sat down on the back steps, took off his black shoes, and shook the sand from them and from his trouser cuffs. His feet looked oddly naked poking out from his suit pants. I'd never seen him sitting on the steps either. We all

124

looked at him. He sipped his beer. Finally he said to my mother, 'I know something you don't.'

'I'll bite,' she said.

'I know the difference between a western noddiwink and a checkered australwink,' he said. He'd been rehearsing this. 'And between a stripe-mouthed conniwink and a furrowed clusterwink.'

He took another sip of beer and wiggled his toes. He was enjoying himself. 'I've been paddling in the sea with Bob Blackwood. His latest craze is shell-collecting.' He laughed. 'Our branch is in his good books because we've got different shells than he's used to.'

My mother smiled. My little sister toddled up behind my father and patted his head.

'And here's my little kiddiwink,' my father said and swung her on his knee.

The big boss's new sea-shell obsession was already the cause of much secret merriment at Dunlop. My father had no intention of carrying his shell bucket a second time, so he volunteered my services. The following early evening Mr Blackwood and I went wading over the Cottesloe reefs at low tide.

Although I spent every spare moment at the beach, I'd never given much thought to shells. I regarded them as better looking gravel. Mr Blackwood had on his baggy shell-collecting shorts. He stooped down and pointed at a shell. 'Do you know what that is?'

I knew the names of about six shellfish – barnacles, oysters, clams, mussels, abalone, limpets. 'A limpet?'

'Correct. There are twenty types of limpets on the Australian coast,' he said. This seemed a lot to me. On the rocks at Cottesloe he pointed out three kinds: giant, banded and flamed limpets.

Mr Blackwood certainly knew his limpets. It was sort of interesting. I hadn't given a limpet a second's thought in my life. I'd never considered them as crawling animals and, what's more, crawling animals with a homing instinct. I found older people's enthusiasm quite contagious when they knew what they were talking about. But as we splashed and slipped about, and he kept going on about limpets, I fell into the sort of information daze that would creep up on me in school.

The limestone rocks here were either jagged and sharp, or flat and slimy with weed. My soles were used to them but I still had to pick my way gingerly across the reef. His middle-aged white feet and ankles were already scraped but he was too overcome with limpet fever to notice that a big toe was bleeding.

In his quiet voice he counted off the twenty types of limpets. He generously left their Latin names out of it. There were keyhole limpets and scaly limpets, star limpets and rainbow limpets. There were limpets named after the limpet lovers who had discovered them. There was even one called a cryptic limpet.

I was surprised there wasn't a Blackwood limpet. I would have been hearing about limpets until Christmas but just then I saw two girls walking along the shore towards us, heads together and arms gesticulating.

126

In the way that a certain type of boy in Aircraft Recognition class in the Air Training Corps at school could recognise the silhouettes of Lancasters and Wirraways and Vampires, I knew and could recognise the outlines of most of the girls I lusted after.

I knew the silhouettes of their particular curves and angles and faces and breasts and legs, and I recognised their swimsuits. They were fixed in my brain. These two girls were Ada and Lola, two legendary beauties. I couldn't let them see Mr Blackwood and me. I couldn't let these girls to whom I had never spoken, and who would look right through me in any case, see me (a) shell-collecting, and (b) in the company of a white-legged senior citizen.

I was desperate. I pointed urgently out to sea and frowned. 'Big evening tide coming in, Mr Blackwood. The tides come in fast around here.'

I didn't wait for him to disagree. I turned and began to hurry back over the reef to the beach. I held the shell bucket against my leg, on the side away from the approaching girls. In my haste, important limpet samples scattered and were in danger of being washed away but I didn't stop to pick them up. The girls, skylarking in the sand, bouncing and jostling each other, came ever closer.

I knew I was brutally ending the only acquaintanceship with an intellectual I'd probably ever have. And he was my father's boss.

'We'd better hurry,' I called back to him.

PROWLER

My mother was lying in bed reading *Peyton Place*. Her friends had been making sly cracks about the book for months so she'd ordered it from the library. It was so notorious and popular that it had taken a while for a library copy to become available. The tale of life behind closed doors in a frosty New England town seemed to have touched a chord in this sandy West Australian town.

I was reading it myself, too, but secretly, making sure I returned it to her bedside table in the same position and with the jacket flap turned to the right page. In this way, perched on the edge of the double bed, ears cocked for approaching footsteps, I'd recently read the 'adult' best-sellers *From Here to Eternity*, *Moulin Rouge* and *Not as a Stranger*, and was still contemplating the vivid images they'd etched in my brain, especially those conjured up by the phrase 'mysterious black triangles' in the brothel scene in *From Here to Eternity*.

It was late at night when my mother was engrossed in the

scandalous lives of ordinary people in *Peyton Place*. She didn't know what made her suddenly look up. It wasn't a noise, more an uneasy sensation. She glanced up and saw an eye at the edge of the bedroom window, watching her through the space where the side of the venetians stood out from the glass.

My father was a thousand miles away, on his annual north-west trip. For six weeks every winter, when the far north-west of the State was warm and dry and the previous summer's tropical cyclones just a memory, he travelled up the coast in one of the State Shipping Service's cargo vessels, calling in at all ports to Wyndham or Darwin, flying the Dunlop flag and taking orders for Dunlop products.

He loved this trip. He relished the hard-drinking hospitality of the north-west. He came back brown and sleek with tales of Dunlop adventures: of crocodiles chasing golfers on mudflat courses and people playing tennis on courts made of flattened antbeds and of finding entire stocks of the company's truck tyres eaten by termites.

He sailed so far north that three other countries, Portuguese Timor, Indonesia and New Guinea, were closer than his office in Perth. He was barely in Australian waters. He was in exotic-sounding places like the Joseph Bonaparte Gulf and the Arafura Sea. My mother couldn't remember which tropical spot he was in at the moment. But the prowler was standing in the front garden.

She could see only this single eye but she felt the prowler was smirking at her. The eye was dark and glinting with interest. It was – she thought, she couldn't be sure – familiar. The eye didn't move for what seemed like many minutes, taking her in, savouring the sight of her in her nightdress, while she stared back, shocked and unbelieving.

She was scared but she was also annoyed. The north-west trip was a peaceful time for us left at home. No one ever said so but the house was much calmer when my father sailed north. Life was less dramatic and emotional. It was like a holiday, and now that serenity was shattered.

The thought also struck her that for the prowler to be looking into the bedroom at that angle he must be standing on the flower bed, crushing her camellias, which were already languishing. She jumped up and shouted, 'Go away! I'm calling the police!'

When she leapt from the bed the face vanished from the window. She said to herself, I mustn't panic, and she acted out a little performance while she ran around the house, switching on the lights and checking the locks on the doors and windows and shutting the doors of the children's rooms.

'I'm getting my husband!' she said, for the prowler's benefit. 'Dear! Wake up! Come here quickly!' Of course he was in Broome or Wyndham or somewhere tropical. And she didn't want to make too much noise and frighten the children. Then she phoned the police.

She didn't tell me about the prowler until the next morning. 'Why didn't you wake me?' I said.

'You might have been hurt. Anyway, he was gone by then.'

She shivered. I looked to see if she'd been crying. She looked drawn but calm.

'The police came and drove around the block once or twice. They told me to leave all the lights on and make a cup of tea. They said he'd be miles away.'

'Did you give them a description? What did he look like?'

She seemed slightly embarrassed. 'All I saw was one eye. I told the police it looked . . . knowing. And sort of amused.' She shivered again.

Knowing? Amused? 'They said, "Not too much to go on, is it madam?"'

BURNING THE *MIRROR*

It was late on a breezy Saturday afternoon in autumn and my father was prowling the front garden. He glared at the hibiscus and oleander bushes and snapped off an occasional dead branch. He glowered at fallen leaves and poked at the sandy patches in the lawn where the superfine couch grass had refused to mesh with the regular couch grass as it was supposed to. But his mind didn't seem to be on the garden.

I was sitting on the front steps convalescing, chewing a gumtree twig and patting the dog. Now and then my father gave me a sideways frown as if to say, *Son, why are you hanging around? Go inside.* But he didn't say anything, and I knew he wouldn't.

I wasn't long out of the Lucknow Hospital's isolation ward, recovering from meningitis. Only a month before I'd been struck rigid and barely conscious from inflamed membranes of my brain and spinal cord. I was screaming with the head pain. My head wouldn't move on my neck. Boiling brain had finally got me.

The family doctor, Dr Owen Synott, had diagnosed influenza. Just in time he'd been countermanded by a second opinion, a lumbar puncture and the quick administering of sulpha drugs.

Now my parents' guilt gave me considerable leeway, at least for the moment. I was supposed to take it easy for a few months. If I wanted to sit on the step, I sat.

I stayed sitting there, tickling Shandy and rolling the chewed twig around in my mouth. I didn't particularly enjoy the taste of bark and eucalyptus but I didn't dislike it enough to spit it out. Now and then I stroked the downy moustache which had miraculously happened, along with the three-inch growth spurt and the big weight loss, in the six weeks I was sick. I was bored but also quite relishing the boredom. I was pale, gaunt, taller, moustached and glad to be home. And I had nothing better to do.

The drama of the illness and my absence from home had given the front garden an aura of novelty. While I was in hospital the seasons had changed, too. Familiar objects, angles and shadows had shifted position. Everything was more sharply defined. The garden and the house looked different to me. I looked different to me. And my father wasn't himself either.

His nervy pacing was making me curious. Ten or fifteen minutes had gone by and he still hadn't said anything. He kept strolling up and down, and now he studiously examined tree bark for borers and tugged runaway strands of couch grass from the garden bed.

After a few more minutes of grass-pulling he sighed and squatted down on the grass verge and half-turned towards the road. He took out his packet of Turf, stared intently into the packet, as if cigarettes came in a varied assortment like Black Magic chocolates, and slowly selected one. Staring into the distance, he tapped it on the packet. *His tapping habit.* He always tapped his cigarettes long enough to drive you nearly crazy, but not usually for this long. He tapped it and kept tapping. The tapping was supposed to pack in any loose strands of tobacco, but I couldn't remember any of the Turf corktips that I'd surreptitiously smoked ever shedding that much tobacco.

No one, I thought now, would keep tapping a cigarette like that unless it was a nervous habit or they thought they looked clever doing it. It was interesting when you looked at it like that.

Before I was sick the cigarette tapping had grated as much as him saying *blah, blah, blah* at the end of a sentence, as if the subject was too boring to pursue. In the past year or so he'd introduced *blah, blah, blah* into his selection of favourite sayings, like *by the same token* and *for crying out loud* and, if we had company and he wanted to sound important, *to cut a long story short*.

In the beginning he'd actually used *blah, blah, blah* to cut his long stories short. But soon he seemed to enjoy finishing nearly all his sentences with it, even short ones. He'd say, 'I've had it up to here with the tyre retailers and all that blah, blah, blah,' or, more confusingly, 'I'm a full bottle on all that blah, blah, blah.' It was like another language and it was contagious. We all picked it up. At the dinner table we'd say, 'Pass me the butter and the blah, blah, blah.'

He seemed impatient with the world, as if he were standing in line and everyone and everything was keeping him waiting. When he was testy and explosive he was a dead ringer for Fred Clark in *The Solid Gold Cadillac* and *Don't Go Near the Water*. Fred Clark always played assertive bald-domed businessmen and politicians with short fuses. Lately he seemed to be in every comedy ever made. I'd squirm when I saw the name Fred Clark come up in the credits. I wasn't the only one who saw the similarity. At the pictures Nick Howell would dig me in the ribs and say, 'Hey, there's your old man again!'

Now as far as I was concerned – and that was strange, too – he could tap cigarettes and say *blah, blah, blah* from dawn till dusk and it wouldn't worry me. I felt magnanimous. Dr Synott's wrong diagnosis and the pain and being rigid were only part of it. The thing was, I'd been sick for two days before my parents had even called the doctor. They'd thought my sudden weakness and severe headache coincided too neatly with my mid-year exams. Now they were feeling so guilty and I had so many credits stored up I felt at peace with the world.

Eventually he stopped tapping and took out his old Ronson and lit the cigarette. Before putting the lighter back in his pocket he snapped it open and shut a few times and examined it carefully as if he'd just got it for Christmas. Then he adjusted his haunches into a new squatting position, leaning his right elbow on his knee to steady himself, and drew on the cigarette. The careful, frowning way he smoked it, you'd have thought he was new to it. You wouldn't have guessed he smoked sixty a day or that he bought his cigarettes not by the packet but a dozen cartons at a time.

He blew smoke self-consciously into the breeze and removed a speck of tobacco from his tongue (even after all that tapping!) and flicked his ash on the lawn. He coughed and cleared his throat right down to the bottom of his lungs, like he did first thing every morning, and then he hawked and spat heavily into the garden bed. He looked at his watch and he looked distractedly up the road again and got to his feet.

Nonchalantly, he began patrolling the grass on the edge of the road, gradually extending the territory under patrol. Soon he was pacing not just our front border but also the boundaries of our next-door neighbours, the Stockwells and the Dolans, on either side. Grimacing with distaste, he kicked a dry dog turd off the Stockwells' buffalo grass into the gutter and gave Shandy a glare. Sighing, he bent down and began plucking stray dandelions and onionweeds from all three verges and throwing the weeds into the street.

I wondered what had got into him while I was in hospital. I also wondered why, even while he paced and tidied and gardened so intently, he kept himself positioned between me and the road.

His community lawn patrol was making me more and more curious. It was enough of a surprise just to see him outside. Apart from Sundays, he didn't often appear outdoors. Sunday morning was official gardening duty, an activity involving the compulsory donning of his old airforce khaki shirt and trousers which showed no signs of ever wearing out.

Otherwise outdoors was considered kid territory. He wasn't the sort of father who threw balls in the yard. Apart from Sunday morning gardening, only once a year did he stay out-doors for more than a few minutes and look calm and happy. This was when he organised my little sister Janet's birthday party in the garden. He directed her party games – the treasure hunts, the pin-the-tail-on-the-donkey, the oranges-and-lemons – with rare patience and good humour.

But this evening, with dusk approaching, there was an urgency in his eyes and movements. He constantly glanced up the hill. He was marking time while he waited for someone or something. Who or what?

Just then I began to smell something burning. I wasn't sure if it was a fire or just me. Since the meningitis I sometimes smelled a graphite smell high in my head. I associated it with electrodes on my scalp and temples, a sensation of flickering lights and a feeling of nausea. The smell and the nausea still returned when I was near fluorescent lights or glaring white sand. Unless I moved away I vomited. They'd even come back the week before when I was watering the garden and staring vacantly at a bed of white daisies. I hoped my brain would sort it out by next summer or the beach would be a big problem. I couldn't let myself think about my brain too much.

A moment later, however, a stream of smoke and sparks gusted past the front of the house. The incinerator at the bot-tom of the back yard was alight. Apparently my father had lit the incinerator and left it burning while he patrolled the front garden. The incinerator was burning briskly.

I was about to ask him if he wanted me to check the incinerator (they would be the first words from either of us for the past half-hour) when a green Austin convertible came down the hill and slowed as it approached our house.

It was the newsagent. The car slowed without coming to a stop, and with his sideways-overarm throw the newsagent flung a newspaper – thin, tightly rolled and bent like a boomerang – up and over his car and over the width of the road and into our garden.

Suddenly the schoolboy high-jumper and footballer he'd once been, my father sprang into the air, an athletic feat I'd never have guessed at, and snatched the newspaper with an outstretched hand. Still on the move, he unfurled the paper and began reading it while he strode across the lawn, around the corner of the house, down the side and into the back yard.

Normally, I wouldn't have dared to be so obviously nosy but I followed him. For three or four minutes he circled the incinerator, reading avidly while he walked and squinted in the fading light, turning the pages hurriedly and never quite coming to a halt or acknowledging I was there. Then he got to the back page, quickly scanned it and dropped the newspaper in the fire.

It was the *Mirror*, the local Saturday sex-and-scandal sheet. The *Mirror* was the only paper that published details of brothel raids and divorce-court proceedings, indeed the only one that printed the words 'prostitute' and 'brothel' and 'co-respondent'. Women and decent people didn't read the *Mirror*. It was never seen in our house.

I stood by the back gate and watched the rising glow of the firelight on my father's scalp as he stoked the incinerator. The *Mirror* had only about twenty pages and the flames jumped up quickly.

There wasn't enough time for my brain to begin to react badly to the flickering. The paper took only a couple of minutes to burn but he stayed by the incinerator, prodding and turning the ashes, until it was dark and I'd gone inside.

THE MORAL AGENT

One morning on Rottnest Island I walked down to the bakery at six o'clock to buy fresh bread and some of the bakery's famous jam doughnuts. In the job roster at the holiday cottage the bread run was my responsibility. You had to get to the bakery before the rush. The fresh loaves lasted until about nine, but the warm jam doughnuts were so delicious they quickly sold out. Despite the necessary early rising – my friends were happy to do the general shopping, washing-up, cooking, cleaning and sweeping in the heat of the day, anything but get up that early – I liked the job.

I enjoyed the quiet walk down to the settlement under the Moreton Bay fig trees lining Thomson Bay. The yeasty smell of the squashed figs under the trees, the salty air of the early summer morning, the overnight coolness still in the sand, even the jarring cries of the crows and squabbling seagulls, charged the day with promise.

When I reached the bakery, the door was open but the

bread-shop section in the front was empty. I could smell the freshly baked bread and the cakes and pastries and I could hear people moving and bumping about near the ovens in the back. I called, 'Hello, there!' but no one answered. A puff of warm floury air drifted out of the bakery into the shop.

I walked behind the counter and peered into the bakery. There was a disturbance in there, in the hot, sweet air. Utensils were clattering and clouds of flour were billowing. Something metallic fell with a clang on the floor. At first I thought it was a fight. A ghostly white figure was straddling another ghostly white figure.

The one-armed girl who helped in the bakery was lying on a table covered in flour. Her white legs were up in the air and the baker was riding her. Or was she riding him? Anyway, they looked uncomfortable and strangely menacing rattling away. They still wore their bakery hats – not chef-type high hats, more like shower caps – and puffs of flour rose as they rode and rocked. Although they were caked white, occasional patches of pink skin screamed out. Against their floury faces their teeth were yellow grimaces. The flour was making their breath wheeze and rasp, but not enough to make them stop what they were doing.

The baker's back was turned but the girl saw me. She didn't stop when our eyes met, however, or indicate to the baker that someone was there. She closed her eyes and shut me out and hugged him tighter to her with her good arm and her stump.

I left the bakery then and went and sat on the seawall nearby and stared out at Thomson Bay. I had a lot to think about. The sun was still low in the east over the mainland. The coastline of Australia was just a thin straight line of yellow light. The only part that stood out was the dark clump of pine trees at Cottesloe. For a few minutes as I sat there I felt as alone as a shipwrecked sailor in a desert island cartoon. I watched a man purposefully rowing a dinghy out to a yacht. He was rowing to the same rhythm as the bakery ghosts.

Half an hour later, when I thought things might be back to normal, I returned and bought my three poppyseed loaves and dozen doughnuts. The door between the bread shop and the bakery was closed and I was served by an older woman with two arms. Our transaction was the same as every morning. I searched her face for some hint of the goings-on in the bakery but it was as expressionless as a cottage loaf. You'd think I'd dreamed everything. I carried the bread back to the cottage and waited for Sten and Dogs to wake up so I could tell them about it. I'd never seen the sex act before. It was even more dramatic than I'd expected.

I loved the smell of ripe Moreton Bay figs on Rottnest Island because they made me think of sex. To a greater or lesser degree, everything to do with the island made me think of sex. Long before the episode in the bakery, any passing mention of the name 'Rottnest' made me think of sex.

This wasn't just my reaction. Everyone I knew associated Rottnest with sex. Just mention the name of this little lime-stone-and-coral outcrop nestling on the horizon and people either winked or looked nostalgic. Or, in my parents' case, disconcerted and suspicious. Rottnest was legendary. Only thirteen miles off the coast, it could have been thirteen hundred miles away. It might have been passed over by the old Dutch explorers, then the French and the English, but now it had a reputation as the most relaxed and seductive place anywhere. People – well, girls – were supposed to do things which on the straitlaced mainland would give them a 'bad name'. Rottnest was different. It was where West Australians lost their virginity.

There was a strange irony in this. The holiday spot had a long dark past as a Devil's Island. It had been a prison and a concentration camp. Its original role wasn't exactly trumpeted by the tourist authorities. But my hosts, Gordon and Irene Schwabb, knew the place intimately and were authorities on its history. They pointed out the old gaol block and warders' houses. They knew where the bodies were buried – Aboriginal bodies. They said proudly that our cottage, overlooking the sea at Thomson Bay, was named Vincent Cottage, after Henry Vincent, the one-eyed Battle of Waterloo veteran who was superintendent of the Aboriginal Penal Establishment for thirty years.

Vincent was something of a Rottnest hero. 'Oh, yes, he lived here,' said Irene Schwabb. 'We get his cottage every year.'

According to Gordon Schwabb, Vincent was a 'no-nonsense

sort of character'. He was suspected of killing some of his prisoners. Others who misbehaved had their ears ripped off. He fed them all on cabbage leaves, quokkas, rice and seaweed boiled up together. 'But he got things done,' Mr Schwabb said.

The Schwabbs knew their island lore. At the meal table they liked to recite the name of every bay and inlet on the island. They worked their way around anti-clockwise, loudly correcting each other if they missed one. When they were done, they named all the lakes and hills. This litany took about five minutes and when they were finished they looked very pleased with themselves.

They were very proprietorial about these places. 'I noticed Coke bottles at Geordie Bay today,' one of them would announce solemnly. Or, 'I spotted six day-trippers at Little Parakeet. I wonder what they were up to?' It was important to display their island knowhow to their guests. I didn't mind. There was a status in knowing these things, in being seen as 'an old "Rotto" hand'.

The early English colonists had thought the island the ideal place to exile troublesome blacks. Then it had doubled as a boys' reformatory. In the early nineteen-hundreds it had been turned over to public recreation and vice-regal shooting parties, but World War One saw it become an alien internment camp for Germans, Austrians and Middle Europeans. The same thing in World War Two: Germans, Italians and Japanese were interned. For more than a century people of various ages and races had been imprisoned there.

Now it was promoted by the State tourist bureau as 'The

Isle of Girls', the most fancy-free place in the country. My parents certainly believed it. They'd never even allowed me to make a day trip on the ferry. Without giving any reasons – and they'd never set foot on the island themselves – they implied I'd get a bad name the moment I stepped off the gangplank.

I couldn't wait. But with their views on bad-name getting, I hadn't expected to see the island's white sands and crystal lagoons, not to mention its easygoing girls, much before twenty-one.

My hopes didn't rise when the Schwabbs invited me and four other friends of their daughter Wendy to stay with them in the cottage they'd rented for a fortnight in January. Everyone else's parents agreed. Mine said no. So what else was new? It was hardly worth it, but I went through the motions.

'Why not? What could possibly happen?' I wheedled, straight-faced.

'Rottnest's got a bad name,' my mother said.

I didn't expect them to give in. But the Schwabbs had a word to them. They impressed on them the high standards required of their teenage guests. No alcohol, of course. We'd have to share chores and earn our holiday. It went without saying the sleeping arrangements would be above board – girls at one end of the cottage, boys at the other.

I couldn't believe it when my parents gave in. They drove me to the ferry wharf at Fremantle and saw us off on the *Islander*. My mother gave the girls the once-over, but she farewelled me with good grace. As the *Islander* headed out of the harbour into a choppy southerly swell I couldn't have been more excited if I'd been sailing off in the same direction to Africa or Europe. Three hours later I was on Rottnest Island kissing Suzette Minchin.

Suzette and I had been viewing the sunset from Vlamingh's Lookout. This was a traditional thing to do and I was happy to observe all the Rottnest traditions. Indeed, I craved to observe them. The lookout was named after the Dutch explorer who'd landed on the island in 1697. Willem de Vlamingh hadn't stayed long. He'd thought the island was infested with rats, so he named it Rat's Nest. The little animals were actually marsupials called quokkas, tirelessly scavenging members of the kangaroo family. Though looking a little moth-eaten three centuries later, the quokkas were still in residence. In fact, they were nibbling and fossicking around us right now.

Poor Suzette had been seasick on the ferry trip across, spewing helplessly over the rail while the rest of us rushed to the other side of the boat. But once the *Islander* was in the lee of the island her colour had come back, and by the time we berthed she was looking her usual sulky, healthy self. A couple of hours had passed. We'd unpacked, settled in to the cottage and had a meal. We'd all set off on an after-dinner stroll, and somehow managed to split up into couples. Suzette and I hadn't exactly gravitated to each other, but Wendy Schwabb was keen on Ross Woolhouse (known, for some long-forgotten reason, as Dogs) and Jenny Steinberg liked Sten Gunn. We were the last two left.

Suzette was a year older, so usually acted rather aloof with me. We'd never spoken more than a word or two. But the way I looked at it, I was on Rottnest at last. She was a girl – big,

146

olive-skinned, sultry-looking. And, suddenly, she seemed quite keen. On our climb up to the lookout, as she reached for my hand, I succeeded in pushing the memory of her retching to the back of my mind. What with the warm pressure of her big, damp hand and the knowledge that we were staying in the same cottage, I was nervy with more or less pleasurable anticipation. I didn't mind what happened. It had to be pretty good.

When we reached the lookout I gave the sunset a long, thoughtful glance. But early Dutch navigation was far from my mind. Neither of us spoke. Suzette was breathing heavily. To steady herself, she leaned against me. She was the same height and about fifteen pounds heavier. I subtly adjusted my footing so I wouldn't topple.

Coming after the extended hand-holding on the trek up to the lookout, I took her leaning on me as a seductive gesture. The sea breeze was blowing in our faces. Quokkas rustled in the shrubbery. My heart was thudding. As the red sun sank romantically into the Indian Ocean, I turned and embraced her. Our cheeks brushed and our lips smeared together and her mouth kept moving sideways as she pushed me aside – but not quite far enough – and vomited over my shoulder.

Fish and chips, coleslaw and beetroot. The quokkas quickly moved in.

After only a week on Rottnest I could look back on the floury fornicating ghosts and my first-night tryst with Suzette Minchin with the sophistication of the seasoned islander. Suzette and I didn't mention the embarrassment at the lookout. In fact, we didn't talk at all. When we passed each other on our way to the bathroom we coughed or looked the other way.

Those incidents seemed centuries ago. Rottnest was like that. Since then I'd turned sixteen, fallen in love and, to impress my new love, killed a shark.

I didn't admit it, but I'd desperately hoped to find my first real girlfriend on the island. Despite our endless talk of sex I was a romantic. If you couldn't get a girlfriend here you weren't trying, it seemed to me. From what I'd gleaned at the dinner table, as Gordon and Irene Schwabb chanted the names of bays and twinkled at each other over the freshly caught crayfish (or crayfish mornay, or curried crayfish), every adult who'd ever been here – since the prison era, anyway – regarded the island in a sensual and nostalgic light for the rest of their days.

I regarded it in a sensual light from the moment I saw Roberta Ainslie's shoulder-blades. I'd never given girls' backs much thought before. I was too busy with the idea of girls' fronts. But she was tall and tanned and elegantly curvaceous and wearing a one-piece turquoise swimsuit cut low in the back. She was walking gingerly over the reef into the Basin, the reef pool which was the island's favourite swimming spot. She looked about seventeen.

'Look at that!' I said to Sten and Dogs.

'Gaol-bait,' said Sten.

'Bullshit,' I said.

In the time it took her to step out over the reef, wincing and giving little squeals when she trod on a sharp rock, then pose at the outer edge and dive elegantly into the sea – two minutes at most – I developed a major interest. When she surfaced dramatically and self-consciously, the way all the girls did, spearing up into the air, chest out, head thrown back to smooth her hair, then opened her eyes and smiled distantly in the general direction of the boys salivating on the shore – and I got a front view – I fell for her.

Sten said, 'She's only thirteen, I heard.'

'So, who's superstitious?' Dogs said languidly.

'Crap,' I said. 'Not looking like that.' But it was a blow. Yet again I pondered how amazingly different girls were. A thirteen-year-old boy was still a kid. 'Anyway, I'm only fifteen myself.'

'Sixteen, when I last heard,' said Sten.

'Only by a few minutes.'

'He's getting over-excited,' said Dogs, 'just because he's legally allowed to do it from today.'

'Only if the bird's sixteen, too,' said Sten. 'Otherwise it's carnal knowledge.' He shook his head sorrowfully. 'Six months inside.'

'You'd do better with the bakery girl,' Dogs suggested. 'You've got a head start there.'

They couldn't put me off. 'Are we going to say hello, or not?' For once I thought I could overcome my usual perverse shyness. I was prepared to show I was as willing as I felt.

'Cradle-snatcher,' Sten muttered. But they didn't need much urging.

We went for the gradual approach. We stood a little way off and skimmed stones in the water. Then we pushed each other

149

in. We progressed to some increasingly reckless dives, somer-saults and bombs off the Diving Rock, and then a dangerous under-the-reef swimming contest. We tapered off by noisily carving our initials on a rock face near her now languidly sun-baking figure.

And at some stage Roberta and I somehow started talking. 'It's my birthday,' I announced giddily. The birthday gambit enabled me to learn that she was actually fourteen. Two years was no great age gap, I told myself. On the other hand it was large enough to give me confidence. I felt mature and relaxed for once. Then there was the extraordinary coincidence of our names. We even lived in the same street, Circe Circle. Were these omens, or what?

I cracked jokes and Roberta laughed. If my sudden urban-ity surprised me, it also surprised the birthday-less Sten and Dogs. Their increasingly grim rock-chipping – their initials were already inches deep – indicated their growing envy. I could see they were mentally extricating themselves from Wendy and Jenny and about to join the fray. They were becom-ing louder and more competitive by the second. Any moment now Dogs would do his chick-trick of walking on his hands.

Hastily, I staked a claim. '*High Society* is playing tonight,' I said to Roberta.

High Society was standard family holiday fare every sum-mer. I'd already seen it three times at different locales – but only when the choice was *High Society* or staying home. For some reason the film made me feel edgy and frustrated. The characters were too flippant. I couldn't believe Grace Kelly would be attracted to Bing Crosby enough to marry him once, much less twice. Or that Frank Sinatra would be such a prim gentleman when tipsy Grace flirted with him. It annoyed me that the lyrics in Bing's song 'Now You Has Jazz' lazily confused jazz and rock 'n' roll. I hated musicals anyway.

'It's supposed to be pretty good,' I said to Roberta. 'Do you want to go?'

'I've seen it, but OK,' she said.

One of the attractions of Rottnest was its old, run-down buildings. The Rottnest Hostel, where Roberta was staying with her family, had once been the Aboriginal prison. It hadn't changed too much over the years. I supposed people paid for the atmosphere. When I arrived to pick her up, her father emerged from their limestone cell in the old Quad and looked me over suspiciously. Back on the mainland he was a leading barrister. He didn't offer to shake hands. 'So, the pictures, eh?' he said.

'Yes, *High Society*.' My earnest tone acknowledged the suitability of this distinguished film. It implied a Royal Command Performance rather than a repeat screening of an old musical in an iron and asbestos shed where half the audience would be barefoot.

'The show finishes at eleven,' he said. He stood on the hostel veranda and looked pointedly towards the picture theatre. It was about a hundred yards away. 'Five past eleven should see you back.'

I heard Dogs, Sten, Wendy, Jenny and Suzette Minchin come into the theatre a while before I saw them. My spirits sank. 'There they are!' Suzette's voice cried out. They moved into the row behind us and the *sotto voce* wisecracks began.

It sounded to me like Dogs and Sten had managed to acquire a couple of hip flasks of their favourite tipple, Beenleigh rum. Suzette, too, was wittier than she'd ever been. She kept cracking them up. When Bing and Grace sang 'True Love' on the moonlit deck of Bing's fake-looking yacht, they crooned along and someone dug me in the back. Then Suzette had a brainwave. In an indignant voice she snapped, 'Hands off, Robert!' and the audience exploded. The usher had to come down and tell them to cut it out.

I turned around to mouth silent threats at them and looked straight into the stony faces of Roberta's father and mother sitting in the row behind them.

Purely as a bitter-sweet masochistic exercise now, I certainly did contemplate putting hands on Roberta, or around her. She sat an inch away from me – and a mile. I could smell her faint lemony perfume and the shampoo in her damp hair. Her face and graceful neck and bare brown arms glowed in the reflected light from Grace Kelly's fabulous gold and silver wedding presents. The whites of her eyes glistened. She looked dewy and polished and edible and slightly startled. I thought she was much better looking than Grace Kelly.

Of course I didn't lay a finger on her. Even so I felt her father's loathing-filled eyes boring into my spine. Stay upbeat, I ordered myself. Girls hated it if you were morose or solemn.

They liked the reckless, relaxed types. Well, OK. Good old Bing sang 'Now You Has Jazz', and got jazz and rock 'n' roll mixed up again, and good old Satchmo rolled his eyes again and wiped his trumpet spit on his hankie, and I feigned cool appreciation and tapped my foot and beat time on my knee.

As we filed out of the theatre both groups seemed to surge around us. Sten and Dogs had cigarettes masculinely lit and sparking away in no time. Suzette was still oddly vivacious, almost bouncing on the spot. For a moment I thought she was going to get us all to sportingly link arms like the just-married couples striding into the credits in *High Society*. 'Who else enjoyed it?' she asked brightly.

We all walked back to the hostel together. Suzette and Roberta seemed to hit it off. Dogs and Sten were puffing away and sucking up to Roberta's mother. Everyone chatted merrily except Roberta's father and me. He was right. Five past eleven easily did it.

Everyone was suddenly behaving strangely. They all seemed to have turned sarcastic overnight. Sten and Dogs went off fishing by themselves without telling me. Suzette Minchin was still aloof with me and hysterical with everyone else. Wendy and Jenny looked old-maidish and disapproving. They were all acting as if

Roberta and I were a hot item but I didn't even know if we were going out or not.

The Schwabbs must have noticed the change in vibes, the sudden rise in emotional levels, because over dinner the night after *High Society* (barbecued crayfish) Gordon Schwabb took it on himself to deliver a caution.

As usual he was able to air some Rottnest knowledge. He told us about someone called the Moral Agent and how, in the bad old days, the government had sent him to the island to watch over the moral welfare of the Aborigines with their degenerate habits. The idea was that the Christian presence of the Moral Agent would also curb Vincent's ear-ripping style of discipline. As a result it would cut the number of increasingly desperate Aboriginal escapes – the stolen boats and suicidal swimming attempts.

Ever since those days, according to Mr Schwabb, successive island managers had taken on something of the Moral Agent's role. Free-and-easy ways might seem the norm, but the island manager took a dim view of certain types of misbehaviour. He was entrusted by Perth's parents with the care of their teenagers. He'd suddenly make an example of some quokka-spearing larrikin or other. He'd pop up anywhere, at any time. He was king of the island. 'He could walk through this front door right now,' said Mr Schwabb.

He took a deep breath. 'Now and then,' he went on, ominously, turning away from the table and gazing out to sea, 'he finds a boy and girl in a compromising situation. Undressed, shall we say. In bed.'

Then, he said, all hell broke loose. Their parents were informed. The boy and girl were escorted to the jetty, placed on ferries – *different* ferries – and thrown off the island. Never to return. Reputations in tatters. Names so bad they never recovered.

I'd been following his gaze out to sea. Reluctantly, I turned back to the dinner table. Sten, Dogs, Jenny, Wendy, Mrs Schwabb and Suzette Minchin were all staring at me over their crayfish. They looked as if they knew this sermon was coming. Suzette arched an eyebrow, slowly forked a lump of crayfish into her mouth and began rhythmically chewing. Sten deftly snapped a crayfish leg and noisily sucked out the flesh. All of them looked prim and smug.

I couldn't believe it. I hadn't even held hands with Roberta yet and now I had to look over my shoulder for the Moral Agent. I seemed destined to have a Moral Agent dogging my heels forever.

Then Mrs Schwabb blinked and gave me a bright smile. 'We seem to be running out of crayfish. Would you be a dear and get us a couple tomorrow?'

They were trying to keep me away from her. 'I'd be happy to,' I said.

I killed the shark instead. I speared it with a *gidgie*, a hand spear, in eight feet of water off Parrakeet Bay. I was looking for crayfish under the reef ledge when I spotted it. It was only a four-foot carpet shark, a *wobbegong*, and resting on the bottom at the time, but it was indeed a shark, I told myself at the anxious and exciting instant of impalement, all my nervous energy forcing the spear through the tough, fibrous flesh of its ornate, carpet-patterned head.

I must have pierced its brain right away. It didn't put up much of a fight. It didn't thrash as they were supposed to. It didn't try to bite me. It just lurched a little bit. Maybe it was sick or asleep.

But a *shark*, I thought, as I dragged it with difficulty up onto the reef. My heart was beating fast. More importantly, it was a shark to show *her*, I told myself as I pedalled slowly back along the hot white limedust road to the settlement. Its big flat head hung heavily across my shoulders and the tail drooped precariously over the handlebars. Its skin pattern was already fading to a muddy brown. Flies clung to the fishy blood seeping down my back and chest.

'Dangerous if molested,' I remembered all the fishing books warned of carpet sharks. 'Aggressive feeders. Formidable fang-like teeth at the front of the jaw.' If those enlarged impaling teeth were strong enough to crush crayfish and hard-shelled crabs they could give you a nasty bite. You could lose a chunk of flesh, maybe a hand or foot. Pierce an artery. Bleed to death.

That made me feel better. That was the risk I'd taken, I told myself. I concentrated on the danger aspect. Look, I thought, it could have woken up at any moment.

It was a hilly road back to the settlement and the limedust made it soft and skiddy. The white glare of the dust was beginning to make my head feel funny. The shark kept slipping and

I had to keep getting off the bike and hauling it back onto my shoulders. It fell in the dust a few times. When I eventually reached the hostel I was exhausted. I got off the bike, hauled the shark up around my neck and shuffled into the Quad.

Now I was there I wasn't sure how to handle the shark presentation. I circled the Quad a few times, hoping Roberta would somehow materialise and catch me casually passing by after a successful day's shark hunting.

The leathery, boneless weight was thudding around my neck. I had to keep hitching it up. Fishy-smelling liquid still oozed down my chest but I didn't mind. I was attracting clouds of flies and a few curious children but not yet the admiring female glances I'd anticipated.

After the third circuit of the Quad I gave up and knocked on the Ainslies' door. Her father opened it. He gave me a disbelieving look. I asked whether Roberta was there. Reluctantly, with a sideways scowl at me, he called her. 'Mr *High Society's* here wearing a fish,' he said.

The shark was beginning to smell bad in the heat. All its weight had dropped into its head and guts were peeping from its mouth. I'd forgotten sharks had no bones to hold everything in. Although it was more elongated and felt very much heavier, it looked wrinkled and smaller. Roberta stepped tentatively outside.

'*Pooh!*' she said.

'Oh, well,' I said. My neck was aching so much from supporting it that I could hardly straighten up enough to look her in the face. I tapped the spear a couple of times on the ground in a Masai-warrior sort of way. 'Sharks, you know.'

'What are you going to do with it?'

It was a shark. It was for display purposes, evidence of the catcher's bravery. I leaned thoughtfully on my spear. 'Maybe I'll keep the teeth as a souvenir.' Then I took the plunge. 'Actually, I thought you might like them.'

'Me?' she said. 'Oh.' Her eyes were darting around the Quad. She was bare-legged and she kept moving from one foot to the other.

'I'll cut them out, if you like,' I said.

'My God,' she said.

With relief I lowered the shark. It flopped to the ground and I squatted beside it on the bare yellow lawn of the Quad. Sticky flies buzzed on us. Roberta brushed at them and took a step back. I noticed I had dusty dried blood streaked all down me, even on my feet. I saw Roberta frowning and wrinkling her nose but I was determined to do this. 'A shark-tooth necklace looks pretty good,' I said.

Actually I'd never seen a carpet shark's teeth before. I jabbed at its mouth with the prongs of the *gidgie*. The mouth was surrounded by ugly, whiskery feelers. The flesh was like scratchy rubber. I prised open the jaws a little. The mouth didn't form the usual sharky oval of jagged teeth that beach-side people kept on their bars or mantelpieces. The teeth were narrow but I could see a couple of big Dracula-type fangs at the front.

At least they looked vaguely sinister. I supposed a fang necklace wasn't out of the question. I kept jabbing away while Roberta looked off into the middle distance. I wasn't making much progress with the teeth. She'd stepped further back. She was now about ten feet from the shark and me. She seemed restless.

'Are you sure it's a shark?' she said. 'It looks more like a flathead.'

'Yes, a carpet shark.'

'They don't have teeth, do they? Aren't they the ones with just gums?'

'No, they do,' I enthused. 'Look at these beauties.' I lifted up the beard-like skin fronds around its lips. To give her a clearer view of the Dracula fangs, I pushed away some of the intestinal matter dangling from its mouth.

'I don't suppose I could borrow a knife?' I said. 'It'd make it easier to cut out the jaw.'

Roberta didn't answer. She said she had to go inside then. She walked back into the cell and closed the door. The shark was hard to lift up again. I thought about carrying it back to the cottage but then I didn't bother. I just dropped the stinking body in the bushes outside the hostel.

THE EYES OF BILLY GRAHAM

One afternoon after school my mother asked me, rather shyly, if I wanted to go with her that evening to hear Billy Graham speak at the Showground. 'I'm curious,' she said.

The American evangelist was visiting Perth as part of his Australian and world crusade. My mother showed me an article she'd torn from the paper that morning which declared boldly that crime in Sydney had halved since his crusade there.

'He must have something,' she said. 'Apart from looks.' Looks? He looked to me like a Christian male version of Bette Davis. I was about to say so but she looked surprisingly girlish and fidgety so I didn't.

Billy Graham was declaring there was a spiritual flame sweeping Australia. He said the crusade's success so far, with tens of thousands of people making decisions for Christ, had made Australia the most prayed-for country in the world.

My father said it was a load of rubbish. 'I'm not going to

any loudmouth Yank's crusade.' Religion at an intense level made him testy and nervous. It opened old wounds, and there were plenty of them.

His father was from a Baptist family, originally strict non-conformist working-class, who'd migrated from Bradford-on-Avon and Trowbridge in Wiltshire in 1854 and quickly prospered in the leafy south-eastern suburbs of Melbourne.

His father, William, my grandfather, was an architect. He helped found Carey Baptist Grammar School at Kew, acquired six properties in Malvern, East St Kilda and Windsor, and during a concentrated burst of energy had designed and built many of the remarkably similar solid bluestone churches around Malvern, Toorak, Camberwell, Kew, Hawthorn and South Yarra, all noted for their small, high windows, starkly functional lines, absence of religious ornamentation, apparently bomb-proof exteriors and well-off parishioners.

At the age of thirty-five, he'd retired to his own functional and gloomy study at 42 Stanhope Street, Malvern, to read biographies, do *The Age* crossword and listen to the cricket on the wireless, remaining there, in retirement and seclusion, except for his nightly foray out to Malvern's Greek cafe for his roast-lamb dinner (having starched his collar and ironed his shirt) and his weekly visit to the bank to deposit his rental cheques, for the next fifty-eight years.

My mother said the reason my grandfather went to his room for so long was my grandmother. Her name was Daisy Mae, the same name, I was delighted to discover, as the voluptuous girlfriend of the comic-strip character Li'l Abner. When

161

the young church architect met Daisy Mae Wells she was working behind the millinery counter at Myer's department store. But not for long.

It seemed impossible to me that two such incredibly different people could have met, much less married and conceived four children. The church architect was dignified, polite, thin, introverted, remote, abstemious and frugal. The millinery assistant was big-boned, square-jawed, bossy, extroverted, shallow and snobbish – almost as far removed from the slender and curvaceous comic-strip Daisy Mae as she was from him.

She was from a family of publicans and racehorse owners. She smoked cigarettes, drank sherry, played poker and ruled the roost. While William was upstairs in his room listening to the cricket, Daisy Mae was downstairs playing five-card stud with her Baptist children – when she wasn't in the members' stand at Flemington races, that is, drinking champagne with her lover, the detective-inspector.

She was also Church of England. She thought, with some justification, that Baptists were boring and tight with their money. Being married to even a well-off Baptist was only marginally better than selling hats at Myer's.

But marrying a Catholic was beyond the pale. The detective's mistress was shocked when my father announced he was marrying a Catholic, even one who herself came from a 'mixed' marriage. My mother, early in her marriage, decided it best not to speak of her mother-in-law at all. When I pressed her about this secret grandmother of mine, she said Daisy Mae had behaved 'snobbishly' towards her on the few times they'd spoken. 'To hear her patronise me,' my mother said crisply, 'you'd think *I* was the one behind the hat counter.'

The problem of their relationship solved itself. By the time I'd begun to inquire about these now unseen and hardly spoken-of grandparents, we were living in far-off Western Australia and Daisy Mae, after a particularly lively day at the Flemington races, had collapsed and died of an enlarged heart.

But at least Daisy Mae had gone to her son's wedding. When my parents were married during the war at the Kew Baptist Church, my mother's mother, Mary, forbidden by her local Catholic priest to attend, had cried for a month before and after her only daughter's wedding to the young Protestant RAAF pilot.

The Catholics were still hard on Mary (née Mary Agnes Bray) over her own marriage to an Anglican bank manager, George Watson, known as Cres, from his second name, Creswick. Mary and Cres had seen plenty of sectarian conflict, usually on a Sunday night when she returned from Mass and he from the bowling club. After one particular bowling-club session he reasserted the influence of the Church of England with a warning shot from the State Savings Bank of Victoria's security pistol. 'Now,' he shouted, fortunately hitting only the kitchen wall, 'I'll get rid of these Catholic kids once and for all.'

To go by all the overheard afternoon-tea murmurings of my mother and her friends, every marriage in our family was a clash of religions and personality types. Weddings were noted for the flamboyant absence of the mother of the bride or

163

groom, for tears with the confetti, for people not speaking for decades. Calm, sensitive non-drinkers married heavy-drinking extroverts. Intelligent, amusing people married boring, angry ones. Anglicans married Catholics whereas the family's Catholics went out on the furthest limb and chose Baptists.

Both sides of the family, however, had an extraordinary ability to keep conflict under wraps. Skeletons remained firmly in the cupboard. 'Shoosh, small ears flapping!' they'd say if a child suddenly hove into view. Not that we cared at all about far-flung relatives. If everyone hadn't acted so mysteriously it would have gone right over our heads.

They were experts at championing traditional behaviour while actually defying it. They didn't realise when they went against the usual grain. My mother's Irish Catholic grandfather and his brothers had been career officers in the British Army, two of them giving their lives in Britain's wars and one of them winning the Military Cross. On my father's side, once away from Wiltshire, its established church and declining woollen mills, the working-class Baptists had blossomed into creative capitalists, started companies and made fortunes – only to give them away to the church, or outsiders, on their deathbeds.

In one generation the family contained members of five Christian religions. My parents' solution to their own Baptist/Catholic dilemma was to have their three children christened Presbyterians. From then on, exhausted by it all, they regarded themselves as Presbyterians too.

At the time of Billy Graham's visit, my father had another religious bee in his bonnet. This was over a decision by St Lawrence's, the local Anglican church, to tithe its parishioners. As we weren't Church of England I couldn't understand what he was getting steamed up about. He didn't even go to church. But as most of their neighbours and friends at least called themselves Anglicans he'd decided to be affronted on their behalf.

He liked to sound off on this church 'blackmail' when these friends dropped in for Sunday drinks. 'Who can afford ten percent of their salary? I like their hide! If the commos did this we'd all be up in arms. I'll say this for the Press-buttons – their pockets might be tighter than fishes' rectums but they'd never dare try it on.'

My mother didn't attempt to change his mind on Billy Graham, not when trouble could erupt at any moment. Religion was both a neglected and a complicated subject in our house. Once our Sunday School years had passed it was ignored. But at some subterranean level to do with past unpleasantness it was always simmering away. If a ruling on Church of England parish tithes could set it off, anything could.

'I think Billy Graham's a Baptist himself,' she murmured to me.

'Really?' I said. I couldn't have cared less. Not surprisingly, I regarded myself as an agnostic. But I agreed to go with her. I was curious, but not for religious reasons. Billy Graham was an American celebrity and, it seemed to me, not too far removed from the entertainment world. We West Australians were starved of celebrities and we revered Americans. As visiting crews of the American fleet always discovered to their surprise and pleasure when they found themselves treated as a combination of film stars and war heroes, we thought of them as the same thing.

It was also a chance for me to go out. I was allowed out only one night a week, either Friday or Saturday. I reasoned that even my parents weren't so unfair as to count a religious evening with my mother as my night out.

That crisp May evening fifty thousand West Australians thronged to the Showground to see and hear Dr Graham prove his claim. He'd promised us the Holy Spirit would travel 'like a radio wave' into his words and then into our ears and minds, to give each of our lives new meaning. Keen to experience this phenomenon, people jammed the admission gates, and when they'd filled all the seats they climbed onto the roofs of the cattle, horse and pig pavilions to watch him through binoculars.

My mother and I were lucky to find a couple of seats beside the disabled section. She said, 'I've never seen so many wheelchairs and crutches.' Hundreds of invalids and cripples had been transported to the Showground and ushered to the front of the crowd, and next to them was another section for blind and deaf people and their interpreters. To the side of the stage was a choir of one thousand singers.

It was the biggest, loudest public gathering I'd ever seen. Even the annual football grand final at Subiaco Oval couldn't muster half this number. Crusade assistants moved briskly up and down the rows collecting donations in buckets. Rumours had spread that profits were going to pay for Dr Graham's 'Hour of Decision' radio broadcasts in America, so the buckets were stamped: 'For Local Expenses Only. All Money Stays in Australia.'

Everyone important was there: Premier Dave Brand, the spotlight glinting on the Returned Services League badge that he never took off his lapel; Lord Mayor Harry Howard, in his Ye Olde Englande mayoral robes and chain; and the Anglican Archbishop of Perth, Dr Moline, in his shimmering purple and mauve vestments.

The star's ordinary grey single-breaster, dark tie and white shirt made the locals look stagey and pompous by comparison, like an amateur Gilbert and Sullivan society. At the same time, as my mother had anticipated, the American was the tallest, blondest, youngest and most impressive-looking man on stage.

'He doesn't look very old,' I said.

'Only forty-one,' she whispered.

He began in a loud, clear, hectoring manner. What he said was at odds with how he looked and how he presented himself. 'May the people see only Christ tonight and not the speaker.' He was using the full force of his crowd-pleasing talents to ask us to forget these talents altogether.

With that out of the way, his face became fierce. 'We cannot shut our eyes to what is going on in the world,' he thundered. His own eyes, as sharp and goggling as Bette Davis's in *The Virgin Queen*, snapped around the Showground, instantly found mine, as I'd feared they would, and bored right into my evil teenage soul.

'What diabolic force drives juveniles, in what should be life's happiest years, to crime, lust and unbridled living?' he shouted up into the gentle Perth heavens.

This struck home. For a start, the scene of my own juvenile crime was no more than a hundred yards from where he was hectoring us. This was the asbestos shed which stored the comic books that were placed in thousands of souvenir showbags before each spring's Royal Agricultural Show.

One day years before, a month before the Show opened, Nick Howell and I had tunnelled under the cyclone-wire fence behind Sideshow Alley, and into the Showground. As if by radar, we'd discovered and homed in on the comic-book storeroom.

We got inside by crawling on our stomachs under the floor and prising apart some floorboards. The piles of comics were higher than our shoulders. Some reached the storeroom ceiling. For boys who loved to read we were suddenly in comic heaven, lounging on heaped mattresses of hundreds, maybe thousands, of copies of the *Phantom* and *Archie* and the *Lone Avenger*. At last we knew how Scrooge McDuck, the comic-strip character we envied above all others, must feel, diving and cavorting among the piles of cash in his vault.

Like Uncle Scrooge, we appreciated our rare bounty and didn't want to spoil it. We didn't vandalise anything. All we wanted was to read comics. Apart from one frightening moment when a motorcycle cop slowly passed by (we held our breath and he rode on), we read comics until dark. Then we re-stacked the piles and replaced the floorboards. We took an armful each, kept the cache a secret, and returned every weekend for a

168

month. By then we'd read them all, even the parent-and-teacher-sanctioned *Classics* series and the soppy English comics. The following year we went back to the Showground, climbed under the fence, came up through the storeroom floorboards, and read our way through a new batch.

But although the Reverend Billy Graham, his shirtsleeved arms raised to heaven, was now standing at the scene of my crime against property and ranting at me, I could put this down to coincidence. What I found more alarming was that the world-famous Christian was also silhouetted against the backdrop of my unbridled lusts.

Only a stone's throw from the stage where Dr Graham stood surrounded by ecstatic cripples, self-conscious bigwigs and angelic singing children was the scene of my crimes against sexual morality: the pavilion and playing field of the Claremont Football Club.

The club abutted the Showground. In the club pavilion – its sloping roof this very moment outlined in front of me – and sometimes also on the cool, dewy but favourably dark surface of the football field itself, adolescent passions simmered every Friday night. To the muted brass, sultry woodwinds and throbbing double-bass of the Riverside Jazz Group, my friends and I pressed our bodies against girls in the almost motionless dance called the Creep. Secure in their armoured underwear, they pressed right back.

The Claremont dance defied the popular music of the era. Rock 'n' roll was daytime, teenage music; it meant high spirits and high school and daylight. Jazz was nightclubs, close dancing, and sexual aplomb. Rock 'n' roll made us feel like the teenagers we were. The Riversiders' slow Dixieland made us feel like tuxedoed twenty-five-year-olds. Rock 'n' roll lyrics suggested milkshakes and hamburgers. Jazz made us feel like Hugh Hefner.

The Hefner feeling was enhanced by consuming male hormones. These were generously provided on two consecutive Fridays by Dave Beetles, whose mother was a doctor. We passed them around. The illicit hormones, with their distinctive salty, floury taste and convenient bite-size stick form, drove several of the more susceptible boys – Craig Vimpani especially – into dance-floor and football-field displays of reckless machismo. Craig's lusty antics only waned on the third Friday with Dave's revelation that the hormones were actually a new snack-food on the market called Slim Jane Pretzels.

The dance was its own aphrodisiac. In the dimmed lights of the pavilion ('Home of the Mighty Tigers'), shuffling my way into the middle of the crowded floor to 'La Vie En Rose' (Don Thompson on trombone, Phil Batty on trumpet) or 'Sentimental Journey' (Brett Lockyer on clarinet), I'd shut out the black-and-yellow Tigers memorabilia, with their unglamorous association with Dunlop's colours, and imagine I was dancing in the Stork Club or the Copacabana or the Blue Angel.

It was dizzying enough to Creep up against the bolstered breasts and pantie-girdled pelvis of a fifteen-year-old normally spotted at the bus stop in a tartan uniform. To tightly clasp a sixteen-year-old stranger, a sweatered stenographer or shop assistant, a girl who *worked*, was a thrill we knew we didn't deserve.

When these worldly, pliant girls, moved by Lockyer's lilting reed and Johnny Van Oyen's sultry piano chords to get better acquainted, asked on their way outside to the football field, 'What do you do for a crust?' and 'What sort of car do you drive?' my half-hearted claim, muffled, I hoped, by Bob Dixon's drum solo or John Bartlett's double-bass, to be a university student (medicine perhaps, maybe architecture) whose MG, sadly, was out of action (anything but an unlicensed sixteen-year-old schoolboy), fell on shrewd ears. They knew the truth.

Even as I sat uncomfortably with my mother at this Christian crusade, drilled by Billy Graham's goshawk eyes and stunned by the proximity of the dance pavilion and the moist shadows of the football field, I remembered with a jolt of pleasure that tomorrow was Friday night. The Claremont dance. Girls. Thompson on trombone. Batty on muted trumpet. Lockyer's sensuous clarinet. 'La Vie En Rose'. Billy Graham versus the Creep. No contest.

I wasn't listening so intently any more. But while his sermon was beginning to pass over me I was still soaking up the atmosphere. You couldn't help it. It wasn't the celebrity with the hectoring voice and the golden mane and the Bette Davis glare making my spine tingle. It was the needy Christian faces, the adoring spastics and nodding blind people, the sweet singing voices. All those Christians who wouldn't be dancing the Creep tomorrow night, or endeavouring to lie on damp grass with stenographers. They'd be back home preserving fruit or making stuffed toys or doing their homework in rural shacks by kerosene lamplight. The armless ones would be painting snowy winter landscapes with their mouths and toes. My mother religiously bought the foot-and-mouth painters' Christmas cards every year and it looked like very hard work.

My heart went out to them. I thought of my Friday-night behaviour and I felt abject and guilty. As low as a snake's der-riere, as my father would say. For the first time I remembered *beforehand* that most Friday nights actually ended for me in a state of guilty anxiety.

If past Friday nights were any guide, I could anticipate parting from my friends and hurrying home alone after the dance, via Cookie's hamburger bar on Stirling Highway, just in time to make my midnight curfew. I could see myself breaking into a jog and tearing handfuls of leaves from the council pep-permint trees along the way and chewing them to mask the cigarette and mouthful of rum or port on my breath.

I saw myself vigorously rubbing my mouth and cheeks on my sleeve (a handkerchief too easily showed powder and lip-stick traces), checking my clothes for grass clippings, sniff-testing my jumper for girl smells, for traces of Gerri's or Trisha's or Someone Unnamed's perfume, and already antici-pating hiding the jumper, with its eternally lingering female scents, from my ever-vigilant mother beneath my socks and underwear in my bedroom cupboard.

Most of all, I saw myself one startling and unique night striding down the Vincent Street hill, now and then sniffing my right hand with mixed awe and pride – and fear. Surely (I could hardly bear to think it), forcing herself to stay awake until I came home, my mother would smell the finger.

172

She would catch the first marine whiff the moment the finger rounded the corner of Adelma Road and turned into Circe Circle, the smell rising higher and stronger as the finger journeyed down the hill, crossed Curlew Road, traversed the lawn and went up the front steps, through the front door and across the hallway (although thrust deep in my pocket as I passed my parents' room and murmured good night), emerging in full intimate bloom as I entered the bathroom, locked the door, gave it a last proud and regretful sniff, then soaped it up and plunged it under the tap.

At the crusade my mother's profile was totally still beside me. She was still hanging on Billy Graham's words. Now he was really in his stride. 'What power is it that breaks up homes,' he cried, 'and causes a man to leave his wife and lovely children for another woman?' His words were like explosions. 'What is it that causes a man to pour his future out of a bottle, and become a partial suicide – to gladly trade all that others hold dear for a few sparkling drops from the vine?'

I sneaked a glance at her. She was looking straight ahead, in direct profile, not moving a muscle. The angle of her nose and chin reminded me of someone. It was remarkable. She looked like the Queen's face on a penny.

Now Billy Graham loosened his tie like Frank Sinatra or Sammy Davis Jr performing at the Desert Inn. 'Is life on this planet an insoluble dilemma,' he boomed, 'and is man destined, like the fateful lemmings, to march to his doom into the sea of oblivion?'

I'd never seen and heard anything like this from the Reverend Gilbert Cameron back at St Paul's, Nedlands. 'Black is always black and white is always white,' declared Billy Graham, 'but above the black and white waves the invisible ensign of Christ's cross and the fact of redeeming grace.'

His arms swept us up. His hands were cupped, seeming to draw us in to him. 'Christ stands with the man and woman in the street,' he said. 'Repent. Believe in Christ the Lord. Be saved.' Then, suddenly quieter now, he invited everyone to come forward and receive Christ.

A tremor flickered through the audience. It seemed a lot of Perth people were aching to be saved. In every row people shifted in their seats and began to stand, to respond, to join him on stage. Soon they were deciding for Christ all over the place – healthy people, cripples, old and young, the well dressed and the casual.

He kept quietly urging and beckoning us to join him. It was hypnotic. It was contagious. The people getting up from their seats didn't look like religious maniacs. They looked like your average movie audience on a Saturday night. I recognised neighbours and a contingent of boys from Wesley College whom I'd played sports against. I saw my friend John Sturkey. I saw the chemist's wife and my old maths teacher. Two rows along I saw Eric, the Dunlop delivery driver, sitting by a sign saying 'South Perth Methodists'. People stood up all along the rows of chairs and people began sliding down from the roofs of the cattle, horse and pig pavilions. The chemist's wife stood up. Eric stood up and joined Billy Graham. People were having conversions all around me.

After a while my mother stood up, too. As she rose to her feet she gave me a small confiding smile. She didn't do anything to try to influence my own decision but I still felt an immense pressure to join her and the serene-looking people on stage. I thought, it's easy. All I have to do is believe in God.

I admired the way my mother calmly rose to her feet, moved determinedly out of our row and walked forward down the aisle, seeking contentment in her life. She looked small but noble, both Dot and Dorothy at once. I felt a protective, almost fatherly love for her. I could see this would be a valuable and adult experience to share with her. I wanted to be a better person, too.

I wanted to follow her into the realm of goodness. I wanted to join her and the Reverend Dr Billy Graham and his celebrated American crusade and the thousand-person choir and the halt, lame and blind, and the Methodist boys from Wesley College, and Methodist Eric with his harelip and funny voice, and the sumptuously robed Lord Mayor, and the Anglican Archbishop, even Honest Dave, the Premier, standing there self-consciously behind his ex-serviceman's badge. I was sorely tempted. But I sat tight.

After a while my mother and the other converted people left the stage and returned to their seats and the crusade was over. Billy Graham said a short prayer for the converted and was easy on the rest of us. People left quietly. We drove home in silence.

THE BRIDGE

On the November day that the Governor officially opened the Narrows Bridge across the Swan River my father was escorted home by police. He'd been to the opening ceremony that morning but it was late, about eleven p.m. by then, and he'd been driving the Fairlane in circles for almost an hour trying to get off the new bridge.

The Fairlane was his company car these days, the model that Janet Leigh drove in *Psycho*. Alfred Hitchcock and my father both favoured Fords. (I'd noticed that the used-car yard where Janet Leigh traded her car for a Fairlane was full of Fords, and that Janet's body even ended up in the boot of her Fairlane – not that her boyfriend and sister looked too upset about it.)

Ever since my father left the saloon bar of the Esplanade Hotel that Friday evening he'd been driving the Fairlane back and forth across the new bridge, and up and down the three-and-a-half miles of the new Kwinana Freeway which led away from it, and around the loops and figure-eights of the bridge approaches and off-ramps. When the police car spotted him heading south for the fourth or fifth time, still trying to find the off-ramp for Mounts Bay Road and home, he was almost out of petrol. They put on the siren and stopped him.

When they walked up to the car he said, 'Much obliged.' He explained that he was endeavouring to get home to Dalkeith, introduced himself and, as he always did, added firmly, 'State manager, Dunlop.'

The policemen said, 'Follow us,' got back into their car and led him north and west and off the bridge. They escorted him home.

He'd obviously been drinking. Perhaps they thought some traffic confusion could be excused on the opening day of the bridge. Anyway, they weren't traffic cops but detectives. They were making yet another random circuit of the neighbourhood of the South Perth flat where Patricia Berkman had been stabbed to death in her bed ten months before. The last thing the homicide squad wanted was some driving-under-the-influence paperwork and their time wasted on traffic-court appearances.

When the cars pulled up outside our house my father showed his gratitude in his usual way. 'You must come in for a drink,' he said.

The younger detective-constable said, 'We're on duty.' The senior detective-sergeant looked at the younger officer, then at his watch and said, 'Just a small one.'

When they came into the house, my father gave an over-cheery rendition of his 'I'm home!' whistle. As if we didn't know that, what with their loud voices and two cars in the driveway. We didn't whistle back. My mother had stopped returning the evening whistle a while back, and Bill and I didn't whistle beyond about nine p.m., especially if there could be trouble brewing. The three men bustled in and, as cops do, immediately filled the room.

My mother modified her surprised look, mustered up some social graces and fetched some beers from the fridge. My father jerked his head at me to turn off the TV. He didn't appear too fussed at having been brought home by the police. He was speaking in his hearty Friday-night voice and acting pretty bluff.

'These gentlemen were kind enough to help me with a traffic problem on the Narrows Bridge,' he announced to us. 'A wonderful bridge, by the way. Top notch. Full marks to Dave Brand and everyone concerned.'

He motioned the cops into the lounge room and began pouring beer into the pewter tankards he reserved for visiting sportsmen and VIPs. 'By the same token,' he said, as they eased themselves into chairs, 'those direction signs are woeful. Definitely below par. I'll be having a word,' he added solemnly, for everyone's benefit, implying Heads Will Roll. The lost-on-the-bridge matter was closed.

I left the room and my mother made us coffee. We sat at the dining table by the open door half-pretending to be chatting while we listened to their conversation. They were on first-name terms already. The detective-sergeant was John McCurry, the younger detective was Max Kommer.

'I know Goodyear supplies the police force at the moment,' my father said, winking and topping up their tankards, 'but we'd be more than competitive. How many vehicles do you run, as a matter of interest?'

He was at ease now, once more the host, in his element. 'Anything Dunlop can do for the police . . .' he went on. 'Tyres, batteries, flooring, footwear, mattresses, sporting goods . . .' He loved this sort of business contact, where two accidentally connected principals were suddenly linked by a mutually helpful form of barter. It was how things worked in this branch manager's town. It was good business and it was also more than that. It was the most common form of male friendship: the generous exchange of assistance, information and wholesale goods. It allowed everyone to benefit.

My father and the detectives drank two bottles of beer in no time and then McCurry sent Kommer out to the car to check the radio. Everyone seemed relaxed. 'Bit of a coincidence seeing you fellows,' my father said. 'We've just had to do a bit of police work ourselves and sack a fellow for thieving.'

They put on polite faces. Theft, eh? 'Is that so?' McCurry said. 'Did you report him?'

'No, no, we didn't want to take up police time with a petty thief. One of our truck drivers. Caught him stealing from his mates' lockers.'

The set of my father's jaw said firm-but-fair, managerial-but-humane. The sack, yes, but not gaol. Anyway, if you brought in the police the company looked bad, too. 'The other drivers laid a trap with indelible ink. They marked a couple of tenners in a wallet. The money disappeared and this fellow had the ink all over his fingers and pocket.'

The cops raised their eyebrows. 'Very impressive,' McCurry said.

'Absolutely,' said Kommer.

'Don't like to sack a family man,' my father said. 'Leaves a nasty taste all round. Heap of kids. Speech impediment. A bit odd in the mouth department.' He tapped his top lip. 'But I shouldn't say any more.'

'Maybe we know him,' McCurry wondered. 'Does he have a name?'

'No names, no pack drill,' my father said. But he kept shaking his head as if he didn't know what the world was coming to. 'A bloke who steals from his workmates . . . Throwing away a steady job like that . . .' He sipped his beer reflectively.

'Pretty low,' McCurry agreed.

'I don't envy what you fellows have to do,' my father said. 'We should all be bloody grateful.'

I'd never heard him say 'bloody' before.

'Nice of you to say,' McCurry murmured over the rim of his tankard.

'What with all you've got on your plate . . .' my father continued. He opened another bottle and topped up their drinks. 'Where would we be without you blokes?'

I waited for McCurry to say, 'Still on the bridge, I suppose.' He said, 'Yeah, well.'

They lowered their voices then. A confiding note crept in. They were onto crime cases. But they didn't waste time on petty theft. They were just chatting generally but they were talking about *actual murders*. My father was pursing his lips and nodding solemnly, like a magistrate, and laughing politely when one of them highlighted what he saw as murder's amusing side.

'What about the Berkman murder?' my father asked suddenly. *The naked divorcee*. My mother and I looked up. We didn't even pretend not to listen. We were all ears. The question seemed a bold and nosy one. I knew he'd had a lot to drink then. The detectives looked at each other. Kommer waited for McCurry to answer.

McCurry said in a low voice, 'Well, I *can* say this . . .'

I was desperate to hear more but my father stood up and said, 'Just a sec, John.' He walked purposefully across the room, gave my mother and me a meaningful frown and shut the door on us.

All we could hear for the next half-hour was a low rumble of voices, punctuated now and then by exclamations of agreement and surprise from my father. Then their voices rose to a normal level again and my father opened the door and they came out. When the detectives were leaving, all the men looked each other firmly in the eye. They exchanged business cards. My father said, 'John, Max. Any time I can be of assistance . . .'

'Same here, Roy,' said McCurry.

Of course the next morning I asked my father who the trapped thief was. He gave me a look. He was drinking Alka-Seltzer. 'Don't like ears flapping,' he said. 'Never have. The matter's finished. The man's lost his job.'

I asked my mother later. 'It was Eric, who comes here, wasn't it?'

'You guessed it,' she said. 'I didn't tell you.'

As it happened, a fortnight later Detective-Sergeant McCurry needed a new Dunlopillo mattress and pillows. My father was pleased to arrange it. Christmas was coming and all parties exchanged Christmas cards. This exchange sealed the relationship. Once you were on the Christmas card list – my parents' list contained four hundred names – you were there forever.

The homicide squad had its hands full that Christmas. Five days before Christmas Day, Jillian Brewer, described in the papers as 'the beautiful twenty-two-year-old heiress to the MacRobertson chocolate fortune', was murdered in her bed in her apartment in Brookwood Flats, on Stirling Highway in Cottesloe.

The killer had begun with a hatchet. He hacked into her face, breasts, thighs, stomach and pelvis. He severed her wind-pipe and fractured her skull and pubic bone. He struck so hard he split the hatchet's wooden handle. Then he snatched up a pair of scissors and stabbed her in the breasts, abdomen, liver and buttocks.

The scissors belonged to the murdered woman, but the hatchet belonged to one of my best friends.

Simon Watson and I were in the same class at school. We swam and surfed together. I crewed on his old plywood

Gwen-12 yacht, sitting out on the trapeze, my arse skimming the waves, while he shouted orders. We went to the Claremont dance. In lifesaving competitions we alternated as Rescuer and Patient, Hero and Drowning Swimmer.

Simon lived at 4 Renown Avenue, a block behind Brookwood Flats. Earlier on the Saturday of Jillian Brewer's murder he'd been doing the gardening chores for his parents, using the hatchet to chip the edges of the lawn. That night, prowling first through the Watsons' property, the killer had picked up Simon's hatchet and taken it with him.

It turned out that the killer had worn gloves in order that any fingerprints at the scene or on the murder weapon would not be his. The next few weeks, encompassing Christmas and the first hot days of the summer holidays, were a difficult time for Simon and his family.

Brookwood Flats was prominently situated on the turnoff to North Cottesloe. I passed the big red-brick apartment building every time I went to the beach. I wanted to talk to Simon about Jillian Brewer's murder. At the same time it was so terrible and gruesome it was beyond my understanding.

Simon was an open, chatty, humorous boy but he wouldn't talk about the murder or even the murder weapon. By now I was thinking about the hatchet as if it were a person – as if it were the murderer.

The police didn't want him to discuss it. Neither did his parents. If and when they caught the killer he'd probably have to give evidence. But . . . but . . . Jesus, Simon! Your axe killed that girl. The murderer was in your yard! He was looking through your windows at you, at your sister! Who do you think did it?

Simon gave a tortured look and clammed up.

⸺

During the holidays an organisation called the Eureka Youth League of Australia wrote to me out of the blue and invited me to join up.

I wondered how they knew me and my address. Why did they want me, anyway? The letter (unsigned) pointed out that my 'sporting prowess' and 'community service' had come to the League's attention. 'You are obviously on the wave of the future,' the anonymous flatterer declared.

How nice of them to say so, I thought. Still, I wondered how I'd attracted their interest. Was it my bronze lifesaving medal (one of only approximately two hundred awarded in the State each year) that had helped me catch the wave of the future? They'd mentioned sporting prowess. Maybe my track-and-field third placing in the second division of the under-sixteen 880 yards had come to their attention. Community service? Search me.

I flipped through their attached newsletter, *Spotlight*, which listed the many and impressively varied things the Eureka Youth League stood for: more swimming pools and recreation facilities for young people; the vote for eighteen-year-olds; equal rights for Aborigines; equal pay for girls and women; a better deal for apprentice tradesmen; adult wages for junior workers doing adult jobs; an end to whipping and hanging; bans on atom bomb tests; world peace and disarmament; and – right at the end – a People's Government to Build Socialism in Australia.

The Eureka Youth League pointed out that if I and the rest of Australia's youth leaders got together (*Australia's youth leaders!*) we could help bring about world peace. We would stop Britain testing any more A-bombs on the Monte Bello Islands, fifty miles off our coast. We would be a friend to all peoples. Yes, I thought. Absolutely. I felt even more virtuous than when I'd signed the lifetime no-alcohol pledge for the Women's Christian Temperance Union when I was eleven.

The Eureka Youth League had picked their youth well. I was a joiner. I'd already joined the school magazine committee and the debating committee and the dramatic society and officer cadets and every sport possible. I was showing leadership and Spartan attributes all over the place – until nine a.m. anyway. In summer I got up at five-thirty and swam laps through the algae and jellyfish in the Claremont baths; in winter I ran cross-country courses before breakfast. Then, ravenous and tired by nine, I ate my lunch under the desk and, to stay awake, wrote imaginary *curricula vitae* in my maths books, listing my marriage to Brigitte Bardot, knighthood and Olympic gold medals in three sports.

I'd always filled in coupons and application forms and sent

away for things. I was ever optimistic that what came back this time would make me stronger and smarter and wouldn't be junk. When I was younger I'd sent my pocket money away to Sydney post-office-box addresses for disguise kits ('Realistic beards, wigs and moustaches! Put thirty years on your age! Fool your parents! Trick your friends!'), Popeye badges, Phantom skull rings, Lone Avenger pistol holsters and Charles Atlas muscle developers.

I'd even persevered with the step-by-step lessons from the Brodie Mack School of Cartooning. Brodie Mack insisted that everything you drew, from animals to battleships, had to start as a circle. It was a pay-as-you-draw system. Brodie Mack didn't want you to rush into the world of cartooning. After two years all I'd learned to draw were circular cats, dogs and rabbits and bald circular businessmen smoking cigars the shape of elongated circles. I began to think that Brodie Mack was scared of the competition. Learning to draw with the Brodie Mack School of Cartooning wasn't cartooning, it was slow geometry.

Earlier, as a reader of *Chucklers' Weekly*, I'd enthusiastically joined the Charlie Chuckles Club and become a Chuckler. Charlie Chuckles's personal signature glowed on my Chuckler membership card and growing number of Chuckler awards. I loved being published and seeing my name in print. I loved the regular five-shilling prizes for my rhyming verse, drawings and competition entries ('Unscramble the Film Stars' Names!'). As long as I was being published and paid I was easily able to suspend disbelief that my publisher was a kookaburra.

I saw the Eureka Youth League as a more serious version

186

of the Charlie Chuckles Club. It made me feel responsible and mature. I would be pleased to bring an end to hanging and whipping and atom bombs and unfairness. I wanted to be a friend to all peoples. I would be a Chuckler for Socialism. I signed up.

A week later my father spotted the membership accept-ance letter from my new idealistic friends at the League. They welcomed me 'into the fold' and urged me to attend a 'special getting-to-know-you meeting' at 75 Stirling Street, Perth. His reaction startled me. He snatched up the letter and began act-ing as if something truly appalling had occurred. He was withering and overbearing.

'How did this happen?' he raged. 'This reflects on all of us.' I knew he meant himself. He had no intention of allowing his son to join the youth wing of the Communist Party of Australia. Finally, he stopped pacing, took a deep breath and said grimly, 'You're still a minor, son. I'll deal with this.'

He was on the phone immediately to John McCurry, his new detective friend. He went into the bedroom and closed the door and made the call from there. But his voice was loud and indignant and I heard him say, 'I want his name taken off the books!' I thought the CIB might have more important matters on its mind, but after about five minutes he came out looking grimly satisfied.

'That's spiked their guns,' he said. 'John's a wake-up to their commo tricks.'

He was right. I heard nothing more from the Eureka Youth League. Soon after, John McCurry called around to our house one night in the middle of a patrol. From his manner I gathered the police hadn't made much progress on either the Berkman or the Brewer murder. He couldn't stop for more than one beer but he went away with two Ladies' Maxply tennis racquets.

A few weeks later, in proud possession of my new driver's licence and in a hurry to get to the beach, I reversed my mother's Renault too fast down the Watsons' driveway and knocked over their brick letterbox where it joined the front fence. Simon's father wasn't happy. His anger at the letterbox demolition took the heat off my questions to Simon on the murder weapon. I was under a cloud. In these leafy suburbs, destruction of property was a serious matter. It was certainly more comprehensible than wilful slaughter.

ON THE BEACH

My father asked me one Saturday evening if I wanted to go and see *On the Beach*. This was quite a surprise but I had nothing doing so I said yes. I'd just turned seventeen, I was his eldest child and I'd never been on an outing alone with him before. Not to the pictures or the football or the beach, not even to the park to throw a ball around. It was such a novelty that in the car on the way I thought I should start some comradely banter.

'What do you hear from the cops?' I asked him.

He gave me a quizzical look as if I had crossed some forbidden boundary. 'Nothing,' he said eventually. Once, long before, I recalled, I'd been reading *Dick Tracy* in the back seat of the car when a question occurred to me. I called out cheerily, 'Dad, what's Skid Row?' He didn't answer. His eyes met mine in the rear-vision mirror. 'Nothing at all,' he said finally.

We drove the rest of the way in silence. It wasn't an unfriendly silence. It wasn't even a neutral silence like when he drove me to school. I was pleased he'd asked me to do something with him. I also had a rich enough store of self-pity to wonder why it took a film about the end of the world for this to happen.

He'd asked my mother first but she hadn't wanted to go. She said she couldn't cope with such a depressing story. But *On the Beach* fascinated him. He'd already read the novel by Nevil Shute. Not only was it about Australians (as well as Americans) awaiting the nuclear fallout which had already wiped out the northern hemisphere, but it was set in Melbourne, his home town.

With most other films I'd have approached the evening more warily, but in a film about the end of mankind I didn't anticipate any embarrassment between us over love scenes. I'd also flipped through the book and couldn't recall any particularly raunchy passages. And I would have.

Usually it was uncomfortable just watching TV with him. Any love scene, in fact any scene at all, even a commercial, featuring an attractive or flirtatious woman, caused a force-field of disapproval and embarrassment to rise from my father's chair and fill the room. The story, the actors, the drama, all became lost and blurred. While I sat there stolidly in front of the television, my face set in an expressionless mask to show how unaffected I was by the woman before us, I was silently urging her to put something on, for God's sake! Do up that button! Pull that sheet higher! Stop kissing that man!

I'd see by the grim set of his mouth and his frowning profile that he was willing the same thing. Of course I really wanted the woman to linger there, preferably with much less clothing on. I suspected he did, too. He never drove past a female pedestrian – as long as my mother wasn't in the car, in which case it was definitely Eyes Front – without swivelling his head to check her out. It was just that neither of us was comfortable sharing the experience.

Still, some progress had been made. I'd grown older. He was still tearing bare-breasted black women from the *National Geographic* in case the younger children saw them, but at least he'd stopped pulling the TV plug on me. Until this year, whenever Miss Kitty had displayed some modest saloon-hostess cleavage on 'Gunsmoke', he'd simply got up from his chair grumbling his catchphrase, 'This isn't suitable for children,' and turned off the TV. Nowadays when faced by titillating television he and I just gritted our teeth and sat it out.

I wasn't surprised to find *On the Beach* moving. But I was surprised it was so sexy. If the end of the world was nigh, Ava Gardner wasn't going to waste a minute on small talk. Whenever she appeared on screen my father cleared his throat. Ava was attractive, tipsy and shameless – three good reasons for throat-clearing. She was unstoppable. She had Gregory Peck in the sack before the nuking of his wife and children and the rest of the northern hemisphere had even sunk in.

You couldn't blame Gregory for succumbing to Ava. Apart from it being the end of the world, he was a widower – if only very recently. But we were meant to agonise with his dilemma and my father did so. When heavy-lidded Ava drew Gregory into the bedroom, the throat-clearing turned into a coughing spasm nearly as bad as his early morning hawking extravaganzas.

When we left the theatre I felt chatty. Stanley Kramer, Ava Gardner and the Cold War had given me plenty to think about. '*Whew!*' I said. 'What did you think?'

His eyes were surprisingly pink and damp. 'Very realistic,' he said.

I had a few queries. When Gregory Peck took his submarine back to San Francisco to see if someone was left alive, and the sailor dived overboard and swam ashore, and you saw the city, it was totally empty. Wouldn't there be bodies lying around?

'Maybe you're right,' he said.

'What are the physical effects of a radioactive cloud, anyway?' I wondered.

He said he didn't know.

I reckoned it was more believable in Melbourne at the end, with the newspaper blowing along the empty street and the camera picking up the religious sign 'The End is Nigh'. It didn't matter that we didn't see any bodies because we'd got to know people living there. 'That was cleverly done,' I said.

He grunted. He didn't want to talk. I remembered that he and my mother had done their own wooing on the same beach as Gregory Peck and Ava Gardner: Frankston, where my mother grew up. The carefree evidence was there in our photograph albums.

When we got home, my mother was making supper for us. She was trying to round off our evening together. 'How was it?' she asked.

'Not too many laughs in it,' my father said.

192

I couldn't wait for her to set the cups in front of us so I could repeat the last line in the movie. She did eventually, and I said it. ' "Peter, I think I'll have that cup of tea now." '

'What do you mean?' she said.

'He's being smart,' my father said.

I explained that the line had been spoken by Mary, the young wife, to her sensitive young husband, Peter. I couldn't remember who played Mary but sensitive young Peter was Anthony Perkins. I told her how Mary and Peter had just quietly poisoned their baby off-screen and were about to drink poison themselves rather than die from nuclear fallout.

I'd thought it was pretty devastating at the time, but I said the cup-of-tea line again, enunciating like a thespian.

'We heard you the first time,' my father said.

My mother laughed nervously. 'It sounds as if I was well out of it.'

'You don't actually see any Melburnians die,' I told her. 'But you get the feeling they're dropping like flies.'

My father sipped his tea. 'Fred Astaire was surprisingly good,' he said.

'Fred Astaire?' she said.

'It wasn't one of his dancing efforts,' my father said. 'None of the old soft shoe.'

'No, I suppose not,' she said.

WINDOWS

Rottnest still had me in its power. A year and a half after my first visit, I went camping there for a week in the August school holidays. On my second day on the island I met a girl and we got on like a house on fire. By the time our final school term resumed two weeks later, Ruth Parnham and I were 'going out'.

'Going out' was a particularly inaccurate way to describe our relationship. We weren't able to see each other. A farmer's daughter whose parents had split up, Ruth was back behind the walls of a Catholic boarding school, Santa Maria College, not to be released into the world until after our final examinations in November.

'Going out', but actually staying in, we ardently pursued our romance by smuggled letter and snatched telephone call. She was imprisoned on the opposite side of the river at Attadale. I could see the Santa Maria tower every morning as I ran my cross-country miles past Sunset and along the foreshore.

I imagined her at those moments waking to insistent bells in a Spartan dormitory. She would wash her pale face in cold water from a chipped enamel bowl. Cryptic Virgins and doleful Jesuses, holding their heads at the passive, oblique angles they favoured, looked down on her. She brushed her fine blonde hair as she re-read my love-letters in the Catholic dawn.

Without Ruth and me present our romance progressed rapidly. It was ignited by the sudden firm opposition of the Santa Maria nuns, whose stool-pigeon network had quickly reported that Ruth Parnham was seeing – although, of course, not *seeing* – a non-Catholic boy.

We did, however, intend to see each other. Ruth was allowed one free weekend in the term. She'd timed it for the boys' interschool track-and-field carnival on a Saturday in late October. That night she would come with me to an athletes' party in South Perth.

This time I was running in the open mile race, the climactic event of the competition. With all the dawn training, my times had improved. But while I certainly liked the idea of her being present if I won, I didn't fancy her being there if I ran last. One way or another, I was feeling anxious about the big day. Running a mile race in front of thousands of people, half of them female, wasn't the least of it. What I was looking forward to was the party afterwards, to seeing her – especially after two months apart – at night-time. (In the best of possible worlds, of course, I would earlier in the day have lapped the field in the mile.)

But the Santa Maria intelligence network had been busy.

The nuns abruptly cancelled Ruth's free weekend. Disapproving of a non-Catholic boy's existence was one thing. Enabling a Catholic girl to watch him in an athletic competition was another.

Ruth couldn't fight it. The Leaving Certificate matriculation exams were looming. The nuns could prevent her from sitting for them. They could blight her future. On the telephone I railed about injustice. How could they do it? She took it surprisingly calmly. She said it was a cinch for teachers who'd removed the Human Reproduction section from their biology textbooks.

So there would be no Ruth at the race. I was relieved of the anxiety of her seeing me fail dismally. But perhaps I wasn't quite so highly charged to succeed either. As a result I ran the race feeling loose and relaxed and did neither badly nor fabulously well: I came third again. Third place was fine by me. Honour was satisfied and Plan B could now swing into operation.

What Ruth and I had planned was for me to leave the party at ten-thirty, drive to Santa Maria and park in a tree-lined street at the back of the school. She would go over the wall and meet me in the car at eleven.

When I arrived at the party it was full of Wesley boys. Most of the boarders had been given weekend leave for the interschool sports day. After a dance or two I announced I was off to Santa Maria. John Sturkey asked if he could have a lift to Dianne Someone-or-other's party. Sturkey was still sixteen, a year younger than the rest of us, and without a driver's licence. He assured me the party was on the way. Absolutely, I said. I was feeling pleasantly relaxed after my race. Bring the bottle by all means.

We set off for Attadale, and we soon got lost looking for his party. It turned out he didn't know the name of the street. Time flew past. The streets seemed to peter out into unsealed bush tracks. The street lights had ended a few blocks back. Whichever direction we drove we seemed to be blocked by the river. We drank beer while he looked for Dianne Someone's party in the street directory. No street there rang a bell. We looked under Tourist Attractions, Nursing Homes and Places of Worship. Strangely, it wasn't listed.

We were laughing by now, and it was hard to see the road with the interior light on. I was still laughing when I ran off the road. I only realised it after fifty yards when the treeline loomed up at me. I braked sharply and bogged the car.

There was one good thing about the Renault: it was so tinny it was light. Sturkey and I picked it up and lifted it sideways out of the mud. 'No more farting about,' I said as we bumped back onto the road. I was getting worried about Ruth. I was overdue at the Santa Maria wall. She'd be frantic. The mother superior, or whoever was in charge, would catch her. I envisioned grim watch-nuns patrolling the perimeter with torches and heavy crucifixes in their belts. I hadn't time to find Dianne Someone's party now. He'd have to come with me.

I said I'd take him where I had to go. Then he'd have to find his own way. 'Fine. I know the way from there,' he said. As I approached Santa Maria, I turned off the lights, stopped, and let him out.

'Say hello to Dianne,' I said.

'Have one for me,' Sturkey said.

I drove there with the lights off. I parked by the wall and waited. In a couple of minutes Ruth appeared. I'd expected to see her in some sort of convent sack-cloth but she was wearing a form-fitting skirt and sweater in smart autumnal tones. Her hair was crisply pulled back. She could have been a sophisticated twenty-five. She didn't look religious or downtrodden. She looked cold and cross.

Her hands and the tip of her nose were icy, but in the car she soon warmed up. It was like being in our own little space capsule, although the Renault was smaller than any spacecraft I could imagine. With its steamed-up windows and the pitch darkness outside it was soon more like a midget submarine. A bathysphere. We could have been down five thousand fathoms.

After maybe an hour of cramped canoodling Ruth asked me the time. It was twelve-fifty. 'I have to go!' she cried. 'I won't be able to sneak back in after one o'clock!' I was supposed to be home by one as well but I had no chance of making it. It would take me at least half an hour to drive across the river.

Just then a footstep crunched nearby. *Nuns!* I nervously rubbed the condensation off the windscreen and a male face loomed out of the dark and pressed close to the glass. '*Yahh!*' growled the peeping tom.

Ruth yelped. I jumped up and knocked my head on the roof. Where was the crank handle when I needed it? I opened the car door and stumbled out into the cold night air.

It was Sturkey. 'Sorry about that,' he laughed. 'Christ, I'm having trouble finding that bloody party.'

—

My mother was lying in bed awake in the dark. She'd turned out the light but she couldn't go to sleep until I came home. My father was away again on his annual north-west boat trip, being a missionary for Dunlop, bringing rubber products to the back of beyond.

She lay there steeling herself to get up and walk to the window in the dark. She couldn't turn on the light because she needed to see out there.

Finally she took a deep breath, got up and walked to the window. She opened a gap in the venetians and looked out into the garden. It must have been after one o'clock because the street lights were out, but when her eyes adjusted she could clearly see the expanse of the front lawn from the Stockwells' fence on the left to the Dolans' fence on the right, and up the short grassy slope to the road.

Dew had fallen and a faint moonlight shone on the damp grass. The dew transformed the lawn from a daytime patchwork of superfine couch, buffalo, ordinary couch and clover into a smooth silvery expanse. You couldn't make out the sandy patch where the builders had mixed their quicklime and

cement five years before and the grass had never grown properly since. It looked like a putting green.

She'd thought she had heard a noise but there was no one
there.

Now she was up she thought she'd go to the lavatory. She
walked back across the bedroom from the window to the door,
and out into the hall. She went to the bathroom. As she came
out, she heard Bill snoring and she looked in on the children.
Seeing my empty bed reminded her that I was now late home,
and she began to worry.

Something suddenly occurred to her. She'd left the back
door unlocked for me. She thought she should lock it. When
I got home she could let me in. She was so fully awake now
there was no chance of her dropping off.

It was on her way through the house to lock the door, as
she turned into the front hall, past the high French windows
which opened onto the back terrace, that she saw the figure
standing motionless on the terrace, pressed full-length against
the glass, looking into the house.

The man was so close to her that she almost missed him.
They surprised each other. He saw her at the same time and
his body squirmed and rubbed against the glass. His body and
her body, separated by glass, were no more than two feet apart.
The dark, blurred shape of him, his brow, was more or less on
her level. He was masked. His hands were up against the glass
and they were what she noticed most. The hands were wearing women's gloves and suddenly they shone a thin beam of
light on her.

She lurched back from the glass, from the big, floor-to-ceiling windows she'd always wanted, the biggest windows in Circe Circle, windows to let the sunlight in, windows that defied the gloomy Leon Road leadlights of Mrs Sefton.

'Police!' she cried. The man had hardly moved. His narrow light beam played calmly up and down her body, her night-dress, around the hall, investigated the room. In her panic she fell back against the telephone table. The phone was right beside her. 'Police!' she yelled again, even before she dialled it.

The light beam picked up her dialling the telephone. She heard the torch tap against the glass as he moved it. The beam seemed to be hovering on her, following her, as if making up its mind what to do now. As she dialled Detective-Sergeant John McCurry's number in the Teledex, waited for an answer, she thought abruptly, *the back door!* But she had to speak to McCurry so she stayed on the phone. The man moved back from the window, turned *towards the back door!* and stumbled into our table-tennis table. The table, divided in the middle in a series of hinges, slid off one trestle, then another, and crashed heavily – in two, three, four stages – to the floor.

In the clatter she dropped the phone. She ran to the back door. (*Big windows everywhere! He'd see her!*) She locked it and ran back to the phone. She thought the prowler had gone then, but as she held on while the police operator was calling McCurry's car the torch beam shone again from somewhere further back on the terrace. Its beam was thin and probing – it must have been one of those pencil torches – and it played over her body once more, as if reconsidering.

Why hadn't he run away? The thought struck her: *He knows Roy isn't here!* He'd already looked in the bedroom windows and seen there were only the two children home with her. The torch went off. She couldn't see the prowler but she thought she could hear him padding around the demolished table-tennis table towards the back of the house.

McCurry was there surprisingly quickly. As his car pulled up outside, its radio crackling, its searchlight beaming into the trees, the man slipped into the shadows of the back yard and disappeared.

McCurry had been on patrol only two streets away, in Minora Road. He sat with her over a cup of tea while the other cop cruised around the neighbourhood. 'Did you see him?' he asked, not too hopefully.

She said, 'He had a handkerchief tied around his face like a cowboy. But I have a feeling he was the same prowler as the other time.'

I arrived home then to see all the lights in the house blazing. I got a fright when McCurry met me at the door. He was wearing a maroon cardigan under his suit jacket, and his buttoned chest and stomach filled the doorway in a proprietorial manner. What had happened? I squeezed past him and hurried into the kitchen. My mother was sitting at the kitchen table in her dressing-gown smoking a cigarette.

'A night-owl, eh?' McCurry said. 'Your mother could have done with you here, son.'

I felt instantly guilty. I also felt like an interloper. 'Sorry I'm late,' I said. 'Car trouble.'

'He doesn't go out very much,' she said to McCurry. 'And he's had a big day running the mile.' She smiled at me wanly and pulled her gown tighter around her. 'I've had another visitor.'

McCurry gave me a last dismissive look and leaned over the table towards her. He seemed to take up the whole kitchen. He told her not to worry, the average peeping tom was pretty harmless. Then he winked. 'A bloody menace to a clothesline full of panties, though.'

My mother shuddered and looked sceptical. She didn't say anything. She seemed exhausted.

That reminded him of something. 'By the way, you don't shop at Shirley's Frock Salon up on the highway, do you?' he asked her. He didn't wait for an answer. He was grinning. 'We've got a charmer who keeps breaking into Shirley's and making love to the mannequins in the front window. We lock him up and the moment he gets out he rides his bike right through the window again, smashes the window with his handlebars. Most times he's still on the job when we get there. In full public view. Light as day. The alarm's going off. I say to him, "Come on, Errol Flynn. Say good night to your girl-friend," and he looks up from the floor and says, "Would you mind giving Sonia and me a few minutes' privacy?"' He laughed and drained his cup. 'True love.'

I stayed up until McCurry's car returned. My mother thanked him and shook his hand and he left. Then she told me what had happened. She said, 'I wish I could be more definite that I knew who it was.' As we walked around the house re-checking all the doors and windows, she said, 'That business about the pervert raping the shop dummies – do you think that was meant to make me feel better?'

Even though she looked drained she laughed then and I laughed with her. We left the lights on and said good night.

In the bright light I suddenly noticed long blonde hairs glistening all over my jumper. If she saw them when I kissed her good night she didn't say anything.

PART THREE

1

THE REAL WORLD

Before my first day at work I went to stay with Simon Watson and his family in Renown Avenue. It was the middle of the summer holidays and my family was holidaying down at Albany. Mrs Watson had invited me to stay until they returned. The Watsons had forgiven me for demolishing their letterbox. And I hadn't brought up the murder weapon again.

Even though the hatchet often crossed my mind, and a couple of times I found myself gazing at the garage wall where they hung their tools, at the empty, hatchet-shaped painted outline next to the occupied outlines of the hammer and saw and chisel and garden shears (the police still had the murder weapon in their possession), I found it easy enough to conduct conversations for a week without the word 'hatchet' coming up.

Anyway, while the Berkman murder was still unsolved, the police had finally captured Jillian Brewer's killer. He was a nineteen-year-old deaf-mute named Darryl Beamish. I'd known Beamish as a rowdy older boy at the Claremont baths when I was younger. Once the police came to the baths to question him. He hung around with a noisy gang of deaf boys who used to touch girls as they swam by. His strange angry sounds and risky behaviour made me think he wasn't right in the head. Using an interpreter, the police had got him to confess. He'd been convicted and sentenced to death.

The telegram from the editor of the *West Australian*, Griff Richards, had arrived three days before we were due to leave for Albany. It said I had the job as a cadet reporter. I was more than happy to miss out on Albany. The starting date was my birthday, a week later. I thought it was a good omen.

My mother and Simon's mother decided I shouldn't have to go home to an empty house on the important day that I both started work and turned eighteen. It was also the day the Leaving Certificate results were announced and Mrs Watson made Simon and me a special dinner that night. Next morning when the paper arrived she complimented me on my first published story. She cut it out and kept it for my mother.

The newspaper cutting was the size of a large postage stamp. In its entirety my story said: *Patrick O'Donnell, 56, of no fixed address, received a broken leg and abrasions when he was struck by a car at the intersection of Murray and William streets yesterday.*

The newspaper's police roundsman, Ralph Wheatley, like many of the senior reporters a middle-aged Englishman, bluff and tweedy and pipe-smoking and proud of his ex-service moustache, had allowed me that filler item from the day's police-rounds grab-bag. I was lucky to get it. Ralph was still reeling from my hard-boiled crime-reporter's small-talk during our afternoon rounds of the Perth detectives.

'This is my new assistant,' he'd said. 'It's his first day.' We were in the vice-squad office. It was hot and stuffy and an old fan whirred and rattled in a corner. Four vice detectives loomed slowly out of their chairs and shook hands. I'd already undone my collar button and loosened my tie so I'd fit in. The detectives remained standing, lounging in their shirtsleeves against filing cabinets full of wicked case histories. I thought of all the vice details stored in those cabinets. All the sin and obscenity they dealt with every day. The detectives stared at me. I felt an air of expectation in the room.

'Tell me,' I heard an unfamiliar voice pipe up, a twelve-year-old choirboy's perhaps. 'On the subject of rape, I read that penetration is enough, legally speaking.'

The detectives stared silently at me. A strange mist floated through the room. Relentlessly, in a sort of suicidal trance, I ploughed on. While one part of my brain was urging me to shut up, another part was dredging up some case I'd read years before while trolling for sex information in Sten Gunn's father's law library. I couldn't stop. I dearly wanted to, but I couldn't.

'This judge said there doesn't need to be ejaculation for it to be rape,' I said. Still no one spoke. A blowfly buzzed and bumped against the vice-squad's dusty window pane. My brain registered a brown leather shoulder-holster hanging over the back of a chair. 'That's what I read in this law book, anyway.'

Ralph didn't say anything as we walked downstairs to continue the round, but he was deep in thought. We walked past the petty-sessions courts to the deserted Press room. Caustic smells wafted up from the holding cells below the courts. Ralph made a noise in his throat. 'Would you mind waiting down here while I see the Commissioner?' he said.

He was gone a long while, more than enough time for me to carve my name beside all the others on the Press-room desk. But I didn't. I was still squirming about my encounter with the vice-squad. I felt too much of a novice to presume desk-carving rights, even to presume I'd have a job the next day.

There was also time enough for me to read all the *Wanted* posters in the entrance hall, even to learn them by heart. Their gritty details cheered me up a little, especially the old, yellowing poster for an American felon, Jacob 'Cheemy' Perlmutter. Cheemy Perlmutter was wanted for escaping from gaol in New Jersey ten years before. He had a record of fraud and racketeering offences going back thirty years. I could see why the New Jersey police or the FBI might want to catch him, but in alerting the West Australian public they seemed to be casting an exceedingly wide net.

A few weeks later, in my own time, I wrote my first 'feature' story. Its subject was Cheemy Perlmutter. I fantasised that Cheemy was indeed hiding out in Western Australia, living the quiet life in some sandy suburb. It wasn't as if he was a murderer or anything. I imagined the retired racketeer pushing a shopping trolley at Tom the Cheap Grocer's, learning to surf, throwing out a fishing line now and again. He might have trouble obtaining his cigars and bagels but I could see him enjoying a nice grilled whiting for breakfast.

212

Ralph snorted in his moustache when he read the published story. He'd passed Cheemy's *Wanted* poster a thousand times. 'Interesting little angle,' he said. The *West Australian* saw itself as the paper of record rather than the paper of interesting little angles. It was more at home with Paddy O'Donnell's accident than Cheemy Perlmutter's long-ago gaol escape in another hemisphere.

The paper of record provided entry into what reporters liked to call 'the real world'. The real world was in a different galaxy to the world of rubber products. It seemed to be populated solely by the police and people in trouble with the police. And reporters, of course.

Despite rare intrusions like the Jillian Brewer murder – now solved at last – it was also situated a long way from Dalkeith and its environs. The real world was somewhere across the river.

When we weren't assisting the senior police, courts, industrial, finance, sport and political reporters we first-years were assigned to back-of-the-paper clerical tasks: collecting and typing up the weather details; the vegetable, fruit, meat and fish market prices; and the television and radio programmes.

Serving in these nether regions, our day's work buried near the classified ads, kept us humble and keen. The repetitive nature of the jobs supposedly sharpened us up and taught us accuracy. In the avuncular, pipe-tobacco-scented atmosphere of the newsroom, these monotonous tasks, like our compulsory shorthand lessons with Miss Pat May, were regarded as builders of journalistic character as well as reporting skills. If so, we cadets were chock full of it.

We also staffed the only fractionally less inferior suburban supplements. I was assigned to the west suburban section, covering the serene suburbs between the river and the coast, my old stamping ground. The middle-class west had even less news than the scruffier points of the compass. My supplement beat was known as eisteddfods-and-shitfights.

Eisteddfod, I soon learned, was the most depressing word in the reporter's stylebook. The Welsh had a lot to answer for. It seemed that every week some suburban choir or twelve-year-old Shenton Park nightingale was competing in one of these tricky-to-spell events. As for the shitfights, shit-scuffles was closer to the mark. These weren't major controversies, although we tried hard to make them so, but the usual local government spats about rezoning and rates and tree removal and preserving old buildings and road widening and how to deal with defecating dogs.

Meanwhile, between eisteddfods and shitfights I covered those sports with a following so minuscule that the real sports-writers shunned them – lacrosse, badminton, Royal tennis.

I hadn't realised how many arcane pursuits there were out in the suburbs. Or how desperate they were for publicity. Previously ignored archers, hurlers, go-karters and clay-pigeon shooters greeted me as a flower does the sun. Soon they were plaguing their new mouthpiece at all hours. I dreaded Monday mornings. Earnest fencing-club secretaries were first on the phone with the weekend épée, foil and sabre results. Then the speleologists brought me up to date on their weekend cavings. (My standard opening question: 'So how deep did you go this week?')

I barely had time to catch up on recent manoeuvrings in table-tennis association politics, and to sympathise with the latest rebuff to go-karting's territorial ambitions, before the newsroom door swung open and my keenest news source, Mrs Thelma Knopp, secretary-treasurer of the Claremont-Cottesloe Croquet Club, arrived at my elbow. Mrs Knopp preferred to personally deliver her weekly six-page, handwritten, blow-by-blow croquet sagas – the headings already written and marked *Do Not Change!*

There was so little real news in eisteddfods-and-shitfights that I walked the suburban streets looking for it. Senior reporters often talked nostalgically about going 'back on the road' but they didn't take it as literally as I did. Every day for a month I caught a bus into the western suburbs, got off some-where along the route in Shenton Park or Claremont or Mosman Park, chose a street that looked as if it might hold a few secrets, wiped my damp palms on my pants, took several deep breaths, knocked on a random door and asked the bemused householder if he or she had a story.

Twice they did. I had a labrador released from the dog pound and 'saved from certain death'. And I found a seventy-year-old primary school cleaner who had taken over coaching the school's girls' softball team. Any day soon they'd win a game.

Even for an eisteddfods-and-shitfights reporter I was

scraping the bottom of the barrel. The supplements editor, Jack Morrison, told me brusquely to 'put Dalkeith under the microscope'. All right, I said, but I didn't expect to find much when I looked through the lens.

Dalkeith people prided themselves on living respectable and modern suburban lives. Modernity was as important as respectability. They lived in the immediate present. The past, as I'd heard it described all my life, went back only as far as the war. But it certainly went back that far. The Circe Circle matrons still ostracised Mrs Brotherson down the road for 'going with' Americans in 1942. Mrs Brotherson was now in her fifties.

In desperation I recalled my piece on Cheemy Perlmutter. At least it had raised Ralph's eyebrows and made a small splash in the office. I'd try to drum up some more feature articles. I started in the newspaper library. And in the library I learned some things. That Roberta Ainslie was working there, for a start.

It was a shock to see my former Rottnest bathing beauty wielding a Stanley knife with the other library assistants. They were mostly older women in their late twenties, jaded stunners with bohemian reputations and sexy smokers' voices. Sarcastic and well connected, they were renowned for the languor with which they cut out and – eventually – filed the stories in the day's papers. They undulated between cutting table, filing cabinet and canteen, trailing cigarette smoke, cynical trills of laughter and world-weary sighs. They had better things to do – gossiping, nursing hangovers, reading magazines, flirting with sportswriters – than assisting apprentice reporters younger than themselves.

Roberta, it turned out, wasn't planning a career as a librarian or a bohemian. She wanted to be a journalist. She'd studied for a year in America and was marking time until she got a cadetship. Meanwhile, it wasn't the hardest job in the world, she said. It hadn't been too difficult to come by, either. Her father was the company lawyer.

For old times' sake she broke ranks and helped me with my research. Well, she stood up from the table, took some files out of a cabinet and showed me how to work the microfiche viewer.

Seeing her out of her Rottnest context was disconcerting. She was wearing a pale blue Angora sweater, dark blue skirt and high heels. Her tan was paler. In heels she was taller, of course. She wasn't showily smoking but I saw a cigarette burning discreetly in an ashtray beside her Stanley knife. She was still beautiful but more jaded. She'd learned to walk the undulating table-to-cabinet-to-canteen walk. She looked like a girl who had travelled. She looked like a girl who worked, but not too hard.

I did learn several things of interest: that Dalkeith's leafy streets were named after graceful racing yachts, *Circe*, *Genesta*, *Viking*, *Adelma*, *Nardina*, *Curlew*, *Minora*, *Iris* and *Beatrice*, which had sailed the river early in the century; that the main street had been named after another elegant yacht, *Westana*. And that, in 1924, a taxi driver, John O'Neil, had been murdered in his Buick cab in Westana Road, 'his head smashed

217

with a heavy instrument until the brain was exposed', and his body dumped in the river at Crawley Bay.

This was news to me. For the apparently motiveless murder, a twenty-four-year-old socialite, George Auburn, had been tried and convicted. Auburn escaped hanging 'because of his youth'. As the *Mirror* pointed out, such an age had never deterred the authorities from execution before. In fact, it was the average age for murderers at time of execution. The *Mirror* hinted that Auburn's 'important connections' had pulled strings.

For twenty days the trial excited the newspapers (*Most Momentous Murder Case in Our History!*). The notoriety greatly concerned Dalkeith's residents and real estate agents. Alarmed at the prospect of falling land values, they moved swiftly to change the street's name. Westana Road became Waratah Avenue. Westana Road and its murder – Dalkeith's bad name – were erased so completely from the public memory that they might never have been.

Learning about the old murder was vaguely exciting. But discovering the main street of my childhood was a re-creation made me feel odd.

Waratah Avenue was the home of Mr Palmer's cinema, the comic-book racks of the newsagent, the Dutch lady baker, the 202 bus route and Eller's Store, which had allowed me to help weigh and pack potatoes into one-stone bags and to deliver groceries, my wage being a piece of cheese, an apple or those

Animals of the World swap cards which had worked loose from Weeties and Vita Brits cereal wrappers. Waratah Avenue had been the central thoroughfare in my life. Now it was revealed as a bit of commercial sleight of hand. The street suddenly seemed as false as a movie set.

And it wasn't the only spot on Dalkeith's reputation. In the files I discovered another violent murder. This one rang a bell. It was the one Nick Howell had heard about from his mother.

It went back to the suburb's beginnings in 1833 as a land grant to a Scottish settler, Adam Armstrong. He'd already been given land on the Murray River, a hundred miles south of Perth, but the farm's isolation and 'the aggression of the natives' had forced him back to town. So on a bend in the Swan River five miles from Perth, where the Aborigines were detribalised and more docile, he took up another grant – of three hundred and fifty acres – instead.

By 1838, with the Murray River Aborigines decimated in the Battle of Pinjarra, Armstrong decided to return there. By then Dalkeith Farm – named after his old home near Edinburgh – was well established, its market garden on the riverbank raising grapes, goats and vegetables. As his *For Sale* advertisements pointed out: 'Its celebrity for Melons is notorious. As a goat run, it is not surpassed by any in the Colony.'

The property passed into the hands of James Gallop and his son James Jr. For the rest of the century the family developed the fruit and vegetable gardens until they stretched for a mile along the riverbank and were the showpiece of the colony. The farm was still isolated from any roads, and access by land was difficult, but in summer the beauty of the gardens attracted boatloads of weekend sightseers and picnickers. The Gallops supplied Perth, Fremantle and the goldfields with plantains, grapes, quinces, apples, figs, mulberries, peaches, pomegranates, currants, watermelons, rockmelons and sugar cane. Fifty tons of grapes were cut each year.

Above the thriving farm and its rare, rich patch of darker soil, situated on a dune of yellow sand at the edge of the bush track which would later become Westana Road (and still later be changed by a taxi driver's murder into Waratah Avenue), there was for more than fifty years a native camp.

The Gallops employed Aborigines from the camp to bang kerosene tins to keep the birds off their ripening fruit. They also armed two of them with guns to shoot the little birds called silvereyes which had developed a fondness for grapes. The men were skilled shots. Despite the small size of the silvereyes, thousands of them were shot each year. One year, the Gallops noted with satisfaction, the Aborigines had killed eight thousand five hundred silvereyes.

When the head gardener's young wife disappeared and a police search for her was unsuccessful, black trackers from the camp were called in to look for her. They found her some distance from the house, chopped to death with an axe. The murderer was never discovered.

In 1920 the old Gallop estate was sold. By then the gardens were overgrown, gone to seed or eaten by birds. The dunes gradually drifted over the vines. The government bought the river frontage for future public recreation and the rest was subdivided into two hundred and thirty-one suburban lots. New streets were named after graceful racing yachts. The blacks' camp was knocked down and the people shooed off.

At last I had something reasonably juicy on Dalkeith. But when I showed this material to Jack Morrison, he passed it back, saying, 'Where's the angle, where's the peg?' He was frowning when he said it. Then he took a deep breath and said it was very interesting ancient history. It would be terrific background if someone was murdered in the same place in the same way tomorrow.

I went back to interviewing twelve-year-old eisteddfod prodigies and fencers and table-tennis players who'd made it as far as the semi-finals in Eastern States competitions. I listened to go-karting administrators griping that horseracing, football and cricket got all the prime real estate as well as press coverage. On Monday mornings I hid in the toilet to avoid Mrs Knopp and her croquet epics. I went back on the road.

It was frustrating. I was desperate to cover real news, yet while I was stuck on eisteddfods-and-shitfights Perth suddenly abounded in big, glamorous stories. According to Premier Dave Brand, the eyes of the world were on us.

Not only was Perth hosting the Commonwealth Games but, more importantly, we had just been dubbed the City of Light. This accolade from the New York *Journal-American* came after the astronaut John Glenn publicly thanked us as he spun overhead in his Mercury capsule. As the *West Australian's* head-line summed up the historic space flight:

> *Glenn Orbits Earth,*
> *Says Thanks to Perth.*

Despite the scoffing of the sceptics, including our Lord Mayor Harry Howard, who said Colonel Glenn would never see them from one hundred and fifty miles up, we left all our lights on all night in honour of John Glenn and the United States space programme – and he saw them. He spotted the tiny glow on the south-west tip of the great black southern continent. 'I can see lights on the ground,' he said. 'I can see the lights of Perth on the coast. Thanks everyone for turning on the lights.'

With the City of Light shimmering in the news, some local boosters even pushed for Perth's name to be officially changed to the City of Light. One canny businessman at the pet-rock end of capitalism made a killing by selling sealed, empty tins labelled *Guaranteed Air from the City of Light.* They gave people a giggle. My father bought a dozen cans of air and gave them away to bigshots visiting from Melbourne.

In this newsy climate eisteddfods-and-shitfights lan-guished even more than usual. But I found one compensation in my beat. Graylands Teachers' College, where Ruth was now studying, was right in the middle of my supplement's area, situated between the Claremont Mental Hospital and the Graylands Migrant Hostel.

The nuns' fears had been realised. With actual personal

222

contact Ruth and I had grown closer. I thought she was warm, attractive and intelligent. She liked philosophical conversations about religion and films and current affairs. I began a routine of borrowing the Renault to do my reporting rounds, picking up Ruth after her lectures, and parking for an hour or two, before driving her home to South Perth, where she now lived, and then parking some more.

I more or less convinced myself I was out on the road. What was parking if not a form of reconnoitring? Movie private eyes did it all the time. The eisteddfod-prodigy mothers and croquet administrators couldn't reach me, and if hard news broke, I told myself, I'd be handily positioned. If a lunatic escaped from the asylum or a shell-shocked refugee went on a hunger strike or set himself alight, I'd be on the spot.

Maybe they did. Madmen and smouldering migrants could have been swarming around us on a daily basis. We were too busy fogging up the Renault's windows to notice. At Cottesloe, Crawley Bay, King's Park, the South Perth riverfront and the Lakeway drive-in we became such accomplished parkers, dexterously maximising cabin space and avoiding handbrake and gearstick, that we were distracted only once, when a peeping tom boldly peered into the car window one night in South Perth.

By then we were bolder, too. There was more to see this time. When the voyeur showed no sign of moving off, we sounded the horn at him and, laughing nervously, covered ourselves and accelerated away.

2

SATURDAY NIGHT BOY (II)

He was peering down into the Swan River from the crown of the bridge and remembering his younger self down there swimming the Narrows with his oatmeal sports jacket gripped to his chest. He was remembering swimming the river before the bridge was built in '59 and recalling things that had happened before and after. He relived every stroke across the river.

He'd calmed down now. Standing there at the rail waiting for the cars to pass, facing east into the breeze, steadying his mind and getting his focus back, he could smell the inland bush and desert, that gravelly eucalypt dryness wafting over the ranges and over the river and out to sea. His people were from the country once upon a time. The York district. Three York generations before his old man, before Snowy, and all of them dust-and-stubble farmers, bad drunks and wife-beaters, Great-grandma Cooke dying suspiciously back then but not enough evidence to put Pa on a charge. So his mother said the

227

time she left and got the legal separation through the courts and changed back to her maiden name. Miss Erica Edgar, a funny name for a mother. It's in the blood, she said, the drink, the violence, the chaos.

And then went back to him! Returned to Snowy, drunk all the time and hating him from the day he was born. *If you think I'm going to keep that misfit all my life you've got another think coming!* Banging his head on the wall. *Talk properly, Uglymouth!*

Anyway, he had bad memories of the country. The country was boredom, booze, car prangs and women who changed their minds when it came to the crunch. He'd known country women, chased a few, and they were trouble. He was more a city boy, a suburban boy. A Saturday-night boy who knew his way around.

Saturday nights had certainly changed since his river-swimming days, he thought, waiting for a lone north-bound car to come off the Kwinana expressway, pass over the bridge and disappear into the freeway roundabout. He couldn't take any chances. He still had on his gloves (ladies' best kid), as he stood at the rail facing the city, a bigger, brighter city now, with a couple of new skyscrapers thrusting self-consciously from the sand flats of the river basin.

He felt its growing power in his own arms and shoulders, a pride in his control of his surroundings. Wasn't he the cat among the pigeons! He could hardly wait to see the paper. He hadn't felt so in command since the Boan's fire, the robbery-arson. When was that – oh, years ago. When he was just a kid. Even if the feeling lasted only the five minutes he'd squatted on the railway-station bench opposite with an old hungover Aboriginal bloke, drinking a bottle of Passiona and watching the smoke pouring under the department store's doors into Wellington Street, seeing the fire trucks arrive, the firemen buzzing around like blue-arsed flies.

He'd heard they always rounded up the onlookers at an arson, checked who was getting the biggest kick out of it, so he'd run home then to his grandparents' place before the cops arrived. Hid the money under the bed. But he'd left finger-prints on things inside. On glass counters, the cash registers. On things not even singed. They looked him up from his other thievings. At least the Boan's business had taught him to wear gloves in future. Always.

He was quite calm now, thinking things carefully through. Again he checked all the approaching bridge lanes for traffic. They were clear. So this particular hectic Saturday night in Cottesloe and Nedlands having come to its natural conclusion, he memorised the number stencilled on the bridge's nearest light stanchion, No. 324. (Was there any point in doing so? Just the pride he took in his memory. He still remembered where he'd thrown the skin-diving knife in the river after the Berkman woman in '59.)

Then he took the rifle out of its newspaper wrapping and threw it overarm into the glowing river.

3

THE FULL MOON CLICHÉ

One Monday morning the headlines in the *West Australian* jumped right out at me. The lead story. The photographs. John Sturkey was dead. He'd been murdered in his bed. He'd been shot in the head. So had two others.

How could this be? The story was jagged, senseless. Sturkey? Funny, good-natured Sturkey. He was alive in my mind sauntering along St George's Terrace. I was waiting for the bus the week before, on my way to see Ruth, leaning against the Government House fence as he strolled by. We talked for a while and he asked after her. He was leaving soon for the East to study veterinary science on a scholarship from the Department of Agriculture. He had a year of straight science under his belt but there was no veterinary school in Perth. He was on his way to pick up his train ticket. I wished him good luck and we shook hands.

Before he walked off down the Terrace he said something that made me feel strangely pleased. I took it to mean he was

233

having to leave his girlfriend behind and that he envied my romantic situation. 'Lucky bugger,' he said. As he strolled off he seemed debonair.

Eventually the blur of typefaces cleared and I took in the words. I took in the police version of events, the Press artist's map of the area with its addresses and times of shootings and the dotted lines linking the shooting sites in Cottesloe and Nedlands. I pictured the panic at the paper on the Sunday and I imagined Ralph Wheatley coming into work on his day off to write the story.

The story said that around two a.m. that hot Saturday night, the night of Australia Day – actually early Sunday – a man had been spying on a couple in a parked car in Cottesloe. They became annoyed at him watching them and threw an empty beer bottle at him, whereupon he drew a rifle, aimed at the man in the driver's seat and fired. The woman shouted at her partner to duck and pushed his head down and saved his life. He was struck in the neck, and she in the forearm, and they drove off, very fast and erratically, to Fremantle Hospital.

Then the voyeur-gunman had climbed into a block of flats nearby and shot a young accountant, Brian Weir, in the head at close range while he slept. He'd then driven three miles to Nedlands, prowled through a couple of properties before he spotted John Sturkey asleep on his boarding-house veranda, and shot him in the head from two feet away. He'd walked calmly into the next street, ejecting the spent shell as he went, rung a random doorbell, taken a bead on the sleepy person turning on the light, and shot George Walmsley, a retired grocer, as he opened his front door.

It was like shooting fish in a barrel. Sturkey and Walmsley were dead, Weir brain-damaged and not expected to live. The victims hadn't known each other. The police had no suspect, no motives and no weapon, although the cartridge cases they had recovered showed the same .22 rifle had been used in all the shootings.

Over the next few days the police followed false trails all over the State. The Police Commissioner, Jim O'Brien, said these killings had nothing to do with the murders of the sleeping women, Patricia Berkman in South Perth and Jillian Brewer in Cottesloe. He reminded reporters that those were, respectively, a knife and a hatchet murder. And the victims, of course, were young women. And they had a conviction for one of them.

In their awe and fear of the mysterious killer, people could speak of little else. The mystified police appeared helpless and confused. Indignant letters-to-the-editor writers demanded they ask the FBI and Scotland Yard to step in. Locksmiths and gun shops did a thriving trade. Dogs' homes sold out of watchdogs. Meanwhile, the papers aired increasingly bizarre theories about the 'maniac slayer'. Soon nut cases were coming out of the woodwork and confessing to the murders. Everyone kept noting that the shootings had taken place during a full moon.

The murder scenes were all in my supplement's zone of operation – though not, of course, in my journalistic territory. A couple of days after the shootings I drove past Sturkey's boarding house at 54 Vincent Street, then drove around the block and cruised past the Walmsley house at 51 Louise Street. For a week I found myself driving past the houses every day. I knew it was macabre but I couldn't help it. I was more than curious; I was compelled.

I expected the murder scenes to be bustling with police activity, but I didn't spot any. When I saw those sedate, single-storey, middle-class houses, typical grandparents' homes, my heart lurched. Over the years I'd passed them hundreds of times by day, and at night hurrying home from the Claremont dance, ordinary 'Californian' bungalows in the faded nineteen-twenties style of our old house in Leon Road. They looked elderly and vulnerable, as if small boys running around them would make cracks appear and sand run down their walls.

The murders immediately changed the spirit of the place. They chilled the warm shadows of the peppermint and box trees and flowering gums lining the streets. The slightly crumbly lines of the brick and limestone houses, the cosy-looking fake-Tudor apartment blocks and shopfronts along Stirling Highway, had a sharper, harsher edge. Their facades looked stony and closed. People's eyes flicked away as they hurried indoors or into their cars.

This eerie feeling hung over the coastal suburbs and over the beaches at Cottesloe and North Cottesloe, and also over Swanbourne Beach, where Brian Weir had been a member of the surf club. (It was only discovered he'd been shot when he didn't turn up for surfboat training on Sunday morning and his Swanbourne boat crew mates, thinking he'd overslept, went to his flat to wake him.)

The same ominous sensation loitered in the beer gardens and bars of the Captain Stirling and Nedlands Park and Highway hotels. It was intensified in the bar of the Ocean Beach Hotel – the OBH, as it was known to generations of coastal drinkers – overlooking North Cottesloe Beach. The feeling was a combination of bewilderment, fear and suspicion. Everyone had the wind up.

It was easy to think of the OBH as an important link in the murders. Rowena Reeves, the woman shot in the wrist in the parked car nearby, was a barmaid there. The man in the car with her, Nicholas August, a poultry supplier, was a regular customer. George Walmsley, a talented musician, occasionally played the piano there at wedding receptions. John Sturkey sometimes drank there, too – illegally, because the official drinking age was twenty-one. But then so did hundreds of university undergraduates, most of them under-age, and lifesavers, and *Daily News* and *West Australian* reporters, and general beachgoers. So did Brian Weir. So did my father. For that matter (though of course at different times to him), so did I.

Now John Sturkey's friends talked constantly and excitedly of him. I supposed Brian Weir's and George Walmsley's friends did the same of them. When we talked of John we were always in awe of fate and luck. Our discussions never forgot how he and Scott MacWilliam, the other student lodging at Mrs Connie Allen's boarding house, had tossed a coin to see who got the bed on the open back veranda for the hot summer nights. John won the toss.

We told and retold Scott's tale of how he'd wandered out

onto the back veranda at one a.m. to escape the heat and to drink a bottle of milk from the fridge. (Coincidentally, he, too, had been drinking at the OBH earlier that night.) John had woken and they'd chatted while Scott sat on the end of his bed and drank the milk before going back inside.

It was an anecdote told because of its ordinary beginning, and its horrible end. Three hours later Scott was woken by Mrs Allen's niece, Pauline. There was something wrong with John. Scott went out to the veranda. Strange gurgling sounds were coming from John's throat. Scott lifted John's head from the pillow, thinking he was choking. His head fell back, and Scott saw the bruising, the powder burns, the point-blank bullet wound through the top of his forehead. There was blood on the bed and on the floor.

You didn't need an overheated imagination to realise this could have been any of us boys. It could have been me. It was easy to identify. I knew John Sturkey; I knew Scott MacWilliam; I knew the house. There was a terrible conflicted, guilty thrill in this familiarity if you were a boy with a taste for the macabre, snuggling down with your girlfriend inside her old house with no adults on the premises. Ruth's parents both lived away: her father farmed in the south-west; her mother was housekeeping for an old woman in Nedlands. Released from the confines of Santa Maria, Ruth lived with her younger sister in South Perth – two attractive girls living by themselves. I kept her company whenever I could.

It wasn't only wanting to be with my girlfriend. Young

women were being murdered again. On a Saturday night two weeks after the Cottesloe–Nedlands murders, Rosemary Anderson, only seventeen, was deliberately run down by a car in Shenton Park. A week after, Lucy Madrill, a social worker of twenty-four, was strangled with a lamp cord and raped in her bed in West Perth. Her naked body was dragged from her house and left spreadeagled on a neighbour's back lawn. The empty whisky bottle which had also violated her was cradled in her right arm.

The police came up with a theory about Lucy Madrill's killer. Because she'd worked for the Native Welfare Department as a psychological adviser to Aboriginal women and children they suggested an Aborigine might have murdered her. There were no grounds for this theory and it went nowhere, except to display their prejudice. They finally admitted they were looking for a prowler. Police Commissioner O'Brien again stressed, however, that there were no links with any other killings. He said the *modus operandi* was too different. Meanwhile, in the Rosemary Anderson case they had charged her boyfriend, John Button, with her murder.

Again the murders had occurred in the sedate suburbs of my beat. And once more, alas, they were front-page crimes, not supplement material. At night I drove past the latest crime scenes on my way to cover one or other of the bickering sessions of the Subiaco or Nedlands or Cottesloe local councils. Insensitive tree-lopping was on one agenda, and beach erosion on another, and quite a bitter fight about whether or not to restore historic Gallop House on the Dalkeith foreshore, where last century a young woman had been chopped to death with an axe by a person unknown.

—

Ruth had two important things to say to me and it was the second one which seemed to cause her more anguish. 'I have to tell you this,' she said. She was actually a year older than she'd claimed when we first met on Rottnest. She was a year older than I was. And – she was weeping now – she'd lied because she'd been scared that her being older would put me off. She was really nineteen, she sobbed, and would I ever forgive her?

She was my first steady girlfriend, we'd known each other a year and I loved her. Of course, I said. I thought, eighteen, nineteen, whatever. I was still numbed by the first important thing she'd told me. She was pregnant.

It was winter. We were sitting on the grass in the middle of the windy Esplanade, the wide stretch of lawn between the river and the city's business district, and in my daze at her news I found myself stroking the big fake-fur collar on her corduroy coat. It was an attractive and efficient coat, mustardy brown, of the sort favoured by stylish students, equally suitable for the coffee shop or sports-watching or the movies, and I sat there soothing the collar as if it were a nervous cat, patting and kneading its fur for ten minutes or so before I realised my distracted attempt at calming pressure was falling totally on fluffy fabric rather than on any part of her body.

'We have to make sure,' I croaked. But I knew she was right. The wind from the grey river estuary gusted into my face. Seagulls and pigeons blew randomly about. Even though it was cold, this felt like it could lead to a scene from *A Summer Place*. As if from a distance I could already see myself and Ruth acting out dutiful movie roles while the world around us gathered momentum. I said things to her from films, the words sounding familiar in my mouth. At the same time I felt far from worldly and knowledgeable. I felt simultaneously much older and younger than my age.

I stroked Ruth's actual wrist. I made a point of finding skin this time. I was stroking her wrist and watching the clouds thickening and blowing north over King's Park, and the late afternoon traffic streaming south over the Narrows Bridge, when it dawned on me why film directors used a sky of scudding clouds to signify a dramatic emotional shift, and that the world and my place in it had altered forever.

⸺

At the instant by the evening stove when she heard the news something happened to the way my mother looked and sounded. One moment she was her smiling and upright self, the next she seemed slowed down and compacted by extra gravity. But her thoughts and tongue were loosened and wildly speeded up.

She took it hard, much worse even than I'd feared. 'This is too much for me!' she said, and began to rage and weep at once. 'This is more than I can handle!' The lamb cutlets were sizzling and spitting but she didn't take them off the grill. I would have leaned into the smoke to move them but I thought she might strike me with her waving spatula. 'I knew this would happen!' She stirred the peas so vigorously some swirled out of the saucepan and rolled along the stove-top. 'This is more than I can bear!'

Ruth and I were hovering in the cramped space between the fridge and the stove. Ruth's face was almost as white as the fridge door. Her fine pale hair was tightly bundled up. She was rugged up in her corduroy coat. For once she looked like a Protestant's image of a convent girl. She'd used a lot of powder but she still looked like a nun, like two of her four sisters. She smiled a wan, churchy smile but couldn't speak.

My mother stared into the spitting and bubbling food and drew deep breaths for a whole minute and then turned off the grill and the gas burners under the saucepans. Ruth was so white I thought she might faint. I steered her to a chair at the kitchen table. I put my hand on her shoulder and patted her. Furious vibrations from the stove area told me I shouldn't be too ostentatiously attentive, or tastelessly draw attention to Ruth's condition and a martyrdom so ill-deserved. So I sat down myself. But sitting felt wrong, too, and it disadvantaged me. It wasn't my usual seat – it was my brother's chair – and all the kitchen angles, even the marbled blue swirls of the Formica tabletop, looked unfamiliar from there.

I stood up again and backed up against the fridge door. I placed myself between the women. It seemed important that I stand halfway between them.

This wasn't like *A Summer Place* now. I felt more pathetic and even dumber than Troy Donahue. Troy handled this sort of thing better; he always looked low-key and sulky but he never looked shamed. I didn't feel low-key. I felt base and somehow abnormal. I was a stranger in our own kitchen. My mother had remained close to the stove but now she turned from it and said to me, 'You know you have ruined your lives. You have wrecked this family.'

'I'm sorry you think so,' I muttered. I felt so wretched I couldn't think of anything more to say. I reached over to touch her arm but she brushed my hand away.

She asked us scornfully what we thought we were going to do.

Ruth looked at me. We hadn't actually discussed it but assumptions had been made that windy afternoon on the Esplanade. Made but not voiced. Alternatives had never been discussed or considered. When the pregnancy was confirmed (by a South Perth doctor who didn't know us), assumptions had somehow solidified. But still not been voiced.

'We'll get married,' I said.

'Hah!' my mother scoffed. 'Not at eighteen you won't.'

She didn't seem the same person. Her usual quiet emphasis on taking responsibility for your actions, facing the music, doing the right thing, the disciplined approach, seemed to have flown out the window. My friends all liked her for her friendly, sympathetic personality. She understood the young. Now she was exactly like a mother from *A Summer Place* – and not Dorothy McGuire, Troy's warm, flawed and understanding mother, but Constance Ford, Sandra Dee's grim mother straight from bitter myth.

I was shocked at how shocked she was. 'You can't go through with this,' she insisted. 'You need our permission. We'll stop it.'

Eighteen was legally old enough to be married, especially if the girl was pregnant. And, anyway, Ruth was nineteen. I felt suddenly much older. I realised that in my life I'd never defied my mother before.

'Well, that's what we're doing,' I announced to her, to Ruth and to myself.

My mother, this sudden stranger to me, said she would be the one to break the news to my father. She told him in the car on their way to a Dunlop function that night. He reacted quite differently. He was fiercely embarrassed. When she told him, he hissed at her not to tell anybody.

She seemed to take a grim pleasure next day in relaying his reaction to me. I was working the night shift on police rounds and sleeping late, or trying to. This enabled my father and me to avoid each other for thirty-six hours. But I couldn't avoid her. I had to get up eventually. Anyway, she woke me in order to continue the agony.

She was still in a spin and spiralling away. As soon as my

brother and sister left for school, she started noisily vacuuming and moving furniture around. When I got up she followed me from room to room. There was no let-up while I was in the house, and when I left the house her bitter remarks and mortifying accusations swam in my head.

'I thought something fishy was happening,' she declared. 'Suddenly I didn't have to change your sheets as often as I used to.' I could have curled up and died.

Then she asked, with an eyebrow arched, whether Ruth had been a virgin. And what about the Catholic angle? Wasn't Ruth's mother a fierce Catholic? With two daughters nuns? She'd never agree to Ruth marrying a Protestant.

'Let me warn you,' she went on, and it was more like a malediction. 'You'll never recover from this. You'll be living in a one-room slum full of screaming kids for the rest of your life.' And, grimacing with disgust, she suddenly thought of something else and called out across the house, 'You'd better not have been doing it in my car!'

I couldn't speak. The ordinary loving son and boyfriend could say nothing; neither could the country's most loathsome sex-pig. I was silent with self-hatred and embarrassment, and furious at being so misunderstood.

At last she seemed to have run out of steam, too. I didn't know this woman any more and I didn't have the words to deal with her. I'd never been in disgrace before. The truth was I was also curious about my behaviour and asking myself questions. I didn't understand myself either.

I'd known the risk involved, yet at a certain point I'd let fate take over. Why had I decided to defy the odds and my own intelligence and be swept away? I was young and naive but I knew better than that. It wasn't just the old uneven battle between balls and brain. For this to happen, I suspected, I must have willed it. How could this be? Why had I lost my reason? Was it just love?

And then the whole sorry state of affairs seemed to abruptly strike my mother once more. She moaned loudly to no one in particular, and it was a sort of angry keening, a deeply female note I'd never heard before. It rolled through the house. 'This is worse than adultery!'

This was too much. I was guilty of making love to my girl-friend, but this was over the top. 'No, it's not!' I snapped. 'We're single!'

I left the house then. I had to get out of there. But her adultery remark kept plaguing me. It was sorrow on an entirely different level. It was kinky. Only much later did I wonder whether I'd got it wrong. It dawned on me that perhaps she was comparing the way she felt now to how she'd felt on another occasion.

I hoped I'd misunderstood her. The look she gave me after my retort about being single was more scornful than scorn. It was more complex than anger. *Furious grief* only began to describe it.

Of course I was also dreading the discussion with my father about the 'situation', as my mother called it. This would be our first ever conversation about life – or sex. I recalled the *Father and*

Son booklet, with its emphasis on scouting, hygiene, swimming in icy creeks, masculine fellowship, abstaining from cigarettes and avoiding 'bad habits', which had mysteriously appeared on my pillow when I first inquired how babies were really made.

I was ten and I wanted the full story. Nothing I'd heard up till then made any sense. And the booklet certainly didn't. I didn't get the cigarette/baby connection, or the hiking and hygiene and cold-water connection, or the bad-habits connection. (Biting your fingernails? Chewing with your mouth open?) Or, for that matter, the photographs of square-jawed, bare-chested boys towelling themselves dry and smiling into the middle distance. *Father and Son* had a distinctly armpits-and-Brylcreem whiff to it.

There wasn't a female to be seen. I thought this was a bad slip-up by the *Father and Son* people. I still didn't understand the male input, but even in my Tarzan kissing period the year before, I'd known women were central to the process.

Our discussion now didn't turn out like a scene from a movie either. It was eight-thirty in the morning; I was still in bed after working the late shift on police rounds. The night before I'd made my first visit to the city morgue with the night police reporter, a debonair gent with the memorable by-line of Donald Dyke. Gary, the cocky little morgue attendant on duty, had revelled in my initiation by suddenly throwing open a refrigerated drawer to reveal a carbon-monoxide suicide.

While I recovered he smoothly pulled out another drawer containing a long-deceased and moulting Muscovy duck: Exhibit A in a bestiality charge. 'A farmer gets lonely down at Manjimup these cold nights,' he said, pursing his lips.

Opening a third drawer with a practised comic flourish, he announced, 'And in this one we have . . . (he paused for effect as I reeled back) . . . ham and cheese sandwiches, Mum's fruit cake and a bottle of Pepsi!' His supper.

When my father's heavy footsteps came down the hall, the visit to the morgue and the stress of the 'situation' were all mixed up in skittish dozing dreams of people chasing me. Even before he reached the bedroom, I woke with my heart beating fast. I lay on the narrow bed of my childhood and pretended to be still asleep.

When we were younger, at a certain late stage of their parties, some tipsy guests would be brought into our bedrooms, amid elaborate tiptoeing and appreciative whispery chuckling, to admire our small sleeping forms. It always woke me but I always feigned sleep.

Now I played possum like a child again while he stood over the bed, breathing impatiently. I could smell the mingled scents of the Johnson's baby powder he dusted himself with after his shower, and the Palmolive shaving cream, and the Vaseline hair tonic he used on the side-wings of his hair and even the Pepsodent on his breath.

It was unusual enough him just being in the bedroom. It was five years since this particular conjunction of him and me: when I lay rigid and elongated with meningitis. He'd stood by the bed weighing up whether I had flu or not. I smelled his bathroom fragrances but I couldn't raise or turn my head to look at him. Now he cleared his throat after a while and rocked on his soles and said, 'I hear you've got yourself into some serious trouble.'

Although his voice was firm and managerial, I realised he felt as sheepish as I did. As I yawned and blinked and acted out the process of waking up, he said, 'What will the company's reaction be?'

This threw me. I snapped awake. The company? What did he mean?

'I wouldn't be surprised if they took a dim view of what's happened.'

Why would they care? It was a newspaper company. Newspaper people were more broadminded than that.

'Well,' he said. 'Don't be surprised. Many companies don't like that sort of thing. It reflects badly on people.' Then, the trouble confronted, he turned and left the bedroom and went off to work.

The marriage took place on a sharp, sunny Friday morning on the first day of spring. The ceremony took only ten minutes at the registry office, followed by an early lunch in a small private room at the Hotel Charles in North Perth. Three photographs were taken on the family camera in the deserted hotel carpark. Ruth wore a creamy beige suit and hat, my mother wore funereal dark blue. Ruth's mother didn't attend. Neither did my brother, Bill.

Bill wasn't being prudish or standoffish; he had no idea the marriage was happening. I'd been warned to keep it quiet. He hadn't been told anything. Just a month off his fourteenth birthday, he was regarded by my parents as too impressionably adolescent to take part in a celebration of flagrant immorality – even one so low-key and doleful. Fortunately it was his schoolterm break and he was holidaying on a friend's farm for a week. Until he returned, and asked where I was, they could postpone telling him we'd suddenly got married, and why.

They were all for putting things off. For keeping things under wraps. On the other hand, Jan was allowed to come. She was only eight, young enough for the occasion to wash over her.

At the Hotel Charles we had prawn cocktails and Chicken Maryland and my mother put on a brave face. There were no speeches. A waiter officially served me beer for the first time. After my first mouthful my mother said giddily, to no one in particular, 'He's getting tipsy!' It's a wedding, I thought. That's what you do. I remembered there was nothing they could do about it. I felt better at that moment than I had for weeks.

In mid-afternoon my parents drove us to the airport where we caught the little plane to Rottnest for our weekend's honeymoon. We were still in our wedding clothes. It was the first time either of us had flown to the island; like most people we'd always made the crossing by ferry. We held hands across the aisle for the whole flight: it took only fifteen minutes.

The room allotted to us at the Rottnest Hostel was the room where I'd called on Roberta Ainslie. I'd never stepped over the threshold then. It felt strange standing inside the room this time. I peered out onto the grass of the Quad where I'd tried to remove the carpet shark's teeth, as if the boy two years younger might still be squatting out there jabbing away with his spear, and appearing too keen, and making a fool of himself. The late afternoon temperature was surprisingly crisp, long shadows fell across the grass, and the Quad itself, off-season, was green and deserted instead of bright and sandy and sprinkled with slow-moving barefooted people.

It was also strange being on Rottnest so quickly, without the gradual transition of the ocean passage, and in a suit and tie, and with a woman wearing a beige suit and stockings and high heels and her hair newly tinted and sculpted for the occasion. And being married to her. All I recognised was the powdered oval of her face. But before we knew it we were in bed.

That weekend while we were at Rottnest my mother found us an out-of-the-way flat up the coast at Waterman's Bay. This was suburbia's northernmost point. Any further away and we'd no longer be living in Perth.

From the small kitchen window we looked out onto a glaring limedust track to the beach and over the rocky shore to the ocean. In front of us, to the east behind us, and to the north, lay white sand drifts which piled up against the fence and shifted in the wind. There were no plants on the property. We had our backs to the desert and we faced the sea. Now we were people of the dunes.

Everything inside and outside the flat was painted green –

the asbestos roof, walls and ceiling and the flat's cement floors. The yard outside was also green cement. Each room sloped towards a drain in the floor so that when old Mr Coleman, the landlord, felt the impulse to saturate his property he could hose down the flat's bedroom, kitchen and dining room as well.

Mr Coleman was rarely spotted without the hose in his hands. He might have been a resident of the dunes but he wasn't one of the Sand People. He wasn't submitting to the sand without a fight, and because he was retired he could give it his full attention. It was a constant battle in the sea wind, with the sandhills hovering and shifting at his borders. But by cementing everything over, painting it green and continually sluicing it down, he not only kept the dunes at bay, he restrained the very idea of the dunes.

His need to defy the landscape started with his own green-painted house at the front of the yard. Inside the house, of course, the carpets, fittings and furnishings and Mrs Coleman's knick-knacks were various rainforest shades. When I came to pay the rent each Saturday morning he gave me a glass of *crème de menthe*.

With its cold cement floors and the constant hosing our flat had the atmosphere of a big laundry. That and the hour-long bus ride to town kept the rent so low that I could just afford it, even on my first-year cadet reporter's wage. In the green flat we went into exile. Up here we were less likely to cause embarrassment to others or incite gossip.

I was sure this had been my mother's thinking when she found the flat. Ruth and I didn't admit to each other that the snubs and giggles and scandalised whispers were happening. But Perth's gossipy, conservative, country-town mindset saw us as seriously aberrant. This was a town where the most talked-about aspect of the Cottesloe–Nedlands murders was a barmaid and a married man being in a parked car together. Ruth and I professed not to care, and were sensitive to every whisper and slight.

At Waterman's Bay we thrived in our breezy, damp conditions. The spring weather was warming up. We cooked on a portable camp stove and treated life like a camping holiday. Sometimes we borrowed the car and went to the drive-in, and on the way home we stopped and made love in the sandhills. We saw *From the Terrace* and, deeply affected by the idea of adultery, sang Ray Charles's 'Hit the Road, Jack' all the way home.

Apart from some early morning sickness, Ruth stayed well. At weekends we swam in the morning, and I pushed her back up the sandhill to the flat. Then, as Mr Coleman drenched the green cement outside, we lay in bed and giggled about his hosing habits and the perfect name of the place.

On the paper I'd returned to the Monday-to-Friday day shift, reporting the Perth police court, and when my older colleagues went to the pub after work I came home early to Ruth. As soon as I walked inside, we locked the door and pulled the blinds in case Mr Coleman thought an interior hosing might be warranted. As the sea wind whistled through the green window frames we leapt into bed at sunset.

One early morning I dreamed I was paralysed down one side –
and when I woke in fright I was. Arm, leg, foot, side of the face,
tongue, cheek, were all numb and floppy. As if my body was
divided down the middle by a dotted line, I could feel my good
half and my bad half.

It took all the strength of my good half to slide and drag my
bad half upright and out of bed. What had happened to my
brain? Revenge of the meningitis? Stroke? I was perfectly conscious but the thickness in one side of my tongue prevented me
from forming words and talking. In a panic, Ruth called my
parents, who called Dr Cyril Fortune, the neurologist and my
meningitis saviour. By the time I saw him the pins and needles
had left my bad side and contracted into a severe headache,
which made me vomit, upon which all feeling and clarity of
speech returned and I felt exhausted but strangely refreshed.

While Dr Fortune taped me up to the electrodes of the
electroencephalogram he questioned me about my recent
health. Any strange sensations and nervous tensions?

It was unnerving to discuss this but I mentioned a sensation
I'd been experiencing lately during sex: a sort of nervous spasm
in the legs, a kind of wild involuntary kick. But I didn't say the
word 'sex'. I cleared my throat and said 'marital relations'. The
only way I could describe the sensation, I told him, was like the
enthusiastic reflex kicks a dog makes when you scratch its belly.

'Hmm,' Dr Fortune pondered. 'Dog-belly reflexes.' How
many times had this sensation occurred?

I was too embarrassed to say how many times a day. 'Every
time lately,' I said.

254

His eyes widened but he didn't say anything for a moment. I had electrodes all over my scalp. He was about to throw the switch and make the flashing lights come on in my brain. Maybe my blushing cheeks would short-circuit the machine. 'Any other changes?'

'Only getting married,' I said.

He looked at me. 'And your age is?'

I told him. I lay there feeling like an experiment. After a moment he said, 'I think I get the picture. No need to go at it hammer and tongs.'

A while later I got the results of the EEG. Dr Fortune said there were no obvious abnormalities indicated in my brain. The kicking-dog reflex didn't return. My good and bad halves merged again.

My mother was occasionally laughing. And for the first time since her children were born she was playing tennis again. She made a wry face at the pat-and-giggle social game she thought she was reduced to these days, but I thought it was a good sign. She seemed almost her old self.

Then one afternoon when I called in unexpectedly at Circe Circle I found her deep in conversation at the kitchen table with the Reverend Keith Dowding. He was the Moderator of the Presbyterian Church of Western Australia. I hadn't thought of her requiring spiritual guidance, or of turning to the Presbyterians, or of going straight to the top when she did, for that matter. But he was the only churchman she knew. His son and I had been in the same class at school. They had met at our sporting events. The Reverend Dowding was a warm, charming man, a liberal, a leading member of the State Labor Party and a prominent anti-nuclear demonstrator. I thought it might have cost her some pride to call him.

Their conversation broke up when I walked in. Although it seemed to end on an optimistic note, I guessed from her full ashtray it had been lengthy and serious and – from the box of tissues by her coffee cup – that she'd been crying earlier. It was a year since the last time I'd walked in on her like this, when the man soothing her was a detective-sergeant.

Shortly afterwards she left to stay with her parents in Melbourne for six weeks. On the face of it this wasn't unusual: she went nearly every year. But not for so long, or so early in the year, or when Bill and Jan were just starting back at school. It was obvious to me – she'd left her return date open – that she'd timed the trip so she'd be away when the baby was born.

Ruth's waters broke conveniently at nine o'clock one Saturday morning at Waterman's Bay and our little boy, a breech birth, was born by mid-afternoon. Afterwards they were both tired but well. Dazed with wonder, I phoned from the hospital with the news. My mother was across the country and my father was at the races. My brother and sister were off with friends. Eventually I reached the elderly housekeeper who was looking after the family while my mother was away, and I told her.

I'd anticipated the scene. After all, I'd seen it many times in films and comics. The glazed and happy new father passes around cigars. His family and friends slap him on the back and ply him with drinks. People toast the baby and congratulate the parents. A fuss is made.

Those movie and cartoon fathers were always much older, of course. Nervous, baffled saps with collars awry and five o'clock shadow, haggard from pacing the hospital corridors. James Stewart and Dagwood Bumstead types. After the birth they celebrated too hard and friends humoured their proud blustering and put them to bed on somebody's couch. The labour-ward nurses didn't frown at them and ask, 'Are you her young brother?'

When he came home from the races and heard the news my father said he was glad 'everyone' was well. He asked what name we'd chosen. I said James. He didn't offer congratulations or open a bottle. He certainly didn't suggest he go to see his first grandchild. He said he had to have a shower and go out again. There was some shindig at the golf club. He was making the most of my mother being away.

I'd decided to stay at Circe Circle to be nearer the hospital, so after visiting hours that night I drove up to Waterman's Bay to get my clothes. The wind had dropped and the dunes lay motionless up against the side and back fences. Mr Coleman had been busy: the usual sheets of water puddled and glistened along the length of the yard.

I sat on the doorstep of the flat and leaned back against the green door and drew breath after the day's events. I was still awestruck at our little boy's existence. I envisaged our lives together. When he was eighteen I'd be thirty-six. In a proud stupor I repeated his name to myself.

The moon shone in the sea below and in the puddles all around me. It was shaped halfway between a fingernail and an orange segment and in my dazed reverie I wondered why film directors never avoided the cliché of the full moon for momentous events. When their romantic or insane or terrified characters looked to the night sky for confirmation of their moods they had only one chance in thirty-odd of seeing a full moon but somehow they always did. A big blue-white bugger of a moon, too, and much closer to the earth than I'd ever seen it. It looked as if it was moored about a mile offshore.

The Colemans' light was still on so I splashed up to their house, knocked on their door and told them the news. It surprised me how pleased they seemed to be. They were in their nightclothes but they invited me in.

'What a lovely day for your little boy to be born,' Mrs Coleman said.

Mr Coleman shook my hand and brought out the *crème de menthe* and we toasted him.

I brought Ruth and the baby home to Circe Circle the next Saturday. My mother then immediately returned from Melbourne. She arrived late on Monday night. We were all in the house together. Ruth and the baby were given Jan's bedroom. Jan was on the spare bed. I was back sharing the bedroom with Bill over the Doghouse, sleeping in my old narrow bed.

The wooden bed-head had been painted over, but under the paint, I knew, were the slightly raised and voluptuous outlines of Brigitte Bardot, Ava Gardner and Marilyn Monroe. Also Marlon Brando, James Dean, Alfred Hitchcock and Paul Newman as Rocky Graziano in *Somebody Up There Likes Me*. I'd thought I was pretty shrewd back then pasting up the pictures of Brando and the other males as cover and balance for Brigitte, Ava and Marilyn. For about a year not a day had passed when I didn't think of Bardot in *And God Created Woman*. But displaying such come-hither-looking women on their own would have been asking for trouble.

The next morning, Tuesday, my mother saw our son for the first time. She held him and said to no one in particular, 'Who does he look like?'

That morning, after nursing him, Ruth slipped into bed beside me. She was wearing again the negligee and nightgown she'd brought on the honeymoon. Seconds later my mother appeared and said we shouldn't cuddle in front of Bill and Jan. She advised us to keep to our separate bedrooms.

That afternoon she played tennis with her friends at the courts behind Dymock's Store in Adelma Road. It was getting into autumn, cooler but still sunny. If it hadn't been for the leaves from the poplars bordering Mr Palmer's summer cinema gardens (recently closed until November) falling on the courts, the tennis conditions would have been perfect.

Early next morning, Wednesday, my mother drove Bill to the school bus stop. She arrived home complaining of a headache and lay down on her bed. She called me into the bedroom and said, 'Your baked beans are on the stove.' Then she fell unconscious.

My father didn't know about her headache. He was busy with his sixty-minute chest-clearing, shaving, toilet and shower routine. When she became unconscious I got such a fright that I phoned Dr Synott at home. But he didn't arrive; he didn't seem to understand the urgency. I phoned him again, and then I interrupted my father's ablutions. He appeared from out of the steam, took one look at my mother and called the doctor himself. This time he came. As soon as he saw her, he called an ambulance to take her to hospital. That afternoon she died. Boiling brain had finally got her.

CHAOS

My mother was a good swimmer. As a young woman she'd been a lifesaver at Frankston in Port Phillip Bay in Victoria, at a time when female lifesavers were quite a rarity. She still knew her resuscitation methods and rescue drills. When I was small I'd play a game where I pretended to be drowning. I'd yell out, 'Help!' She'd throw her left arm diagonally over my chest and under my armpit, or cup my chin in her hand and, breathing steadily, sidestroke me to the safety of the shore.

Some grown men and women remember their mothers as the scent of face powder, or the mingled scents of the inside of a handbag, or perhaps as a particular rustle of fabric after the good-night kiss. My mother was the smell of salt water, warm tanned flesh and the satiny femaleness of her bathing costume. She was the faint perished-rubber odour of her bathing cap.

The family albums showed her vigour and athleticism. She'd played competitive tennis, recovered from a broken pelvis in a show-jumping accident and enjoyed highboard diving. The diving came as a surprise to me when I was twelve and old enough to have few illusions about parental heroism. She'd never mentioned it.

We were picnicking one Sunday at Yanchep, north of Perth, and had gone swimming in the pool of the Yanchep Inn to cool off after lunch. My mother swam her usual laps, then suddenly she left the water, climbed the high diving tower, stood poised way above us, frowning slightly, and jack-knifed perfectly into the pool. The rest of us were bobbing in the shallow end – my pale, outclassed father, my brother and sister and I.

No one spoke for a moment. When she surfaced and swam to the edge of the pool and jauntily hoisted herself up she was grinning. She dived again, a perfect swallow dive this time. After that, whenever I saw the Jantzen swimwear trademark of the diving woman in the bathing cap I thought of her.

What astonished us was her apparent good health until that day, her sporting ability and agility – and, of course, her relatively young age. She'd turned forty-seven three weeks before.

How instantly those attributes and impressions fell away. Fitness. Youth. The Jantzen diving girl. As soon as she lapsed into unconsciousness the resilience left my mother's flesh. Her body was already transformed into something else. Her shoulder muscle didn't give when I squeezed it. Her cheek was cool to my kiss. Her eyes weren't quite shut. The open bits, grey and cloudy where they were supposed to be green, didn't look like normal eye tissue.

At the hospital I felt self-conscious talking to her. It was like acting. It was like saying loving farewell things to a picture or a statue of her. By now she wasn't noticeably breathing. You would have had to hold a mirror to her lips to tell. She was lying on her side, her knees jack-knifed under her, and her hip beneath the hospital blanket felt like wood.

Cerebral haemorrhage, Dr Synott said. 'We can't do anything.' Her brain was swimming in blood, boiling in blood, and he stood there. Dr Fortune had also been called. He stood there, too.

I willed them to do something brisk and efficient, to undertake revolutionary brain surgery, to connect her to some lifesaving machine, but I didn't say anything to them. I felt as helpless as they looked. The two doctors, my father and I stood around her bed in the Bethesda Hospital on a sunny autumn afternoon with Freshwater Bay gleaming below the window. Yachts bobbed and rattled at their moorings at the Claremont Yacht Club. Their stays tinkled merrily against their masts. It was a fabulous view.

After a while the doctors faded from the room. In my mother's unconscious presence my father and I suddenly embraced for a moment. Tears exploded as he cried out, 'What will I tell Jan?' Then we drew apart again and stood around and waited for her to die. It was hard to tell when. The moment after seemed exactly the same as the moment before.

For a while I was too numbed to be aware that life was in chaos. The orderly world seemed turned on its head. Nothing about her death or its aftermath was appropriate. Not my father putting off for a week telling Jan that her mother had died – by sending her to stay with friends. Certainly not the men-only funeral, that mid-morning gathering of my father's business associates around my mother's sandy grave.

My brother and sister weren't there, or any of my mother's friends. I wondered whether this was a Presbyterian habit, or maybe a Baptist rule. Or just my father's belief that funerals were men's business, and businessmen's business at that.

There was no church service. As the Reverend Dowding led the brief Presbyterian service at the graveside I looked across the grave at the half-circle of men in business suits, forty or fifty of them, all standing superstitiously well back from the hole. Their smug, recently shaved faces stared back. To them Karrakatta Cemetery was just another ten a.m. business appointment. Some of the faces showed a mild curiosity and a willingness to be entertained by the possibility of untoward emotional reaction from the only family members present: my father, my mother's brother Ian and me.

My father kept his composure. I wept as the first clod of dirt hit the coffin and saw, astonishingly, that a couple of the men seemed cynically amused at my emotion. The stab of hatred I felt for these businessmen then was so sharp it instantly dried my tears. I wondered whether she would have found it ironic that even her funeral had ended up as a Dunlop function. They were burying Mrs Dunlop.

264

Over the next few days I was desperate for sentimental stories of her, for tales of their early love. I couldn't ask my father. Ian told me how dashingly my father had wooed her. How he'd buttered up Nan, their Catholic mother. How he'd bribed Ian, then aged thirteen, two shillings a time to go to the pictures and let them canoodle on the couch in peace. We laughed as if the tales were much funnier than they were.

I wanted to hear of the Jantzen girl and the bomber pilot. There was the old family anecdote I'd always found funny and romantic: that my father, while in pilot training at Point Cook, had broken low-flying regulations and buzzed my mother at Camperdown in his Avro Anson. He'd flashed her a message, but no one ever said what it was.

Ian said I'd got it wrong. The message was for him. He was a teenager in the Air Training Corps by then and my father had told him to watch out and he would fly low and signal something to him.

'What did he say?' I asked.

Ian said, 'He signalled "TIT" and then he signalled "BUM".'

Back at Circe Circle there was a sudden influx of concerned, bossy, nosy women with stews and steamed puddings and casseroles. Concern for the widower and his family was stretched pretty thin when it came to me, Ruth and the baby. The women stopped talking a little too readily, or loudly changed the subject, when we walked into the room. You could see them absorbing material for later gossip. When they spoke it was to patronise us or question Ruth's mothering techniques.

All this made it hard to be publicly joyous about the baby

without feeling guilty. The two events had clashed too dramatically. My mother's death had well and truly trumped his birth.

Nevertheless, for Jan's and Bill's sakes, my father asked us to stay in Circe Circle for the time being. We gave up our exile in the green cement flat in Waterman's Bay. Every day I went off to report the police courts, and at night we stayed up and watched television until my father came home. He would call for the hairbrush and brush Jan's hair for an hour or so, until she was falling asleep, and then she and Bill were allowed to go to bed. He sat up and drank Dewar's.

I stayed up with him in front of the dead television while he drank whisky and occasionally muttered something. Even though we had no conversation it seemed the right and companionable thing to do. It was understandable that his moods were up and down. I'd sit through the various stages – the silence, the abrupt declarations, the teary reminiscences, until he began getting caustic with me. When his eyes turned cold and savage I begged off just in time and went to bed in my old bedroom under the painted-out bodies of Brigitte and Marilyn and listened to the mother-and-baby noises in the next room.

Another girl was murdered in the next street shortly afterwards. It was another Saturday night and Shirley McLeod was baby-sitting for Carl and Wendy Dowd in Wavell Road. She was eighteen, an exceptionally bright and pretty girl and, like her friend John Sturkey, a science student on a scholarship at the university. By now these links, or coincidences, if that's what they were, seemed hardly worth noting.

A thunderstorm was raging. She was studying on the couch in the Dowds' living room, her books on her lap. The killer parked his car near the top end of Circe Circle. He strolled up and down the street in the storm, then walked quietly into the house through an unlocked connecting door from the garage, and shot her in the forehead.

In the storm no one heard the gunshot. When the Dowds returned home at two a.m. they thought Shirley was asleep. Their baby, Mitchell, was sleeping in his bedroom. It was a cold night and the heater was on. A record was still spinning on the record player. A cup and saucer were beside Shirley. She still held her pen poised in mid-word.

My father and I learned some of this from the papers and some from the detectives who arrived on our doorstep next day to interview and fingerprint us.

The police had found one fingerprint they believed was the killer's. They wanted to eliminate all prints that weren't the Dowds'. They also wanted to know our movements that night. As it happened, my father had socialised in the Dowds' house in the past. Carl Dowd was a business associate of his, another branch manager sent from Melbourne, the State manager of the Berlei-Hestia lingerie company. (It was famous for its Hestia brassiere range. A generation of Australians believed

Hestia was an acronym for Holds Every Sized Tit In Australia.)

'It could be my print,' my father helpfully told the detectives. They were suddenly grimly attentive. 'Do you know John McCurry?' he asked hurriedly. 'A good friend of mine.' But the fingerprint wasn't my father's. Or mine, of course. Why then did I feel so strangely guilty as another cop in a grey dustcoat pressed my fingers carefully one by one onto the ink pad? Why did I half-expect the dustcoated cop to take off his glasses and say quietly to the detective in charge, 'Bill, could you have a look at this?'

But every neighbouring male was a suspect. The police were clutching at straws. They ended up fingerprinting my father and me twice, the second time with every other male over fourteen from our side of the river. At this stage they were only fingerprinting males from our side. For some reason they thought we were killing our own.

It was on our way home from the Claremont police station after our second fingerprinting that my father broke into the old Crosby song, 'Where the Blue of the Night'. I hadn't heard him sing anything in a long time. Not since the tranquil days of *Carousel* with the Sunday roast. It was so inappropriate I wondered whether he was all right in the head. But we weren't ourselves. It was a Friday night. He'd had a few drinks after work.

We were driving along Victoria Avenue, past the Claremont baths. I recalled skinny, deaf-and-dumb Darryl

Beamish skylarking in the baths, grabbing at girls' saggy swimming costumes as they climbed up from the river. He was a big-eared, glittery-eyed, toothy boy who cackled gibberish. The pylons and wooden ladders at the baths were encrusted with mussels and barnacles so the shrieking girls couldn't rush it, couldn't get away too fast without cutting their hands and feet. And now Beamish was on death row for murdering Jillian Brewer.

He was still protesting his innocence. So was the other nineteen-year-old, John Button, convicted on circumstantial evidence of the manslaughter of his girlfriend Rosemary Anderson, of running her down with his car. The Press and the community were in no mood to hear his protests either. The local feeling was that he was lucky the jury had gone soft on the wilful murder charge. Lucky to get just ten years' hard labour. It was terrifying that all these different murders were happening in the area but at least two of the killers were off the street.

A couple of blocks past the baths my father stopped singing. He must have realised what he was singing, and how ominous the words sounded, because he stopped abruptly, set his face in a frown and we drove the rest of the way home in our usual silence.

4

SATURDAY NIGHT BOY (III)

He read the social columns without envy or malice. On the contrary, they made him smile the way they advertised who the rich people were, who of them were getting married or attending charity events and wouldn't be at home. They were a very useful service. His favourite section of the *West Australian*, however, was the Saturday architecture page written by Frank Platell. Platell's articles were another good guide to people with money. Better still, they provided a helpful plan and address of the particular house. It was handy to know the layout before you went in.

When he left the house this Saturday night he took in his pocket that day's architecture page, a recent social column item about a wedding on this night, his kid gloves, a handkerchief to cover his mouth and his pencil torch. That was all. None of them could be described as house-breaking implements. He didn't need those; he opened unlocked doors. So he travelled light. A bit later he did have something else in his pocket. A pair of women's panties from a house in Peppermint Grove, plus money from there and other houses in Claremont and Nedlands. Well, he had to fill in the time somehow until the street lights went off at one a.m.

PART FOUR

1

PHENOBARBITONE

When Bill Hawker grabbed him in the dark as he reached for the rifle Hawker wondered what sort of weirdo he'd caught. This creature was burbling strange nasal sounds and when he went to handcuff him the hands felt slick and smooth, almost slimy. Eric was wearing the kid gloves, of course, and in the policeman's anxious mood the skin of the gloves felt creepy, other-worldly. But Hawker held on. He handcuffed him to the fence. He had him.

It wasn't until they turned a light on him that he saw the slimy skin was fine kid gloves. And the harelip explained the incoherent speech.

It wasn't detective work as much as sheer luck. Luck and a little help from the Press. An old couple, William and Leila Keehner, had been out for their daily afternoon stroll by the river in Rookwood Street, Mount Pleasant, when Mrs Keehner decided to pick a sprig of Geraldton wax from a thick bush growing on the sandy bank of the road. As she leant on the bank to reach up for the flowers, the sand shifted slightly and something heavy slid out from under the bush. It was a rifle butt.

After the Cottesloe–Nedlands business he'd thrown the rifle into the river, but this one he'd hidden to use again if he felt the inclination.

It was the rifle used to kill Shirley McLeod. After they'd tested it, the police put the rifle back in the Geraldton wax bush, and waited. They set up camp in a camouflaged pup tent and watched the bush day and night for two weeks. No one came to get it.

They decided to let the papers in on the discovery. It was a risk but the police had the papers well trained. Ralph Wheatley and Jack Coulter, the *Daily News* crime reporter, not only agreed to keep mum about the rifle discovery but to run a story saying the police would be turning their inquiries to the Mount Pleasant area at the end of the week. This gave the gunman time to worry about the safety of his hiding place.

He came on a Saturday night, of course.

———

When he was committed for trial on the charge of murdering John Sturkey, Eric had nodded politely to the magistrate. I thought he also murmured, 'Thank you,' but with his indistinct speech, and the scraping of chairs and the shuffling of the police guards in the dock as they moved towards him, I wasn't sure enough to write it.

Anyway, despite his Hollywood-gangster appearance he certainly looked resolved about the decision. He was on authority's side. *Anything I can do to help? Just ask me the questions.* Short of holding a smoking gun, he looked as much a serial killer as anyone could. Yet he didn't appear to feel any guilt at all.

Not like me. As I finally drove back across the Narrows Bridge and headed towards my evening appointment, the guilt kept rolling in, steady as surf on a sand bank. Along with those other recent feelings: grief, confusion, embarrassment. And now a special sort of childish shame and anxiety as well. The feeling of being called to the principal's office.

I was anxious about Dr Synott summoning me this evening. I'd intended to go home first, to see Ruth and fortify myself for the ordeal. But having wasted time driving dazedly around South Perth I was running late. I hadn't seen him since the funeral and, before that, standing helplessly by my mother's bed at the hospital. He was the family doctor, the family friend. The man who'd made a mistake with my meningitis. The man who could come around to Circe Circle for drinks on Sunday evening, then professionally examine my mother's body in his office on Monday afternoon. In retrospect this seemed very peculiar to me.

Some family doctors had offices of cheery disarray, with hunting prints or Rottnest Island scenes hanging beside their medical degrees. For decoration Dr Synott had the gloomy *Stag at Bay*. Otherwise his office was as bare as an operating theatre, with sharp silver instruments laid out, and coils of vaguely obscene rubber tubing and concave metal appliances like little stacked bed pans. It smelled of methylated spirits. On the wall Landseer's hounds were about to force the stag over the cliff.

The doctor told me to sit down. He was frowning. 'I thought it was time to discuss your mother's death,' he said.

I waited, more a dismal child again than a father. My head swam in methylated spirits. 'You've probably been wondering,' he said solemnly, 'whether you killed her.'

I'd discovered that morning it was possible to faint or black out and yet appear to be conscious. This sensation was like the one in court, only sharper and more precise. I realised after a while that Dr Synott was still speaking. I rose from a great depth to the surface. The meths fumes brought me round. 'I want you to know this wasn't *necessarily* the case,' he said.

I remained sitting on the cracked leather chair in front of his desk, regressed to a nervous eleven-year-old, while he sat there fingering some silver probe or other and gazing at me with steady disapproval. Over the years I'd sat on that chair many times while he peered into my ears, eyes and throat, listened to my chest, tapped my knees, gave me injections.

'What I mean is, we can't tell for sure.' On the one hand, he said, these cerebral haemorrhages were usually congenital. If he were thinking along the lines of a congenital condition, he'd be looking at her family history. 'But I think I'm right in

282

saying her parents, brothers, aunts, cousins and so on are all still alive?'

I nodded. My heart was thumping.

On the other hand, he went on, he'd been treating her for depression, anxiety attacks and insomnia brought on by my 'actions'.

Make up your mind, I thought. Her friends already blamed me. I suspected my father did, too. Did I do it or not? Am I a murderer?

'I think we're looking at a sixty/forty situation,' he said.

Which way? I wondered. For the life of me I couldn't ask. I realised this was all he was going to say. This was the best and the worst he could do – call me in and act as if he were doing me an undeserved favour by saying the answer to whether I killed my mother was on the affirmative side of maybe. The jury was going to stay out on me forever.

By now my face must have told him what was going through my mind because he ended our meeting by taking my blood pressure and prescribing phenobarbitone for me as well.

I drove home to Circe Circle with my head and heart pounding. *So I killed her . . . didn't I?*

Everyone except Ruth and the baby was sitting in front of 'Bonanza'. A flouncy middle-aged woman was flirting with an uncomfortable Ben Cartwright. The Cartwright boys were all grinning. My family's faces were all expressionless. My father was brushing Jan's hair and a Dewar's was beside him. I didn't know whether he knew about my being summoned to the doctor's office. I didn't mention it.

It was very rare that he got home before me. 'You're late,' he said.

I thought that was a bit rich. 'Work,' I said. 'I'm covering the court case. Your man Eric was committed for trial.'

He had parted Jan's hair and was attempting to make two plaits. The three hair divisions on either side of the part were uneven, some thick and bunchy, others sparse. I didn't say anything. She looked up as if she knew her hair felt wrong but she was being patient. He loved her more than anyone on earth. Neither of them knew how else to deal with this. None of us did.

He stared up at me, too. Suddenly I was the big crime authority. I was the one in the know. He was dying to learn more but he didn't want to ask. He shook his head slowly and pressed his lips together as if he'd predicted it back then when the petty thieving started. 'What's the next step?' he said eventually, in his Dewar's voice.

I said Eric would now go to trial. There was no doubt he'd be found guilty of murdering John. 'They hang you for murder in this town,' I added.

Well, sometimes they did.

'Not in front of the children,' he said.

NEWS SHARK

I followed the pack north up the West Coast Highway, well outside my territory, with the two-way radio crackling in the Ford Anglia and the sun glinting off the white dunes and sandy verges, off the roadside bottles and approaching car windscreens and the glassy sea itself.

Along the way I kept the news editor primed with the progress of events. I called him from City Beach and Scarborough and a couple of stops in between. He didn't remind me that my territory stopped at Cottesloe. He liked reporters sticking to a story.

'Tiger sharks,' I said knowledgeably, trying to keep the self-consciousness out of my voice when I said 'Come In!' and 'Over and Out!' Then I stomped through the pigface and sandhills once more, training the office binoculars on the unbroken sea just beyond the surfline. Where were they?

On the western horizon as usual Rottnest was mysteriously transformed by summer's atmospheric conditions into a misty string of mirage-islands. They hovered like spacecraft above the ocean, well south of the island's real whereabouts. As I searched for fins in the rise of each breaking wave, for those sinister, thrilling shadows in the swells, glistening women smelling of coconut oil glanced drowsily up at me from their towels. Children squinted into the glare to see what this fully clothed boy was peering at. Languid adults' faces said: What do you think you're doing?

Willing you to be eaten. The sooner the better. Well, not a kid, but definitely a well-known businessman or sun-dried old socialite. If possible, I wanted even more than a shark attack on a noted victim. I'd learned my news values. The shark should be of record size and rare species. And I needed a garrulous old-timer as a witness. Someone like Ted 'Sharky' Nelson, every reporter's favourite contact for shark stories. ('It rushed at him like a Metro bus, bit him in halves and swallowed him in two bites. Never seen one that big this far north. Poor bastard never had a chance. I'll never forget the look on his face.')

In the best possible world there would be still more. And not just that this excellent tragic day (Black Sunday? Bloody Sunday?) was the victim's birthday or golden wedding anniversary or that he'd just won the lottery. (News editors adored the poignant coincidence.) I wanted more than to break news. I wanted to be the news.

My fantasy front-page lead – shark attack or boating disaster or freak rip-tide – was a watery adventure story where I became the hero and got the scoop as well. Naturally it would take unusual circumstances for me to step outside the traditional role of neutral observer and modestly but heroically intrude. (Frantic captain of surf lifesaving club, through loud-hailer: 'There's still a little girl on a floatie out there! All my guys have major arterial bleeding. Does anyone on the beach have their bronze medallion for lifesaving?' Me: 'Well, if there's a kid's life at stake . . .')

Just as my dream scoop required loss of life, it required me to save lives, too. And, importantly, to risk my own. Then, dripping water, and possibly blood, over the Anglia's dashboard, shrugging off medical attention, and modestly keeping news of my own heroism until the fourth or fifth paragraph, I'd dictate the story over the two-way for the first edition.

<hr />

Despite the phenobarbitone, I was driven to keep busy. I couldn't sit still. Ruth and I were now living near Swanbourne Beach in the one-bedroom, lamb-smelling 'residence' attached to the butcher's shop in North Street. The butcher chose not to live there, and after a few weeks I could understand him needing a meat-free home life. But the lamb smell kept the rent down. We became used to the sight of the abattoir truck pulling up outside in the early morning and the men dressed like medieval executioners in leather caps and shoulder aprons lumping carcasses into the cool-room. We were fond of the

House of Meat. When Ruth and I weren't marvelling at our boy or making love, I was submerged in work or in the sea. I swam each morning before work. I was doing a stint in Fremantle, only six stations down the railway line, in the *West Australian's* branch office.

Fremantle was rarely short of news of a raffish sort. The previous century, Fremantle harbour had been blasted out of the limestone seabed where the Swan River estuary suddenly narrowed and twisted and flowed into the Indian Ocean. Ever since, as Australia's first port of call for shipping from Europe, Asia and Africa, as well as the home of the State's fishing fleet, it had been a rough-house town.

A young chaser of ambulances and fire engines (as well as police-court reporter and shipping-list compiler) walked the windy night-time wharves and streets with caution. The water-front pubs were bloodhouses. Most mornings Polish and German seamen appeared before the court for the previous night's assaults with marlinspikes and vodka bottles on each other or the prosti-tutes in the Cleopatra Hotel. At nights and weekends the sons of Italian and Greek fishermen, Irish wharf labourers and Yugoslav vegetable growers circled the port in their V8s looking for girls and fights. At least one of their desires was usually met.

But by day its population, maritime aspect and leached limestone buildings gave Fremantle a calm and distinctively Mediterranean character. It was a cohesive, strangely old-fashioned place, proudly independent for a town situated only thirteen miles downriver from Perth, with power more or less evenly divided between the Waterside Workers' Federation and the city councillors (mostly second- and third-generation shipping and general merchants), between labour and capital, between Catholics and Masons, between the South Fremantle and East Fremantle football clubs.

Its most imposing building was the old Female Insane Asylum, which had switched from madness to romance during World War Two when it housed US naval officers and became notorious as a sexual rendezvous. But the dominating structure was a high wall, quarried from the same local limestone as the old asylum, which seemed to ring the town like an ancient fort. The wall formed the boundary, warders' quarters and gatehouse of Fremantle Prison. The prison had a grim history dating back to the earliest days of European settlement. Executions sometimes still took place there, for some reason always at eight o'clock on a Monday morning.

I remembered four Monday-morning executions. Especially the first one. I was waiting for the school bus. I was nine, and I'd just seen the story in the paper, *Killer to Hang*, with a photo of him. I couldn't believe this dark thing was happening. In the photograph he had black hair and eyebrows. The headlines were blacker than black. He was twenty-two, a migrant from Czechoslovakia working on a farm. One night he and the farmer got drunk, and he threw a stone at the farmer and hit him on the head. I'd thrown stones and hit people on the head myself.

As eight o'clock approached I was staring so hard at the second hand of my watch ticking away that I didn't notice the bus pull up. My ears were thudding as I counted down the seconds. The air held a different light. The shadows fell longer and darker on the road. *They* – someone, the government, important forces – were killing this man. *Five, four, three, two, one – now!*

I felt an eerie vacuum, a black absence I hadn't known before. The 202 United bus, with grinning boys pressing their faces against its back window, was already chugging away down Waratah Avenue.

On my reporting rounds I passed the prison several times a day and each time it gave me a jolt. I never got used to it: its gates always closed against the gusty port; its clock always stopped, bizarrely, at either 12.05 or 10.15. The greyish-yellow wall was as sombre and ageless as murder and retribution. It seemed appropriate that over a century the sea winds had given it a patina of salty misery and that it looped around the neck of the port like a noose.

In the *West Australian* office on the corner of Adelaide and Queen streets, the reporting staff of two senior and two junior reporters worked out of a back room on the west of the building behind the classified advertisements' counter and the ad salesman's and typists' tea-room.

The other junior reporter's name was John Dare, in my mind the perfect by-line for an intrepid journalist. Each afternoon either Dare or I prised the daily shipping list from the reluctant sausage fingers of the harbourmaster, Captain Oliphant, whose phobia – the waterfront equivalent of worrying whether he'd left the gas on – was checking and re-checking the sailing times in case four hundred passengers missed the *Fairstar* to England. Then, in the two hours where our day and night shifts crossed and the late afternoon sun made our shared desk uninhabitable, Dare and I played office cricket in the back corridor, with a ruler for a bat and a ball made of copy paper and Scotch tape, and cheerfully pondered ways to scoop each other.

A good fellow and a Fremantle boy himself, Dare had the advantage of local knowledge and an easier way with the cops. My own relations with the local police hadn't recovered from my inquiries into the aftermath of a retiring senior inspector's farewell party. The party boy's car had jumped the pavement near Fremantle Hospital, struck an Italian family of four, seriously injuring a little girl, and accelerated away. I spotted the distraught family at the police station making their complaint. I couldn't open my notebook fast enough. 'Tell me about it,' I said.

If the drunken, hit-and-run senior cop wasn't *the* story, it was a good story. An earnest young constable had reported it in the Incident Book. I took down the details. I interviewed the witnesses. I got details of the farewell booze-up and the child's admission to hospital. I felt indignant on the family's behalf. So was the story I wrote.

I was surprised not to see it on the front page next morning. I flipped through the rest of the paper. It wasn't there. I guessed they had to run it past the lawyers. Such a strong story would need some legal tinkering here and there. I envisaged Roberta's irascible father, R. I. Ainslie QC, the company's lawyer, perusing it.

But it wasn't in the paper the next day either. Two days later I was summoned back to Perth. The chief-of-staff, Mr Goldsmith, told me that he, Ralph Wheatley and I were to attend a meeting with Police Commissioner O'Brien. Of course. I was awestruck. The power of the Press!

On the way to police headquarters in Ralph's police-rounds car no one spoke. I'd been expecting congratulations all round. I supposed they were holding off until publication. I reminded myself this was the newspaper world. Praise was rationed; envy was everywhere. I should be content that my exclusive story was finally getting serious attention.

As we entered his office the Commissioner was frowning. That was to be expected – his force was in a spot of bother. He already had a copy of my unpublished story in front of him. He flipped through it dismissively and then tossed it aside.

He didn't look at me. He looked over and around me. He said it didn't happen like that. The child's family wasn't unhappy with the police. Anyway, the officer had officially ceased to be a policeman at five p.m. that day. He'd retired an hour before the farewell party began. He was a member of the general public. So no story.

Again the feeling of being in the principal's office. I took a deep breath. My voice was husky; I cleared my throat. What about the little girl in hospital? Her condition was still critical. She could die. The hit-and-run was entered in their Incident

292

Book. The driver was named. What about the official complaint? Charges must have been laid?

The Commissioner still didn't look at me and he didn't answer. I looked at Mr Goldsmith and Ralph. They'd back me up. The Commissioner looked at them, too, and smiled grimly. 'You teach your juniors the defamation laws, do you?'

'Just doing his job,' Mr Goldsmith said. His tone was soothing and confiding. 'You know how it is.'

'A new chum,' Ralph muttered in his moustache. 'Keen as mustard.'

The Commissioner appeared slightly mollified. He picked up my story again, held it in the palm of his hand as if weighing it, then let it fall. 'There's nothing on our books about this,' he said. 'Nothing at all.' He stood up. 'I'll handle it from here,' he said. 'I'll calm down the Fremantle blokes.'

We got into the police-rounds car and drove back to the office. I was in the back seat. I didn't say anything. Ralph drove through the city like an exasperated uncle. 'Thanks very much,' he snorted over his shoulder. 'I've got to deal with those bastards every day.'

Mr Goldsmith turned in his seat and smiled at me, coolly but not unkindly. He was a gentleman. He summed up my scoop. 'It was your job to report on the matter, Rodney, and you did. You got the facts. You did your job as a reporter.' He could have been addressing a new boy scout who'd attempted a badge test way above his abilities. 'And it's our job to decide whether to publish it.' *Rodney?* He'd got my name wrong, too.

Now I needed my big coastal story more than ever. My hunger for it easily matched Dare's amiable street-wisdom and cop-friendly banter. I even thought about the story in my own time, jogging along the beach each morning from Swanbourne to Cottesloe and willing a passing container ship or crayfish boat onto the reef. I wanted the story so badly that I *studied* for it.

I went up to town on my day off, and in the *West Australian's* library I got out all the files on shark attacks and shipwrecks and coastal disasters since the colony's first European settlement. The more marine mayhem the better.

'How's married life?' asked Roberta, as she passed me the files. 'How's the baby?'

'Terrific,' I said. Was she smirking? She seemed very confident all of a sudden. I could feel my cheeks burning. I still couldn't tell whether girls were needling me, or gathering gossip, or genuinely passing the time. She was wearing an engagement ring. I'd read about her engagement to a young grazier, Digby Lee-Steere. It had made the social pages.

'By the way, congratulations,' I said. I couldn't wait to get out of the library, out of the city and back to Fremantle where no one knew me or cared less. Where teenage fathers weren't such a novelty, for that matter.

And in the Fremantle City Library, a hundred yards across King's Square from the office, I read up on local history, too, right back to the early Dutch mariners, the Dutch East India Company, the mutinies and marooned sailors.

There were tragedies I'd never heard of. Like Charles Robertson being taken by a whaler shark near the Claremont

Jetty in 1923. He was a thirteen-year-old coxswain thrown laughing and kicking into the river by the crew of his Scotch College rowing shell. Straight into the shark's mouth. There was the middle-aged bookmaker's clerk, Simeon Ettelson, who died after a twelve-foot tiger shark mauled his thigh down to the femur in the shallows at Cottesloe in 1925.

I was surprised I'd never heard of them. I'd swum heedlessly in those places for years. Maybe they'd happened so long ago they'd passed out of memory. Or maybe they'd been regarded as bad for the real estate market.

While I liked this sort of grisly information I had no idea what to do with it. But I was getting my optimism back. Parenthood was part of it. I was happily dazed by marriage. I adored our little James. He was a card and the apple of my eye. Being a father and breadwinner made me feel more mature and responsible.

And a germ of an idea was growing. In the way that John Dare's Fremantle background helped him understand the port better, this coastal knowledge could perhaps give me a background of my own. Maybe it could help me make sense of events in my own life. I'd spent my childhood and adolescence on this sandy moonscape. I was sure I had something to say about it. I just didn't know what.

For a year after my mother's death my father lost himself in work. He made risk-taking business decisions. He pulled off a major deal with the government: he would build the State's first tyre factory if the government gave Dunlop all its business. His standing in the local business community had never been greater. He was made an executive councillor of the West Australian Chamber of Manufactures and a committeeman of the Perth Chamber of Commerce. He was always hosting receptions and giving speeches. He was a leading branch manager in a branch manager's town.

In the evenings he still came home late, brushed his daughter's hair in front of the television, then drank Dewar's until after midnight. But by day he seemed fired with energy.

Dunlop head office, sensing a national economic slump, had announced a motivating contest with the prize of a trip around the world for the State manager (and his spouse) with the best figures for the year. The recession came as predicted and car sales plummeted – and the sale of fewer cars meant the sale of fewer tyres. Western Australia was the only State to actually increase sales. My father won the trip hands down.

He refused to take it. He didn't say he would be lonely travelling by himself. He said the company was too important and the economy too chancy. He said he didn't want to be away from the office for too long while things were busy. Instead he took his first time off since my mother's funeral and flew to Singapore for ten days.

He brought us all back duty-free gifts. Mine was an Olivetti *Lettera* portable typewriter. I was surprised and delighted. It was the best present he'd ever given me. The office typewriters I used every day, the industrial-strength, cigarette-burned Siemens machines chained to their wheeled metal stands, were tools of the trade, as useful and as mundane as a telephone or a desk. What those heavy-duty models plodded through – their punctuation marks and lower-case *e*s and *o*s punching holes through the copy paper – was *work*. What the little blue-green Olivetti began to write at home was everything else.

The Olivetti began tapping out magazine stories of shark attacks and Dutch shipwrecks and mutinies along the west coast. I sent them off to barber-shop magazines like *Australasian Post* and *Weekend* and *People*. *Australasian Post* in particular liked shark attacks and it liked the maulings to be described in gruesome detail. For badly needed extra money, I was happy to oblige.

The *West Australian*, stern paper of record, frowned on its staff doing outside work for racy Eastern States magazines. Even its stablemates across the office corridor, the lighter afternoon *Daily News* and Saturday *Weekend News*, were regarded as barely proper. So the Olivetti and I indulged in this hack work under various writerly *noms de plume* (Scott Conrad, Joe Fitzgerald, Ernest Forster) and with a delicious, illicit sense of freedom.

With my first writing cheque from *Australasian Post* I took Ruth to dinner at the Sea Crest, on Cottesloe Beach. The high tide lapped on the sand below us as we ate Steak Diane and drank Porphyry Pearl and watched the sun sink like a red whale into the horizon.

We were commenting favourably on the glorious sunset

and behaving like sophisticated restaurant patrons when it suddenly occurred to me that our meal had actually been paid for by the unfortunate Simeon Ettelson, mauled by the tiger shark just below our table.

I looked down at the inoffensive waves breaking on the soft sand below and raised my glass to Mr Ettelson. I began this small toast feeling amused at the coincidence, but by the time I put my glass down I felt unsteady and quite moved. Almost misty.

As I headed to the Gents to splash water on my face, I wondered if it could be the Porphyry Pearl. A minute later I knew it was. I hadn't drunk wine before. I was a father, a husband and a newshound but I was still two years off legal drinking age.

—

I'd grown up on the ocean and river shores. In younger days my friends and I had crabbed and prawned and fished, patrolled the rock pools and reefs with our *gidgies* and *kylies*, our versions of Aboriginal fish-spears and boomerangs. We knew the tides and reefs, the hot easterlies and blustery westerlies of our coast. We swam in competitions at the Crawley and Claremont baths, earned our lifesaving bronze medallions, skin-dived, paddled canoes, built rafts, rowed boats and crewed on ancient varnished Gwen-12s and VJs and fourteen-footers. I'd even rescued a couple of swimmers in trouble in the surf – one of them a sportswriter who was so embarrassed he never forgave me.

Everyone I knew lived near the riverbank or seashore. Some came from families who'd been boatbuilders for four generations. Two brothers, Kim and Richie Male, even came from a pearling family who operated luggers out of Broome in the far north-west. They'd come south to school where Richie and I had been in the swimming team together.

All this coastal experience and I'd never seen a man-eating shark in its natural habitat. Nor had my friends. All I'd seen were potential man-hurters, plenty of them, but nothing that looked as if it could devour me even if it wanted to. Every summer, of course, there were 'sightings' of man-eaters reported in the papers. But never by anyone I knew.

So why did I think of man-eating sharks every time I dived into the sea? Not that it prevented me swimming every day. I thought about them, then tried to put them out of my mind. But coming over the hill at North Cottesloe any still, hot, mid-day and seeing the human bodyslick floating out to sea, all that sweat and suntan oil, I thought of berley, the rich, greasy groundbait that fishermen tossed in the water to attract fish. Same principle. And sharks were supposed to have a miraculous sense of smell.

I favoured the idea of shark nets, like the ones I'd read they used off the beaches of Sydney and Durban, South Africa. They set the nets off every beach and moved them each week. The success rate in Sydney was one hundred percent; no one had been killed on an ocean beach since the nets were installed in 1931. It wasn't just that the nets trapped sharks, but they prevented them setting up a habitat. Intruders were kept out. A shark never got to feel at home and establish territory. I liked the certainty of nets. If our beaches were netted I knew I'd be a more confident person, happier and calmer. Then again, I might lose the shark-attack scoop of my life.

It had to be that sharks were buried deep in my collective unconscious. I'd read this somewhere in my research, too, and I believed it. Clearly some of us were born with it – like the chicken's instinct for the shadow of the hawk. It was amazing what I saw in the back-froth of a snapping wave, in the darker patchwork ripples of weed and reef. Was that surge just a diving shag? Was the shadow really a passing cloud? Or the first and last hint of the white pointer's charge? This, I thought, was obviously the underlying anxiety of my life.

One blustery Saturday afternoon in mid-November I was bodysurfing with Richie Male and three or four other fellows at North Cottesloe. Richie was seventeen, two years younger than I. He was a joker and a good swimmer, an easygoing boy. He was in good spirits that afternoon because his final school examinations had finished the day before.

The early summer breeze was chopping up the beach surf so we thought we'd try the waves on the Slimy. This was a limestone and coral reef between Cottesloe and North Cottesloe carpeted with spongy, mossy weed. Even at low tide when only a few inches of water covered the reef you could usually bodysurf on the Slimy, skim over it with no worse injury than a grazed knee or stubbed toe.

I was there for a quick surf. With my new responsibilities I'd only an hour to spare. Of course I didn't mention this to Richie or the others when I spotted him and began chatting. I shut up about it. Even twelve months later the whispering and gossiping were continuing, from my mother's acquaintances, from girls I knew, even from ones I didn't know. The reaction from boys wasn't so bad: just simple teasing and total incomprehension. None of them, certainly not a kid like Richie, would understand.

Conditions at the Slimy weren't good, but at least there was some surf – a small reef-break at the Cottesloe edge. By about three-thirty, however, the tide was rising. The surf rolling over the reef was cloudy and swirling with kelp and sand. I'd never seen so much seaweed. Then the surf began to dump heavily on the back of the reef.

There were four or five of us crowded together out on the reef, stumbling and splashing and getting in each other's way. Richie and I started using the back of the reef as a foothold to launch ourselves into the waves breaking on the southern rim. The idea was that they'd carry us diagonally off the rocks and over the safer sandy-bottomed basin beyond.

This plan wasn't a success. The waves had too much water in them; the tide was too high and the waves had no shape. The water was now shoulder-deep and murky. You had to feel for the reef with your feet, thrust them blindly down into the kelp and search for a crevice with your toes and heels. Who knew what was down there? In the currents the kelp seemed alive. One moment it was pressing against you all sleek and silky, stroking your thighs and stomach; the next it was scratching and lashing you.

We soon got tired of being buffeted by the surf and the undertow and the rolling kelp. All of us were swearing in exasperation and dancing and stumbling on the slippery weed and rocks. It was hard to get a grip on the reef, much less position yourself on a wave. And yet you needed to catch a wave to get in to shore. To think about anything other than the next breaker and your own sudden intention was impossible. You had to concentrate.

As if conditions weren't difficult enough for bodysurfing, three board riders paddled out on heavy plywood boards and began cutting in on us. Those knife-nosed monsters were the last straw. They could slice right through you. With every wave-surge one or other of us gave up and swam, staggered and rolled through the froth to the shore. When I got to the beach I saw a straggling line of figures trudging back ahead of me along the shoreline to North Cottesloe. I headed back, too, and kept walking home.

Night always changes the sea. Next morning it was calm and slick as I cruised the coast road in the Anglia, desperate for a shark story to make this humdrum Sunday day-shift worthwhile. Sharks were in the news. There had been several 'sightings' already this season and it was only mid-November.

Passing Cottesloe, I noticed four surfboats strung out in a

line beyond the reef, riding the light swell. The sweep oarsmen were keeping them parallel to the beach. On the boats there was no sign of physical effort or excitement. Their movements were so calm and measured they could have been fishing. As I passed, I wondered if the crews were trying some new training manoeuvre. One thing was sure: if they weren't rowing they weren't chasing any sharks out to sea.

I drove further along the West Coast Highway, and from a sandy rise where suburbanites were beginning to build new brick houses in the dunes, I looked out into the low swell. And I actually saw dark shapes gliding there. Perhaps five or six of them. Gliding, not rolling and surfacing. There was no doubt. Not dolphins, sharks. I couldn't have been more pleased. All morning I followed them north.

Then a motor sounded above the shallows. The shark-spotter plane, a little show-off Cessna, was after them, too. There went my story. I could have cried. Even if the plane didn't herd them out to sea, the local surfboats would give chase. The shark alarm was already sounding back on Scarborough Beach.

I lost them then anyway, somewhere in the dunes between Scarborough and Trigg. The new breeze was just beginning to shirr the surface of the ocean. Once that happened you couldn't see anything from the shore. Through the binoculars I saw the pattern and colour of the sea changing fast: small choppy waves darkening from turquoise to blue and losing their clarity. I saw that Rottnest Island had shed its mirages and returned to its proper anchorage. The sou'westerly had lifted the heat haze and brought reality back.

On the two-way, the news editor was philosophical. 'You've still got a story. *Shark Pack Threatens Beaches*. Get some quotes. Over and Out.'

Somehow my shark story grew from a snappy news item into an information-choked feature article. Of course I had my background material already. My story was bursting with historical knowledge. For 'colour' I dropped in a couple of quotes from the obliging Ted 'Sharky' Nelson. But my coup was to bring in science.

I got 'the State's leading ichthyologist', Dr Byron McIntee, to leave his Sunday barbecue and come to the phone to declare that the sharks I'd followed up the coast were probably from the family *Carcharhinidae*, otherwise known as requiem sharks. Requiem sharks included some of the biggest and most voracious sharks: the tiger, whaler, bull shark, blue shark and grey reef shark. Dr McIntee said, and I duly wrote, they were characterised by 'a nictitating membrane and a heterocercal tail'.

Requiem sharks were everywhere, he said. They travelled long distances each day and migrated according to seasonal changes. They had a huge range of habitat: river estuaries, tidal pools, the open ocean, muddy bays and coral reefs. They weren't put off by fresh water or hypersalinity and were found in all tropical and temperate seas.

The biggest requiem sharks were the tigers, reaching about twenty-four feet. They were among the most important marine predators and scavengers, eating a 'broad spectrum of prey':

bony fishes, other sharks and rays, crustaceans, carrion, sea-turtles, sea-snakes, sea-birds and large marine mammals.

At last. 'And humans, of course,' I said.

'Let's not sensationalise that aspect.'

Naturally I asked him about the name. He said that with its funereal associations *requiem* was more stirring than *tiger* or *whaler*. Exactly. I asked him to elaborate. He said it was from the obsolete French *requiem*, a variant of *requin* – 'shark'. And obviously influenced by the gloomier associations of the word *requiem*.

Gloomy? This was more like it.

'A requiem, as you know, is music for dead people,' he said.

'So,' I asked eagerly, 'their name comes from their habit of killing people?' I quickly added the obligatory question. 'What are the chances of a West Australian swimmer being killed by a shark?'

His sigh was loud in my ear. 'You've got more chance of dying from a bee sting or a lightning strike or murder. You've got several hundred thousand times more chance of dying in a car crash on the way to the beach.'

Did scientists have no imagination at all? While he talked I was thinking up a heading. *Requiem For WA Swimmers?* sounded pretty good to me.

He sighed again. 'I hope you people aren't going to beat this thing up.'

When I arrived back at Fremantle, Dare grunted, 'There you are. I need the Anglia,' and speeded off down Queen Street. In the two hours when his and my shifts would normally cross he was nowhere to be seen.

Next morning I was at the newsagent's early to get the paper. The sub-editors had cut my thousand words to ten paragraphs. *Cut* hardly describes it. My shark story was more than filleted, more than slashed. It was *flensed*. The story ran on page seven with a single-column, much-used stock picture of Ted 'Sharky' Nelson, not a word from my ichthyologist, and the heading *Shark Hunter Warns of Beach Threat*. Dare, meanwhile, had got himself a story on page two.

How did I know Dare's story would be about Richie Male? I felt a complete lack of surprise. My brain turned the shock around, took it back a stage and changed it into something like retrospective premonition.

At once my brain was saying I'd always suspected what had happened. I'd suspected it in the lessening of our numbers when we were out on the reef. I'd suspected it when I kicked the weed from around my legs and stumbled ashore. I'd known it for sure when I saw the searching surfboats.

Student Drowns at Cottesloe. I felt no surprise at all. It seemed like I'd known many things like this for the past year or more, things I'd mysteriously witnessed, or hadn't acted on. I didn't feel numb either. Frankly, I had to struggle to keep my attention on it. My mind was already veering away and racing towards some other narrative.

Dare's piece was jammed into a longer story on the weekend's rough seas and surf rescues. It was obvious his source had been the police. There was nothing of Richie's family's background in the pearling industry, no reminder that a pearler's livelihood was always at risk from sharks, tropical hurricanes and a multitude of disasters on and in the sea. It didn't mention the irony of the pearling industry's youngest son drowning on a suburban beach down south in the city. Nor did it say who his companions had been when he drowned.

It said his body, trapped in thick seaweed, had been found by a surfboat crew in knee-deep water only fifteen yards from shore. He'd been missing since Saturday afternoon. The police thought he might have become dazed after being dumped by a wave. The police officer in charge of the search said the seaweed was so thick near the shore it was 'suicidal' to swim there.

The body had received a knock on the head and other abrasions which may have been caused by rocks. It had not been disturbed by fish. This surprised me. I'd always believed there were these tiny sea-lice that could reduce a body to a skeleton in twenty-four hours.

CHEERING UP

My father's hard work was paying off. His tyre factory was well under way. Head office increasingly sought his opinion on a range of matters. But as he now told the friends and neighbours who dropped around on Sunday evenings to cheer him up – the men with beer, the women with a week's supply of his favourite offal treats (tripe, kidneys, brains, lamb's fry) – there was one question worrying the company that they might be able to help him with.

Although he quickly changed the subject if Bill or Jan, or even I, the married man, drifted in, I overheard him several times, after the third or fourth round of drinks, canvassing opinions on this curious matter. He put the question deadpan, and phrased it carefully, and his solemn expression didn't change when they guffawed or, in the case of some of the women, affected shock.

'Should Dunlop get into condoms?' he'd ask.

What? I couldn't believe I'd heard right. I couldn't imagine him asking this if my mother were around. But I had to admit it was an attention-grabber.

When the tittering stopped, he'd tell them stoutly how Dunlop had once made condoms for the nation, but had been forced to dump them fifty years ago when a Catholic became chairman.

'Shame!' someone always cried.

He'd relate how one of the shrewder employees, Eric Ansell, a former ship's purser with an eye for an opportunity, had bought Dunlop's condom machine, resigned from the company, and started making them himself. Over the years Ansell Rubber had kept making them, but had also branched out into less secretive latex products – surgical and household gloves, babies' feeding teats, party balloons, hot-water bottles and so on. But naturally Ansell was best known for its condoms.

Here Hilton Wittaker or some other life-of-the-party felt bound to butt in: 'Let's hear it for French letters!' Some other fellow muttered, 'Hooray for Frenchies!' Then Gordon Beavis or Jim Lehmann or Ken Dengate would join in the hilarity by chortling, 'frangers!' and 'raincoats!' and 'rubbers!' and 'safes!'.

'I prefer sheaths,' some woman invariably said, to the raised eyebrows of the other women and the winks of the men.

'"Today you'll use a Dunlop product!"' declared Mr Wittaker, saying the slogan in a radio announcer's voice.

By now everyone except my father was red-faced and chuckling. Having gained their attention, he told them the Ansell family were looking for a buyer. Should Dunlop buy them out? His advice to head office, he said sagely, was that they should. But they must jettison the condom. There was no money in it. The contraceptive pill was coming in.

'Condoms?' he declared decisively from centre stage. 'Not this boy! I was put on this earth to sell tyres and tennis racquets!'

'He's a one!' the women murmured.

'Just talking business,' he said, twinkling at everyone.

What was all that about? I wondered. What had got into these middle-aged folks?

After overhearing one Sunday evening's anti-condom declaration I went into the kitchen to get a beer and he was standing by the fridge with Mrs Gwen Halliday from Minora Road. He was holding a bottle in one hand and studiously examining her necklace with the other. She was patting his head. Then the hand fingering Mrs Halliday's necklace moved down and solemnly cupped one of her substantial breasts.

This was the man who tore Zulu and Tahitian breasts from the *National Geographic* and tossed them in the garbage. Who, one January, had thrown away a perfectly good *Countryman* calendar because September featured a billabong full of adolescent Aboriginal girls, bare-chested, beaming and waist-deep in water lilies. The man who, for that matter, avidly waited for the *Mirror* to be delivered so he could burn it as he was reading it.

I wondered whether this hypocrisy happened to you after you got married and had children. I wondered whether the Prudery/Lust roundabout came from the clash in his nature between the church architect and the Myer's millinery assistant,

310

the Baptists versus the pub and racehorse owners. Birth and death were making me think a lot about genetics lately.

They kept standing by the fridge. Mrs Halliday continued patting the skin of his head and he kept holding her breast – not squeezing it, just cupping it reverently.

He was too absorbed in treasuring this precious artefact to notice me, but Mrs Halliday broke away gently and came out of the kitchen then, and as she passed me on her way back to the party she smiled at a spot a few feet from me and said, 'Isn't he looking much better lately?'

After surfing with Bill one Saturday afternoon, I drove him and his surfboard home to Circe Circle. I thought I'd go in for a coffee and to say hello. The Fairlane was in the driveway but the front door was locked. The back door was also locked. We rang the doorbell, and knocked, but no one answered. The curtains were drawn and so were the venetians in the main bedroom.

Strange, we thought, and decided to get inside by our old death-defying method. We climbed up onto the narrow brick wall of the Doghouse stairwell – on its outer side a garden bed, on the inside a risky drop of twenty feet onto a damp square of cement – and I pushed up the window into our, now Bill's, bedroom and began to hoist him through.

He was almost inside when the back door opened and my father called out, 'Oh, boys, there you are!'

We clambered down and went to the back door. He stood

in the doorway beaming at us as if we'd just returned safely from Antarctica. He seemed very chatty. From behind him appeared the manageress of his favourite pub. 'I'd like you to meet Mrs O'Hare,' he said.

She was just a middle-aged woman, round-faced and placid-looking, but she was smiling insanely at Bill and me like meeting us had realised all her dreams. Neither of them could stop jabbering. Something about a business meeting and home-decorating tips. I hadn't heard such twaddle since I'd delivered it myself. Coming home earlier than expected, my parents had almost sprung Ruth and me a couple of times. I'd tried to brazen it out, too.

We backed off. Bill and I muttered something and made our excuses and left. We couldn't wait to get out of there. Bill looked confused. A few days before, Betty, their new, officious housekeeper, had found a copy of *Playboy* in his desk. In the row that followed, he received the grim warning: 'You don't want to end up like your brother, do you?'

'What do you reckon?' he said.

'Of course they were,' I said. What the hell. He was a widower.

Quite abruptly, it seemed, my father was promoted and trans-ferred back East. He was made the Dunlop manager for New South Wales, the biggest State branch. He sold the house in Circe Circle. His resignation from all his business and service associations was accepted with regret and congratulations on his new posting. He put Bill into boarding school for his last two years of school, and he moved to Sydney with Jan.

It was hard to imagine him in a different setting. He'd seemed so at home here. Such a big fish. I wondered whether he would have accepted the posting if my mother had been alive. I wondered whether he'd sought the transfer.

Perth was a branch manager's town. Men like him from head offices in Melbourne and Sydney ran the business of the city. As young men they had brought their initially complaining wives and families across the Nullarbor to the most remote city in the world and deposited them in its leafier and more tranquil middle-class suburbs. And then something happened to them. Resisting national advancement and calls back to head office, they were seduced by the light and the landscape and the promise of something as intangible as 'a way of life' and stayed forever.

But he was returning. The greatest fear of our childhood had been realised. The three of us had always worried that one day he'd be brought back East. We'd be dragged away from our friends and from the beach, torn out of Western Australia and sent to austere new schools, to live among pale, citified Easterners with no appreciation of the casual coastal life.

I used to indignantly tell my mother, 'You can all go, but I'm staying right here.'

'Don't worry, dear,' she'd say. 'No one's going anywhere.'

2

TRIAL

This time Eric was looking very spruce – clean-shaven and grey-suited. I thought he looked like someone who read electricity meters or sold fabric lengths. He could have been a Watkins man, worried about cochineal and thimble supplies. He didn't look like an insane serial killer, someone who had recently confessed not only to the murder of Shirley McLeod but to the additional murders of Patricia Berkman, Lucy Madrill, Jillian Brewer and Rosemary Anderson. Someone who had shot, stabbed and strangled eight people, who had struck them with a hatchet and a car.

Nor, with that mild appearance and demeanour, and his indistinct, nasal speech, heard by his public for the first time, did he resemble someone who'd felt – so he told the court – that when he shot the sleeping John Sturkey a power was operating upon him as though he were God.

His trial in the Criminal Court was proceeding swiftly. The prosecution concluded its evidence in only one day. It called just fourteen of its twenty-one listed witnesses and not many of them were even cross-examined. His only chance was to plead not guilty to John's murder because of insanity. He told the court, 'I thought I had power over life and death and must use that power.'

That was his feeling on the night of Australia Day, he said, after prowling around Cottesloe with a stolen rifle and spotting the couple, Rowena Reeves and Nicholas August, the barmaid and the poulterer, in the parked car. He didn't know them and he had no animosity to them. In the beginning, when he walked towards their car, he was only holding the rifle by the sling. 'My desire was just to be a peeping tom or a pervert and look into the car,' he said.

Then something made him raise the rifle. 'It wasn't an impulse. It was stronger than an impulse. I brought the rifle up and put a bullet in it. It was then that this power came over me. I felt as though even if there was an army in front of me they could not have shot me – as though I could have walked through a brick wall.'

Not that you could always go by appearances, but I kept glancing at the jury – eight men and four women – and they didn't seem to be buying insanity. They looked as if they would have been happy to give their verdict as soon as they were sworn in. The judge, Mr Justice Virtue, just looked sanctimonious. Only in real life, I thought, could a judge in the State's most notorious murder trial be named Mr Justice Virtue. You couldn't get away with that name in a movie or a novel. It was too much.

318

But in the real world there was Virtue on the bench. And there was Evil in the dock, the man who had brought fear and chaos to Perth, trying earnestly now to oblige his lawyer, Ken Hatfield QC, by politely stressing how insane he'd been.

'What came over you?' asked Mr Hatfield.

Eric frowned thoughtfully. He said, 'I had full possession of my faculties, like speech and hearing, everything like that. But there was a power. I can't say whether it came from my heart or my head, but it was a very, very strong power – as though I were God and I had power over life and death.'

'And were you able to combat this power?' Mr Hatfield asked.

'No, sir. I wish I had.'

'Did you feel any change take over you?'

'I felt these people in the car were not people in the sense of the word. I did not regard them as human beings. I started to laugh.'

Eric said the power had remained upon him while he walked into Brian Weir's flat and shot him, and then while he drove to Nedlands and shot John Sturkey. The power only lessened after he shot George Walmsley. 'While I was walking back to the car the power left me altogether.'

If this were so, it seemed to me he'd been very selective about using the power. He hadn't shot the milkman he'd said he saw making deliveries along the way. He'd decided against shooting the man he spotted in the front window of Shirley's Frock Salon (Detective-Sergeant McCurry's regular client!) making love to his girlfriend the shop dummy.

Mr Hatfield skated over that. He said, 'Can you tell the judge and jury how you felt after the power left you?'

'I felt deflated, like a pricked balloon. I knew what I had done but it was too late. I could not make amends.'

Mr Hatfield got him to tell the court of his miserable childhood: the mockery from other children, the savage beatings from his drunken father, the expulsions from every school he attended, and his many accidents and head injuries and hospitalisations. He told how he had suffered headaches, blackouts and 'grey-outs' since he was fourteen, when he knocked himself semi-conscious in a high dive. He'd had exploratory brain surgery and had spent six weeks in a psychiatric hospital.

Mr Hatfield asked him about his family. He said he'd been married for ten years and had seven children aged between two and nine. His eldest boy was mentally retarded. His eldest daughter, a twin, had been born with her right arm missing below the elbow.

While Eric was talking, Mr Justice Virtue was cradling his fingers like a judge in an English film when someone from an inferior class was in the dock. He rested his chin on them, then stared over them at the far wall. Eric's voice sounded eager and peculiar. The jury were shifting in their seats. Their faces said they thought this litany of genetic misfortune was in bad taste.

The prosecution called the State's Director of Mental Health Services, Dr Aren Samuel Ellis, to rebut the insanity plea. The defence had asked, in fairness, for a psychiatric assessment of Eric to be made by a psychiatrist from another

State, or by one not employed by the government. The Crown had refused. The Crown had also refused permission for any government psychiatrist junior to Dr Ellis to examine Eric. The only psychiatrist to examine him would be their man.

Dr Ellis told the court, 'My examinations indicate that this boy has a chronic long-standing resentment against society.' He said he wasn't suffering from schizophrenia. He had an abnormality of character as distinct from any question of mental disease. It possibly stemmed from being born with a harelip and cleft palate and from the maltreatment he'd received at home. His self-esteem was very shaky and he would go to any lengths to bolster it and get the attention he required.

'Attention is another name for what some people call love and affection,' said Dr Ellis.

Mr Hatfield did his best in the circumstances. In cross-examination he asked whether patients suffering from schizophrenia sometimes regarded themselves as being driven by an outside power or an outside force.

Dr Ellis said yes.

'And if a patient said he thought he was God, would that be a relevant sign or symptom?'

'No. If he said he was God, it would be. But not if he thought he was God. There is a distinction there, sir.'

The *West Australian* had anticipated a longer, more complex trial than this. Mr Goldsmith had assigned a team of reporters to cover it in shifts. The usual Supreme Court reporters, the shorthand whizzes, took down the evidence and addresses to the jury and the rest of us ran their copy back to the office. But no one minded being relegated to copy boy this time.

This was the biggest local story in memory, even though Eric suddenly had his thunder stolen by two other murderers. The report of his trial's first day was pushed off the front page by the dramatic news and picture of Jack Ruby shooting President Kennedy's assassin, Lee Harvey Oswald. The second day's trial report was shunted back to make way for the photograph of three-year-old John-John Kennedy saluting his father's casket.

But the trial's final day made the front-page lead. In his summing-up, Mr Hatfield told the jury, 'You are as capable as a psychiatrist of forming an opinion of a man's mental condition at a particular time.' It would be difficult for them to forget the emotions they felt at the time of the crimes, he said, but they must consider only what they had heard during the trial.

It was asking a lot. The jury retired for only sixty-five minutes. This was almost as brief as court decorum allowed, a retirement of less than an hour suggesting rashness and impoliteness, even an insult to the legal process. The jury rejected the insanity plea and found Eric guilty of wilfully murdering John Sturkey.

Mr Justice Virtue complimented them and said the verdict was the correct one. From somewhere close at hand he produced the black cap, elaborately placed it on top of his bewigged head and sentenced Eric to death.

Eric took the death sentence like someone who had won a

handy lottery prize. Not first prize exactly but a perfectly acceptable third. He said, 'Thank you, Your Honour. Thank you.' His voice was surprisingly clear. For a moment I wondered if he'd misheard the verdict. If he hadn't, this was taking good sportsmanship and grace under pressure to the lengths of absurdity. He winked at the Press table and at the detectives who had arrested him and at the police as they led him down the stairs. He was winking all over the place. This time I didn't wink back. I wouldn't accept the gesture. I was stunned. The verdict was hardly a surprise – he'd killed and killed without remorse; he'd shot my friend dead – but I felt burned out and nauseous and I could hear my pulse thudding in my ears.

Maybe the government psychiatrist would have said he was enjoying the ultimate in attention. But this reaction to a death sentence, especially from a man of thirty-two, a father of seven, looked bloody insane to me.

3

THE BOY THE COLOUR
OF SAND

While Eric was on death row, his mentally retarded eldest son, Michael, who was in care at the Nathaniel Harper Home down at the river bend at South Guildford, was taken on a picnic to Sandy Beach. He became separated from the other children, wandered into the river and drowned.

When the prison authorities told Eric about his boy's death he broke down. He cried and talked about him all that night and next day and read his Bible. He asked to be buried alongside his son's ashes. The authorities were non-committal. 'You're jumping the gun a bit,' they told him. In the meantime, he asked to be allowed to attend the funeral. This was denied. He took the decision surprisingly calmly.

In his last days, according to those who saw him in the condemned cell – the prison superintendent, the Methodist chaplain, his lawyers, his mother, and his wife, Sally – he again apologised for his crimes. He repeatedly said that Darryl Beamish and John Button were being punished for two murders

327

he'd committed, the hatchet murder of Jillian Brewer and the running down of Rosemary Anderson. He swore on the Bible they were innocent. He seemed relieved to get it off his chest.

His visitors remarked on how philosophical and uncharacteristically talkative, lyrical, even optimistic, he seemed since his son's death.

He said lots more things went through his head these days, as you'd expect. Reading the Bible started off all sorts of thoughts and regrets. But what he kept thinking of was the day his boy said 'starfish'.

When he remembered that day it was stretching out in three sharp colours – yellow and blue, and then the river a milky green like an aquarium, with things in it you couldn't quite see. A warm Saturday afternoon in late January.

They were at Crawley, sitting on that strip of sand between the grass and the river, near the tea-rooms. There was quite a crowd, mostly families, with old people and little kids and a few New Australian boys showing off with a soccer ball. There were radios playing. The people who preferred the river to the ocean – people with little kids, New Australians, old people and other people scared of the surf – liked to take a radio to the river.

They were half in the shade of a big flowering gum. He'd sat his boy in the shade so he wouldn't get burnt. But there were tree roots poking up, and ants, and the shade kept moving, and the boy kept squirming out into the sun again, so he'd had to spread zinc cream on him. The other kids were way down the beach by now, doing bombs off the jetty.

The Paddle Pop he'd bought him was melting fast. He'd got it all over himself, all mixed up with sand and zinc cream. He was a mess. He'd tried to wipe him off with a towel but of course he was twisting away. Anyway, all of a sudden the boy stopped wriggling, looked him in the eye and said 'starfish'. Clear as a bell.

What? He couldn't believe this was a proper word he'd said. 'Yes!' he agreed quickly. 'Right! Starfish!' Then he took a breath and asked him quietly, 'Where's the starfish?'

Crawley was nine or ten miles upriver. Not many starfish that far from the sea. He'd never seen one anyway. None there this day either, and nothing on the shore you'd mistake for one. But hearing him say the word got his hopes up, even after all that time. It made him think things might be changing in the boy's brain. Maybe a little cog had adjusted itself and moved back into place.

For a few seconds there on the beach things were pretty strange. Despite the mess of the icecream and the zinc and sand, the boy's face had changed. He seemed on the ball and older than nine, even a normal nine. There was another thing. When he'd said 'starfish', he'd stared deep into his eyes. His look was sort of wise, like he was gazing right into his soul.

Eric told them this wasn't just him looking back all regretful and imagining things after they'd happened. The picture was so clear. It was still as sharp to him as five minutes ago. He said he bet his nerves showed that afternoon. In a way he'd been more jumpy then than he was now.

'Good boy!' he'd said. His own voice sounded enthusiastic and fake to him, like someone in a commercial. But he'd never been more deadly serious. 'Thinking about starfish? That's the boy!' He was desperate to keep the mood and the moment going. Draw it out. So he quickly scratched a star in the wet sand.

'Look, a starfish.' But his starfish didn't seem to register. The boy's wise look was fading. He quickly drew another star shape. It was a pretty panicky star he scratched out this time. But the blind was already coming down. That's the only way he could describe it. Like shutters. The focus had gone again. Now the look in the boy's eyes was just his old lights-on-but-nobody-home look. Then he started making the old bossy noises that meant he wanted something right away, and hurry up about it.

Everything hopeful drained out of him then. He could've cried at the *nnh, nnh* bellowing noises and those *gimme, gimme* grabbing motions. It was like when they first realised he was not progressing. It was like seeing his little girl's arm the first time. He cried and then he was angry. He couldn't be bothered trying to catch on to what it was he wanted. It was always something impossible. Bring me those seagulls! Hand me that cloud! Let me drive that speedboat! Make it happen!

This one was a real tantrum. He was like a two-year-old in a supermarket. You couldn't ignore him, of course. Icecream in his eyebrows and ears and trickling down his chest, people turning around at the racket, seeing a screaming boy and giving the father disapproving snaky looks. After a few minutes of this, he grabbed him up, a bit roughly, carried him in his arms into the river and kept walking.

The boy kept screaming. The river was just stirring up with the sea breeze and afternoon tide. Underfoot it was all oozy silt and algae, and colder than it looked, but he was determined.

For a while the boy kept up the ruckus, then when the river got deeper he clung on tight, moaning and grimly hanging on. It took a while but he carried him out until the water was up to his own chest and deep enough to submerge them both, and he did.

When they came up the boy was coughing and sobbing, but then he went quiet and just clung on tight all the way back to shore. He felt like a bastard doing it, but he was still so bitterly disappointed he was numb. As he waded in to shore he felt like he'd been teased and swindled by the world's most twisted conman. A real sadistic, mocking bastard, that God.

Back on the beach the boy stayed quiet and well behaved, squatting at the water's edge, playing his sandy little games while he took some deep breaths. Get a grip, he thought. The little fellow couldn't help how he was. He was his boy. Be thankful for small mercies – at least the bloody icecream had washed off him!

Those games were such solemn bits of nonsense you couldn't help your heart going out to him. First he carefully placed mussel shells in a hole and covered it up, and then he jabbed jellyfish with a stick. Watching him so busy and frowning away to himself with the shells and jellyfish, he'd really tried to understand what made him tick. He studied him real hard.

Small for nine. Thinner than the younger kids, more pointy-looking and slightly paler. Not abnormal to look at – just the far edge of normal. You noticed his knees and elbows more, and the way his legs bent out to the sides. The other kids were as brown as berries but watching him it struck him that he was the same colour as the sand.

Everything about him – his skin, even his faded khaki shorts – blended right into the sand. He was like one of those little ghost crabs. Now you saw him, now you didn't. If you leaned back a bit and half-closed your eyes, the beach absorbed him. It soaked him up. He hardly had an outline. He was nearly invisible. If it wasn't for his jerky little movements and his noises now and then you wouldn't know he was there.

⸺

As the murderer waited for the morning of his hanging the people of Perth tried to outdo each other in their claims, if not of kinship (no one wanted to claim that), then at least of a firm and everyday connection to him.

332

Suddenly there was a kudos in having once worked along-side him, or even being related to someone who had, at one of his many brief jobs: at Krasnostein's Scrap Metal, for instance, or the city fruit and vegetable markets, or indeed at Dunlop Rubber.

There were at least another four people, all women, more reluctant in claiming an association, who eventually came to the realisation that it had been he who'd assaulted them in their beds in Nedlands. One he'd hit with a fire poker and turned into an epileptic, another he hit with a knuckle-duster, one he was trying to strangle and rape until her cat attacked him and he ran off, one he stabbed with an umbrella.

And then there were the other women, some badly injured, whom he'd run down with cars at night.

Many hundreds of West Australians, from Premier Dave Brand down – and my family, of course – had unknowingly had him in their homes, scores of them more than once, many of them several times. He had entered so many houses that the police gave up trying to collate all the offences.

Two other people had a strong connection to the murderer. Darryl Beamish's death sentence was commuted to life, and John Button served all his ten-year term. They would think of him every day of their long sentences. And for the rest of their lives, even after their innocence was officially recognised.

4

THE MURDERER'S WIDOW
RECALLS THE EXECUTION

I felt compelled to ask Eric's wife, Sally, about her life with him. She had been loyal and attentive during his trial and imprisonment – never missing a visiting day – but had never spoken publicly. For years there was a great curiosity in the community about their relationship. (Did she know or suspect?) But there was also a deference to her own suffering and her unique position as the Nedlands Monster's widow.

Eventually, much later, I would ask her how she'd been able to cope with her husband's execution. I especially wondered about her feelings in the minutes before his hanging.

A remarkably light-spirited and generous woman, her Liverpool accent still pronounced after many years in Australia, she didn't seem to mind me asking. She served me tea and a freshly baked cake and as a cuckoo clock ticked loudly in her cheery front room I told her how the terrible suspense of watching the clock as the seconds ticked away to the execution was fixed in my imagination. Even thinking about it

337

now made me feel nine years old and anxious again. Had she counted the seconds?

'No, no, dear,' she said. 'What with feeding the kids and getting them ready for school and all the rest of it, eight o'clock sort of went past without me noticing.'

I looked at her. Surely she was joking.

'Then the next-door neighbour came over and said, "Don't you feel like crying?" And I said, "No, no, maybe later." Actually I . . . Life wasn't easy with Eric Cooke. He killed every bit of trust. Every bit of respect, admiration, love, was gone at the end. I was there just because I was his wife and that was it. It made it easier to cope, it made it easier. Oh yes, oh yes.'

Sally and Eric met at the metropolitan markets in West Perth. She was a waitress at the market cafeteria. She'd been there a year when he started work over at the market store. 'I was swept away, the same as any teenager. We went out on the eighth of June and we got married on the fourteenth of November the same year, 1953. A whirlwind romance. I was nineteen, he was twenty-two.

'He was Methodist when I met him. He'd been in trouble, so he'd got involved in the Methodist church when he was a teenager. He told me he'd been in bother. He didn't tell me about arson or life bonds or anything like that, just that he'd stolen. He went from stealing, arson, right through to killing people. In all different ways. Incredible, really.'

His eight murders had never dawned on her. 'He was never home; he was never a husband, put it that way. If he'd been home and then suddenly started going out I would've realised he was doing something, but he was always going out womanising all our married life, and in some ways I was just so relieved that I was going to get a break from all the hassle, the arguing. We were always arguing about the going out. In the end I knew I couldn't change him, so I just let him go. He'd always have big excuses when he came home. He'd been out to a nightclub or whatever. If he said he'd been with somebody it was always somebody you could check up with, therefore you don't check up. You let it go.

'I suspected him of infidelity rather than crime, oh yes. I mean, I lost count of how many women he'd been with. From a year after we got married right to the day he was arrested. Sometimes he'd go away for a week and then come home and I'd think, "He's been with another woman!" That's all I used to think. I thought it only concerned us, really. Nobody else.

'If I'd cared a lot it would have been harder at the end. It made it easier. To be able to just go out and talk to a neighbour, which I'd never been able to do, to be able to go out for walks without his permission. Oh, yes. Possessive! I could never have any money. He used to lock the wardrobe with the money in it and take the key to work with him. One day I took the children to the park and he was at work and he knocked off half an hour earlier than I thought and we got home a bit later than him, and he said, "Do I have to lock you and the kids inside when I go out?" I wasn't allowed to do anything. When he was arrested it was such a relief just to be able to go for a walk and buy the kids an icecream and . . . you know.

'I often thank God I didn't ever try to leave him. I mean, I didn't know he was killing and all that, but now that I know he was killing I think he would have killed me, because I was his possession. I wasn't allowed to leave. And yet he was out with every woman and never home. He was a liar. A very good liar. I think he even believed his own lies, I really do. He could repeatedly tell the same lie and never trip up. So convincing. He'd say, "You can check with So-and-so."

'I was real green, talk about naive. I'd always lived with Mum and my sisters, never gone out. I was thirteen when we came to Australia. Mum brought myself and my two young sisters out from Liverpool after the war. Dad had just died and her mother and family were already here. We were Ten Pound Poms. I love Australia. I've never been back to England, even for a visit. I love the Australian people. I love everything about it. Great country.

'Eric's father was Australian and his mother was Scottish. His father, Vivian, known as Snowy, was violent with the drink. Eric never drank, never smoked. Coca-Cola, that was his drink. He loved Passiona and Coca-Cola. Never drank tea, never drank coffee. No hot drinks of any kind. No religious reason for it. I used to think it was because of his harelip, his cleft palate.

'He loved any sport – hockey, swimming. Very particular about his skin. Never a mark on him. He used to swim across the river, a very strong swimmer. A member of the Scarborough Surf Lifesaving Club, but he stole money from there and was tossed out. Before I met him, before we were married. I don't think he'd actually gone to prison before I met him but he'd come close. They'd put him on a life bond a couple of months before I went out with him. He'd stole money and then set fire to the building to cover up his tracks. The old Boan's store. He got away with a fair bit of money. He had it hidden under his bed but they found it. He'd had a lot of small crimes but that was a big one for a boy. After I married him he got caught for loitering and being a peeping tom and did a month on each charge. And then of course he stole a car from the markets and did two years, one for stealing and one for breaking his bond.

'When he got caught for stealing the car I woke up that he was a thief. He stole it to go and see a girl in Bunbury. She was in town with the country women's hockey team. He didn't make it. He crashed the car in Yarloop and finished up in Royal Perth Hospital. Completely wiped the car off. Brand new car. The boy in the markets he'd stolen the car from, who'd known him for years, felt bad about it. He came to me and said, "Sally, we could've worked something out," thinking about me and the kids, and Eric in gaol. I said, "Don't worry about it. He committed the crime and he's got to face the sentence."

'After that he was good until he had this rampage and he started killing people. It never dawned on me, all the killings I'd read about, and I even said to him one day, "God, I do feel sorry for this poor fellow. They must be desperate. They must have nobody to go home to, nobody who cares." And he said, "Sally, it could be somebody with everything to live for." Never ever dawned on me he could kill anybody. I knew he was a liar, a cheat, a thief – you couldn't do anything about that. But not a killer.

'When the police came Tony answered the door and said,

"Mum, there's a big man with a hat at the door." And I thought, "Oh my God!" and I went to the door and I said, "What have you got him for this time?" thinking stealing, and he said, "Can I come in, Mrs Cooke?" Detective-Sergeant Bill Nielson and another detective. They sat at the table and asked me a few questions. "When did he go out?" And I said, "Yesterday morning." They said, "You didn't worry when he didn't come home last night?" They had him in the lockup, of course. And I said, "I don't worry if he doesn't come home for a week or a fortnight, he's only with other women. There's nothing I can do about it. I've got seven little kids here." I said, "What have you got him for?" and he said, "Well, we're still questioning him. We've got a warrant and we want to search the place." I said, "Go for your life." And with that I've never seen so many detectives. They were everywhere. Up in the roof, going into the cistern in the toilet.

'Anyway, they went away and they came back and said, "You'd better sit down." And they told me Eric had confessed to doing the boy Sturkey. I said, "Oh, dear God!" And Mr Nielson said, "You can come and see him tomorrow. Can you get a sitter for the children?" and I said yes. When he came and got me, Mr Nielson said I was going to get a terrible shock when I got to the lockup because Eric had confessed to all the others. Right back to 1959 when he killed Patricia Berkman. Mr Nielson said, "It shocked me so it's going to shock you. The poor girl Lucy Madrill, he strangled her, dragged her out into the back yard and raped her and she was already dead." I said to Mr Nielson, "No, he couldn't!" and he said, "Well, he's confessed to it, told us everything just the way we found her."

342

'It was all proven. He did all of them. Oh, Mr Nielson said, "Why couldn't he have been on the police force? What a memory." He was a mastermind for detail. He remembered everything – where he'd thrown the skin-diving knife in the river the night he killed the woman in 1959. He said, "It'll be down there," and they dived down there and brought it up. He said, "I've thrown the rifle off the bridge. It's down below that post. I've memorised it." And there it was. The evidence was down there. So it was all proven. Mr Nielson said to him, "Did you realise you'd be caught?" and he said, "I knew I would, one day."

'I don't know why he did it. People say a grudge against the world because of his harelip. Kids were cruel to Eric. He never talked about it. I did hear he was beaten a lot and that he used to jump in between his mum and dad when they were having a row and that's how he got himself hit, trying to protect his mother. Whether Snowy actually set out to belt Eric or he just got in the way, I don't know. I don't think he had a very nice life. Snowy was always drunk. Eric never spoke about it, never ever. But he always visited his father on Father's Day and birthdays, hardly the thing to do if you'd been beaten a lot. Maybe he blocked it out as he got older.

'His mother never spoke about it either, or the life they had. And she had a bad life with Eric. He was expelled from school in first grade. First grade, mind you. He was expelled four or five times, until in the end she just pulled him out of school. He was always getting in trouble. There was no point leaving him there. But my eldest daughter was born with one arm, her right arm missing, and she had no difficulty at school. But talking. I mean, he was a pretty bad talker. They called him Birdmouth. And his father did too. His mother told me that when Eric was born he was very ugly and his father said, "If you think I'm going to keep that misfit all my life you've got another think coming!" He was really an alcoholic, and she left him. She changed her name back to Miss Erica Edgar and got a legal separation through the courts, and then went back to him. Eric was twelve and he never forgave her for that, going back to the same environment. But she lived under the name Miss Edgar until she died.

'As a family we don't talk about the bad days at all. It's as if they never happened. When tragedy hits we all stick together. It was hard when Michael drowned while Eric was in gaol. But I don't know, I've always believed we're born to a life and we're born to a destiny. And you've just got to not ask questions and keep going. We lost my youngest daughter, Rosalie, with cancer on her twenty-first birthday. And my little grandson has cerebral palsy, can't do anything about it. A nurse told me once I had a special gift – the gift of acceptance. And I said I'd often wondered why I react different to other people. When my daughter died I went out and planted a bed of petunias. When my sister died I went window-shopping. That's the thing I do. I do feel a lot, I just react different. The nurse said, "Not many people are born with that gift. Don't knock it."'

Eric Edgar Cooke would be the last person hanged in Fremantle Gaol, on 26 October 1964, and the second-last person to be executed in Australia. (Ronald Ryan, hanged in Melbourne's Pentridge Gaol in 1967 for killing a prison warder during an escape, would be the last.) Fremantle Gaol would be closed to prisoners and become a historic site. Former prison warders would become tour guides at this popular tourist attraction.

Sally Cooke would visit the gaol again – with her grandchildren in their school holidays. 'The littlest one, Brodie, he was about six, and I kept losing him, and he's in all the cells, and I find him in the death cell, and he's sitting on the seat, and I said, "Get off there!" and the poor guard, he knew who I was, and he's trying to keep it hush-hush, and of course Brodie's calling out, "Is this where Grandpop sat, Grandma? Did Grandpop die down there, Grandma?" This poor guard, his face is getting redder and redder, and I said to him, "Just forget it." I couldn't help laughing because kids are kids, aren't they? He's a character, that Brodie. He couldn't have got closer to the gallows if he'd fell over it. Fascinated, he was. They don't realise the seriousness, you know.'

The Sunday the police came to the house in Rivervale to tell them his father had been arrested for murder, Tony Cooke, the second son, was eight and he and his brothers and sisters were waiting to give him his Father's Day presents.

His father had warned them one night about the murderer.

'At the time it was a very warm and secure experience, and maybe it expresses his sense of humour, but he said no one was safe and we had to lock our doors. All the boys used to sleep out in the sleep-out, and it was a small house – well, it's got to be a small house, there were seven kids – and he put all the mattresses on the lounge-room floor and we all slept in the lounge room together and he was there to stand guard over us.'

I had to ask Tony, too, about those final minutes before eight o'clock on that Monday morning. He said before he left for school he was watching the Tokyo Olympics on television with Ron Woodward. Woodward was the young policeman assigned to guard the family while the father was on death row because they had been getting prowlers and curiosity seekers hanging around *their* house. 'Dawn Fraser was swimming for Australia and it was pretty exciting. I forgot eight o'clock. The next time I looked at the clock it was ten past eight.'

He said no one was watching the clock. 'I mean, I'm sure the neighbours were. The day is a blur to me. I can remember the whole day being very, very quiet. I can remember that unearthly quiet. People came. It wasn't like people stayed away. People offered some comfort, people just making sure she was OK.'

I told him I was watching the clock.

5

THE VIEW FROM THE
ESPLANADE HOTEL

I agreed to meet Graham Perkin, the news editor of *The Age*, the venerable Melbourne daily, at the Esplanade Hotel. He'd written to me first from Melbourne the week before, then he phoned me on his arrival in Perth. He was on a recruiting mission. The *West Australian* was regarded as a good training ground for young reporters and the big city papers had begun poaching them.

My name had been one of those mentioned to him, he said mysteriously. Would I be interested in talking to him about joining *The Age*?

I guessed a couple of former Perth reporters currently on *The Age* had given him my name. I was flattered as much as interested. On my way to the hotel, however, passing the usual open-faced, slow-strolling pedestrians and considerate motorists, I wondered vaguely what I was doing. Life was calming down. The paper had promised me an early upgrading. In a month I'd be a graded journalist. I was getting bigger assignments. I had good friends here. It was a cosy place to work. And how could I ever leave the beach? All I wanted was to hunker down in the dunes with Ruth and James and gather my scattered wits.

But I was curious to meet Graham Perkin. He was only in his early thirties and his reputation had even crossed the Nullarbor. The grapevine said he was *The Age*'s editor-in-waiting. I said I could see him in my lunch hour.

We met in his hotel room. I found him friendly but also slightly intimidating, with a brisk sophisticated manner, high colour and fierce, protruding blue eyes, not unlike Billy Graham's. Although he was better groomed and dressed than Perth's crumpled and tweedy newspaper executives, his collar and small tie-knot seemed too tight for his neck, and his over-flowing cheeks and laconic, down-turned mouth gave him an air of exasperated amusement. Even in this relatively calm situation his speech and gestures were clipped and speedy.

To see if I was on the ball, we batted around some current news events. When a topic made him mildly emphatic his eyes bulged even more, his colour rose and his nostrils flared back towards his cheeks. He referred to leading newsmakers by their first names – 'Henry' and 'Bob' and 'mad old Arthur'. His whole impatient, insider manner said there were things to be done, changes to be made, stories to be covered and uncovered. And if they weren't – and soon – he would burst.

He was sitting with his back to the view and I was facing it. The wide Swan River estuary filled half the window. There was no wind and I couldn't remember the river looking more placid and scenic. In the picture-frame of the window one small yacht sat becalmed, so still it could have been painted on the glassy surface. Not a wisp of cloud, not a bird or plane or puff of smoke marred the sharp blue sky. Below the river, crossing the crisp green stripe of the Esplanade, parallel lines of sprinklers sprayed high into the air. In the absence of wind the silver sheets of water dropped directly to the ground. The whole familiar scene was bathed in a generous golden light.

I knew a more newsworthy and urbane world lay east of this glistening view. But as we talked I felt a growing conflict. I felt sentimental and nostalgic about the river and the sky, as if I'd already deserted them. Being impressed by Graham Perkin's big-city presence seemed treacherous. It denied their unique charms.

Some sort of loyal West-Australianness on my part wanted him to turn and glance at the view. Congratulations were in order. Crazily, I wanted him to pay the view and the climate and topography – the very elements – the lavish compliments they deserved. (What fabulous water! What great sunny weather! What white sand! Keep up the good work!) Especially the view. Then I could let them go.

He continued to ignore the view. He wanted to let me in on his plans to revitalise *The Age*. He implied he'd be editor before long. A changing of the guard was imminent. He spoke of bringing in keen young reporters and changing the paper's fusty layout and content to make it a great newspaper. As he did, he stared at me even more intently, as if only the participation of a naive and untested youth from the boondocks could help him bring it off. Then he swore me to secrecy. It was a shrewd and seductive recruitment technique. I bought it entirely.

'Well,' he said then, briskly lighting a Kent. 'Tell me about yourself, chap.'

I'd planned none of this but I suddenly realised the extent of my frustration and it shocked me how stifled I felt. I wanted to stretch my wings. I wanted adventures. I was tired of being the black sheep, and of supporting three people on a teenager's salary. Far too much had happened here. It was holding me back and perhaps it would hold me back forever. I had to get out.

His enthusiasm was catching. As soon as I started speaking I forgot the halcyon West Australian way of life. I lied about my age. I put it up three years and said I was twenty-three. I upped my status, too. I was a third-year cadet but I said I was a D-grade – a graded reporter. I didn't feel bad about this exaggeration; I'd been promised my grading next month. But I raised my actual current weekly salary by ten dollars.

He bought it. If he didn't think I was really twenty-three, he didn't turn a hair. He said he'd give me a C-grading, with an extra margin of ten dollars a week. He was offering me thirty dollars more than I was getting! 'When can you start?' he said.

I didn't think to ask for moving expenses. When it occurred to me later, I thought better of it. I already had an amazing deal. I didn't want to seem greedy.

'One more thing,' said Graham Perkin. 'What's the best fish restaurant in town? Not a grease-trap. Something classy.'

352

Naturally once I'd made the decision to go to Melbourne and join *The Age* everything became settled in Perth. As I served out my notice, life seemed more serene than it had for years. Instead of being swept along in a torrent of dramatic events I felt in charge for once.

Being recruited by an Eastern States newspaper gave me more confidence. It also brought a new respect from my old bosses on the *West Australian*. I stopped taking Dr Synott's phenobarbitone. (I'd never noticed any sedative effects anyway.) And Mr Goldsmith suddenly got my name right. After three years he stopped calling me Rodney.

With a huge sense of relief Ruth and I found we weren't self-conscious exiles any longer. We discovered we were sociable. We began holding regular keg parties at the House of Meat. Suddenly we enjoyed having lots of people around – all those amusing, argumentative journalists who had become our friends.

All the reporters came to the House of Meat parties, the suavest, Harry Potter, often arriving with an actress or a Beachgirl Quest contestant, and once with the female chorus from *South Pacific*. Even library girls turned up. Not Roberta, of course. Nowadays she was twice removed from the smoky, languid world of newspaper files and Stanley knives. After a brief stint as a reporter on the *Daily News* she'd married her grazier and moved to his country property.

We pooled our money and bought kegs from the brewery and set them up in the small cement yard between the butcher shop and the house. In high spirits we drank under- or over-gassed beer and argued animatedly about news events (whether South Vietnam was a bigger story than the Profumo/Christine Keeler affair) and stomped to surfing music in draught-beer froth and the watery blood seeping into the yard from the butcher's cool-room.

A party generally lasted until dawn, or until the neighbours called the police, or the cigarettes ran out and the smokers reeled off in search of more. After it broke up, our clothes always smelled of lamb fat as much as cigarette smoke. The smell hit hardest in the fresh air of the Swanbourne sandhills when we peeled off our clothes in the glary dawn and rushed into the surf.

But a party got a new lease of life when the night-shift reporters and sub-editors arrived. They brought cigarettes and the first edition of the paper with them. The smokers fell upon the Rothmans and Kents of the recent arrivals; everyone grabbed the fresh, inky newspaper, and several more hours of circuitous bantering argument began.

So it was late one humid summer night, a week before we left, that I learned from the still-warm front page that Roberta had been decapitated that day.

My eyes moved back and forth from the heading to her picture. It was a relaxed, smiling photograph, probably snapped originally for her Press pass or a story in *House News*, the staff magazine.

She'd been flying with her husband, Digby, in his single-engine Victa Airtourer from their property at Northampton to his parents' place at Toodyay. Caught in an unseasonal summer storm, he landed in heavy rain. Upset, shaken by the turbulent flight, Roberta rushed from the aircraft. Apparently blinded or confused by the rain, she stepped off the leading edge of the wing instead of the trailing edge and stumbled into the propeller.

—

My father telephoned from Sydney out of the blue. He sounded very hearty as he asked after us all, but he seemed to have something else on his mind. I detected an anxious note. I wondered if anything was wrong. Finally he blurted out that he was getting married.

I didn't even know he had a girlfriend. As usual with an important emotional event, he'd left it until the very last minute to tell us. He said he'd send us the wedding details. They'd already booked the church and made the arrangements. I must have sounded stunned because he was at pains to stress that he'd known his fiancée for some time.

Even though he was talking in his bluff managerial voice he started to explain their meeting as if our situations were reversed, as if I were the parent needing convincing. He said they'd met when he was in Singapore and had hit it off immediately. She lived in Sydney, as it happened. She was a nursing sister. It was a stroke of good fortune we were moving to Melbourne because we wouldn't have so far to travel to the wedding.

I recalled how swiftly and efficiently he'd pulled out of Perth and moved to Sydney. Things suddenly fell into place. He'd been in quite a hurry. 'Congratulations,' I said.

'So we'll see you soon,' he said. But he seemed to be lingering on the line. Was he worried how I felt about our mother being replaced? Did he want the blessing of his eldest child?

'We'll be there,' I said.

—

Three years to the day after I started there, I finished work on the *West Australian*. It was my twenty-first birthday. We were leaving town that evening on the Trans-Continental to Melbourne, travelling second-class across the Nullarbor Plain and changing trains at Kalgoorlie, Port Pirie and Adelaide. We'd already packed and sent our few possessions ahead. We were paying our own fares. *The Age*'s largesse didn't run to air tickets.

I didn't have a twenty-first birthday party. My father, brother and sister were all in Sydney now. And the rush and hubbub of departure got in the way. In any case, the traditional coming-of-age celebration – the proud parental speeches, the presents, the champagne toasts, the ceremonial passing over of the big cardboard key to the door of adulthood – seemed ludicrous in the circumstances. I'd been supporting a family for nearly three years. It seemed like I'd been an adult forever. As a special ritual, my twenty-first birthday could slide quietly past like our wedding and the birth of our first child. That was fine by me. I'd had enough of parties.

Early in the morning, I walked to Cottesloe Beach for a final swim. The idea of turning twenty-one this day and leaving my job and hometown and taking my family across the country to a bigger, busier, colder city had me feeling somewhere between elated and already homesick for Perth. Something struck me for the first time: I'd thought of us as intrepidly setting off, but wasn't I actually returning? Hadn't I come full circle?

Walking up the hill to the beach, I couldn't help imbuing everything I saw – the suburban houses with their dogged gardens, the jaggedly pruned council street trees, even the dry veldt grass and dandelion weeds on the sandy road verge – with great seriousness. Every object was a symbol of my life so far and a portent of all the travelling ahead. I mused on how mature and intelligent it was of me to think like this, to wonder and worry about the lasting nature of things but to press on. I didn't consider this focus on myself naive or imagine that my optimism couldn't always be replenished by a good story, a glimpse of the sea and a particular angle of sunlight.

The way the early morning summer light struck the surface of North Street, the outlines of houses, the first scruffy dunes, and then streaked across the beach and the glassy ocean, was the way sunlight always fell on the last day of the school holidays. It was the way the rays slanted through the

Moreton Bay fig trees on Rottnest Island when I trudged back to the *Islander* with my bag on my shoulder. It brought the same pangs of romance and remorse. It was an achingly familiar and sentimental tableau. But it was all used up.

At Cottesloe Beach I dived under a couple of waves and tried to catch a few more but they were breaking too close to the shore. Then again, I thought, they always did. I had my last swim and walked home.

When I got back a truck was pulling up outside. It wasn't the usual morning carcass delivery by the medieval executioners; the truck was yellow and black. Two men got out and opened the back tray of the truck and hauled something out. It was my father's twenty-first birthday present to me. The nature of the present made me wonder whether he perceived me differently these days. But then the company had long ceased making the Bumper Leisure Shoe. His gift was a Dunlopillo mattress.

As we set off that night for Melbourne the sunset was at our backs and the lights of the suburbs fell away surprisingly quickly behind the train. A young couple, a small, sand-coloured boy and a double-bed mattress, we hurried across the coastal plain, up the steep gravel slope of the ranges and into the desert.

Author's Note

This is both a book of memory and my portrait of a place and time. Memory may falter and portraiture is a highly subjective endeavour, but I have tried to tell a truthful story. A handful of names have been changed for the usual reasons.

Early drafts of some parts first appeared in *Granta*, *Westerly*, *A Sea Change*, *Toads* (Allen & Unwin) and *My One True Love* (Random House). The song 'Where the Blue of the Night' was written by Bing Crosby, Roy Turk and Fred Ahlert in 1931.

I'm deeply grateful to Sally Cooke and Tony Cooke for their time, patience and memories, as I am to Jan Purcell, Ian Watson, Nicholas Hasluck and Loss Whittig. None of these generous people, however, can be blamed for the track I've chosen to take through the sand dunes.